STUDIES IN

ECONOMIC
NATIONALISM

PUBLICATIONS DE L'INSTITUT UNIVERSITAIRE
DE HAUTES ETUDES INTERNATIONALES - N° 35

MICHAEL A. HEILPERIN

STUDIES IN
ECONOMIC NATIONALISM

LIBRAIRIE E. DROZ   LIBRAIRIE MINARD
8, rue Verdaine   73, rue Cardinal Lemoine
GENEVE   PARIS V•

1960

THE LUDWIG VON MISES INSTITUTE
2010

To the Memory
of my Teachers and Friends
WILLIAM E. RAPPARD
and
PAUL MANTOUX
Founders of the Graduate Institute
cf International Studies

Where there is much desire to learn, there of necessity will be much arguing, much writing, many opinions; for opinion in good men is but knowledge in the making.

John Milton: *Areopagitica* (1644).

I shall ... venture to acknowledge, that, not only as a man, but as a British subject, I pray for the flourishing commerce of Germany, Spain, Italy, and even France itself.

David Hume: *Of the Jealousy of Trade* (1742).

Das ist die Eigenschaft der Dinge:
Natürlichem genügt das Weltall kaum;
Was künstlich ist, verlangt geschlossnen Raum.
(Such is the nature of things: the universe is barely sufficient for what is natural; but what is artificial requires closed space.)

Gœthe: *Faust*, Part II, Act 2.

There is no social phenomenon more universal in its incidence, nor more far-reaching for the future of mankind in its consequences, than economic nationalism to-day.

William E. Rappard: *Economic Nationalism* (1937).

I desire freedom as an end in itself. I desire order as a means to freedom. ... I hold that if freedom is to be preserved and progress assured, we must look outside collectivism for an answer. We must look to a system in which there is truly independent initiative and truly dispersed power. ... If we did not know a better system than overall collectivism, we should have to create it.

Lionel Robbins: *Freedom and Order* (1955).

PREFACE

This short and unpretentious book is a by-product of the comprehensive — and as yet unfinished — inquiry into economic nationalism in the twentieh century which I have intermittently conducted for many years. The chapters of which it is composed were written in the first place in order to clarify my own ideas; and they have also served me for some of the lectures delivered at the Graduate Institute of International Studies during the academic year 1958-59.

My reason for deciding to publish what is assuredly an incomplete treatment of a most important subject, is that apparently no volume of this particular scope exists today. I have also been prompted by the encouragements given me by my friend, Professor Jacques Freymond, Director of the Graduate Institute, and by his hospitable offer to include the book in the series of the Institute's publications. Thus provided with an opportunity to render at this most appropriate place my heartfelt homage to the memory of two great and ever-regretted friends and teachers, Professors William E. Rappard and Paul Mantoux, who founded the Institute thirty-two years ago, I owe to their eminent successor a debt of gratitude very large indeed.

The content of this book has been the subject of conversations and discussions with scholars of many countries, to all of whom my warm thanks are here expressed. As it is a highly controversial study, however, no names are mentioned and I alone bear the responsibility for what it contains.

To my wife go my affectionate thanks for her encouragement and a moral support that never falters.

✻

As I write this preface on the day on which the University of Geneva is four hundred years old, I wish to pay my grateful tribute to my famous and venerable Alma Mater, to which I owe both my academic training and my first teaching experience and with which I have been again associated, albeit somewhat indirectly, over the past few years.

Four hundred years: what a span of experience this covers in the history of economic nationalism! When Calvin's Academy was founded, mercantilism was in its youth. It grew, flourished, declined, and fell; then came the age of liberalism and free trade and the great expansion of international commerce and economic development. World War I destroyed the liberal world trading system and there followed the ill-fated efforts to rebuild it in the twenties. The Great Depression of the thirties ushered in the most virulent forms of economic nationalism the world has ever known. As these pages go to press, liberalism and internationalism are triumphantly returning in Western Europe, the struggle against protectionism in the United States is rife; but in most of the underdeveloped countries economic nationalism prevails, as it does, of course, in the totalitarian countries of the communist bloc.

The balance of this century will be of vital importance for the future of international co-operation, which, to a large extent, will depend upon the fate of economic nationalism. It is my hope that this slender volume may help better to understand the issues involved and the stakes which are so high in terms of individual happiness and of peace and welfare for all.

M. A. H.

Geneva, June 5, 1959.

CONTENTS

PART I

IN QUEST OF PERSPECTIVE

CHAPTER I

WHAT IS ECONOMIC NATIONALISM?

I

C. K. Ogden, the great semanticist and inventor of "Basic English", is reported to have commented on the saying: "words are convenient noises" by remarking that no more than one thousand of them have any precise meaning. This is particularly true of words relating to human affairs! The reason for this unsatisfactory state of affairs is not hard to find. Social relationships (political and economic) are extremely complex and involved; social "realities" are changing almost as fast as a student can commit their description to paper — or faster; emotions become involved in matters affecting the happiness, the prosperity, and the future of individuals and groups; and words often acquire explosive political qualities even before they are clearly defined. Add the fact that the situation, condition or relationship covered by a term changes frequently — and often imperceptibly — thereby causing an eventual need for redefinition, recognized only after more or less delay — if at all. Life has a way of breading homonyms without anyone becoming aware of them for a long time. The verbal jungle in which the man in the street and the social scientist both live has become in recent decades a very dangerous place indeed.

Words, as was well observed during the past war, are weapons. Indeed, there are words which are sticks of dynamite, just awaiting detonation. The "dynamite words" are the stock-in-trade of the demagogue and the scholar's nightmare. Among them there are words which exist for evil purposes alone; and there are words which have a Jekyll-and-Hyde existence, now respectable terms with every appearance of objectivity (if not always of clarity), now slogan-like fighting words with which to inflame the mob. It has been my endeavour to avoid, as far as possible, all such terms. In this book, the principal theme of which is *economic nationalism,* I am concerned with the problems of collectivism and liberalism as well, an area in which many emotional words are in current use. For my part I use the term "collectivism", rather than "socialism", "fascism", or "communism". And I speak of "free enterprise", of "liberalism", and of the "market economy", but avoid using the ambiguous term "capitalism", especially without qualification. Concern for the clarity of the terms used in this book leads me, as I have been led in earlier writings, to devote particular attention to the problem of definitions. Both this and the following chapter have unavoidably a considerable "semantic" tinge. Yet to avoid misunderstanding is worth a moderate amount of what may strike some of my readers as excessive "pedantry". Indeed the use of ambiguous words without a definition ought to come to be regarded as intellectual bad manners, and this not in academic circles alone.

II

After these preliminary observations, my first task is to define the term *economic nationalism.* Let us note in the first place that it relates to a set of national policies which regulate the relations between a country and the rest of the world. The policies covered by this term are very ancient, the term itself is of very recent origin. In the seventeenth and eighteenth centuries — indeed from the sixteenth century onward — one spoke of mercantilism or of the "mercantile system". When the system was dismantled in the early part of the nineteenth century, the opposite to free trade was known as "protectionism". During the reconstruction period which followed the end of World War I, "protectionism" was still the most widely used phrase. Although there may have been earlier uses of the term "economic nationalism", the first instance that I have found, prominently displayed, is in the title of a book by Leo Pasvolsky, published by the Brookings Institution in Washington in 1928: *Economic Nationalism of the Danubian States.* It was after the outbreak of the Great Depression and the collapse of the precarious reconstruction of world economy achieved during the twenties, that the term *economic nationalism* began to be more widely used. It is found for example — and this is symptomatic — as the title of a small volume published in a reference series in New York, in 1933. [1] It was in the thirties that the term *economic nationalism,* and the concept it covers came into general use as something considerably at variance with what was called "protectionism" during the nineteenth and the earlier part of the twentieth centuries. Wherein the difference lies will be seen presently. It may be briefly suggested here that the new notion of economic nationalism is closely bound up with the new collectivist philosophies — and policies — of the inter-war decades and expecially of the decades following 1930. *Protectionism,* in the older sense of the word, *belonged to a liberal age.* It was in conformity — and not in contradiction — with the operations of the price system, of the market economy and of individual private enterprise. Collectivism, as will also be shown below, is based on a philosophy of society at variance with the entire liberal tradition of the West.

III

To revert, however, to the task of providing a definition of the phrase: *economic nationalism.* We can do no better, to begin with, than to turn to the most authoritative student of this subject, Professor William E. Rappard. In his address on "Economic Nationalism" delivered at the Harvard Tercentenary Conference of Arts and Sciences, he made the following pertinent comments:

> To define economic nationalism as the economics of nationalism would be neither accurate nor illuminating.
>
> It would be inaccurate, because the policies which some acclaim as economic nationalism in their own country and which all denounce as such in their neighbours' are today practised by all nations, not all of whom are animated by the spirit of nationalism. Nor would such a definition be illuminating, because nationalism itself would

---

[1] G. G. Hodgson: *Economic Nationalism,* The Reference Shelf, New York, The H.W. Wilson Company, 1933. This short book is a compilation of texts from the economic literature relating to economic nationalism. The experimental character of the terminology used appears from the following sentence in the introduction: "At best economic nationalism is an indefinite term, used by its opponents, more than by its proponents." It is of interest to note that any texts reprinted in the book which use the expression "economic nationalism" are posterior to 1930.

remain to be defined. Economic and political nationalism, if they cannot be regarded merely as two aspects of one and the same reality, are, however, so closely related one to the other that we can in no case avoid the necessity of defining the latter if we wish fully to understand the former.

Nationalism, then, is the doctrine which places the nation at the top of the scale of political values, that is, above the three rival values of the individual, of regional units, and of the international community. [2]

Professor Rappard goes on to say that "a nationalistic ruler of a nationalistic state will be more tempted to practise economic nationalism than a liberal ruler of an individualistic state", but also observes that "contemporary economic nationalism... is by no means characteristic of nationalistic states alone." It follows that "it can obviously not be correctly defined solely by reference to [political] nationalism." [3] And so, having discarded the "obvious", but incorrect, definition, our author pursues an inquiry into the economic literature of the past two centuries, and finally arrives at the following definition:

Il we wished to define economic nationalism by its underlying purpose, we should say that it was a doctrine destined to serves the nation by making it not richer, but freer, by promoting not its material welfare, but its independence of foreign influences. Economic nationalism is the policy of national self-sufficiency. [4]

Professor Rappard then proceeds to show how this definition of economic nationalism as a policy destined to promote national self-sufficiency may be justified both by the pronouncements of its leading exponents and by the analysis of the measures taken to attain its aims. The latter are summarized as follows:

First, economic nationalism seeks to limit the nation's consumption to those goods which are the fruit of its own soil and labour. By appeals to patriotism, as well as by the more drastic and effective means of tariffs, quotas, exchange controls, and outright prohibitions, nations are urged to prefer national products and

---

[2] *Authority and the Individual,* Cambridge, Mass., 1937, pp. 77-78.
[3] *Ibid.,* p. 80.
[4] *Ibid.,* pp. 83-84.

constrained to forgo the enjoyment of foreign commodities and services.

Secondly, economic nationalism seeks to promote the domestic production of all those commodities for which the national needs are imperative. ...

Thirdly, ... economic nationalism is apt to raise the cry for more space, that is, for annexations of neighboring or colonial territories. ...

As no measure of restriction of imports, of stimulation of home products, and of territorial expansion can possibly make any state entirely self-sufficient under modern conditions, economic nationalism seeks, fourthly, to secure a favourable balance of payments, and thereby to promote an influx of gold. In this, as all other respects, present-day economic nationalists show themselves to be the legitimate offspring of their mercantilist ancestry. [5]

Thus *economic nationalism* is not only defined with precision but also illustrated through its major policies. Some further elucidations may, however, be in order. In the first place, let us distinguish between self-sufficiency (or autarky [6]), as an objective of policy, and self-sufficiency as a by-product of a policy which has primarily other objectives in mind. Thus, for example, tariff protection granted to some industry for the sake of conciliating politically influential elements results in reducing the country's imports of corresponding foreign-made products and, accordingly, increases the country's self-sufficiency — but autarky is not the deliberate *aim* of most policies of "straight" tariff protection. The protection of "vested interests" apart (which, although it leads to an aggravation of economic nationalism, is not essenially an expression of it), these are the three principal reasons why a country might strive for self-sufficiency:

(a) The desire to be as independent as possible of sources of supply that lie outside the country's control, in order to be strong in war. For most governments which contemplate aggressive warfare, autarky is a prelude to conquest — and,

---

[5] *Ibid.*, pp. 85-87.

[6] Autarky — a word of Greek derivation — is the technical term for self-sufficiency. It will be used frequently throughout this book. See A.G.B. Fisher: *Economic Self-Sufficiency*, Oxford Pamphlets on World Affairs, No. 4, Oxford, 1939.

as will be shown later[7], conquest is a means to achieve autarky.

(b) The desire to achieve a greater degree of diversification of production and a better-balanced national economy. Such diversification is here regarded as a means of increasing both national prosperity and national power. These policies are often considered by their advocates to be temporary, albeit of indefinitely long duration. [8]

(c) The desire to plan the economic life of the country as independently as possible of the condition of the world economy. Here autarky becomes a policy, if not of economic isolation, at least of economic *insulation*.

These motivations and their implications are examined in later chapters of this book. For the present it will suffice to identify each line of thought by the name or names of its leading exponents. Thus the autarky of power and conquest goes back to the days of the mercantilists, but its most consistent intellectual framework was formulated by the German philosopher Joham Gottlieb Fichte (1800). Policies aimed at developing a country's industries by deliberately restricting its imports were first consistently formulated by Alexander Hamilton (1791) and later — and more fully — by the German economist Friedrich List (1841). The concept of economic insulation is much more recent and has many modern advocates, none of whom has been more brilliant or more influential than the la Lord Keynes. [9]

In this century, argument (b) was very often used in the twenties, argument (a) in the thirties (especially by Fascist Italy and Nazi Germany, not forgetting the Soviet Union, which uses it still), while a combination of arguments (a) and (c) is a "creed" very widely accepted since the Great Depression and to the present day. It is a combination typical of the contemporary convergence of economic nationalism and collectivism. Its adherents favour policies of autarky not so much because they desire national insulation for its own sake

---

[7] See Chapter V.
[8] In textbooks, this line of reasoning is usually called the "infant industries" argument for protection.
[9] His principal writings along this line were published in the thirties. See below, Chapter VI.

as because they want to be free from the "disturbing effects" of international economic interdependence. Believing, as they do, in the virtues of States control over economic life, they distrust economic developments which, because they occur abroad, cannot be subjected to national control in the way in which purely domestic developments are so subjected.

IV

Before pursuing any further this inquiry into the nature of economic nationalism, let me comment very briefly on nationalism *tout court*. The subject is wide — too wide indeed to be treated here in any detail. The following two quotations, however, taken from the writings of careful and profound students of nationalism, express a point of view which should be submitted to the readers of these pages.

The first quotation is from Professor Toynbee's *A Study of History:*

Industrialism and Nationalism, rather than Industrialism and Democracy, are the two forces which have exercised domination *de facto* over our Western Society in our age; and during the century that ended about A.D. 1875, the Industrial Revolution and the contemporary emergence of Nationalism in the Western World were working together to build up "Great Powers" each of which claimed to be a universe in itself. Of course this claim was false... Every Great Power also aspired to be a substitute for Society in the sense of being self-contained and self-sufficient, not only in politics and economic but even in spiritual culture. The state of mind thus engendered among the people of communities which constituted Great Powers spread to communities of lesser calibre. In that age in the history of our Western Society all national states, from the greatest down to the least, put forward the same claim to be enduring entities, each sufficient unto itself and independent of the rest of the world. [10]

This tendency, Professor Toynbee noted, was checked through the consequences of World War I. Writing in the early thirties he found that "all States alike are feeling less and less able to stand by

---

[10] Arnold J. Toynbee: *A Study of History*, London, 1934, Vol. I, pp. 9-10.

themselves economically", and that "all but the strongest or the most recalcitrant states are also beginning to feel the same lack of self-sufficiency on the political plane and are displaying a readiness... to accomodate their sovereign independence to the international procedure of the League of Nations Council and Assembly or to some other form of international limitation and control..." [11]

In the later thirties this hopeful tendency was again reversed and *autarky* became the most potent and widespread slogan; and since the end of World War II the quest for a revival of an international consciousness in all nations is marred by the virulence of nationalism in general and economic nationalism in particular.

The second quotation is from the pen of Professor Rappard:

> Nationalism has been defined as a scheme of moral values in which the nation or the nation state stands supreme. On the one hand, the nation is superior to the individual—hence, in totalitarian nationalisms, the repudiation of all political freedoms and the denial of all constitutional rights. On the other hand, the nation is also superior to humanity—hence the opposition to all efforts to organize the international community, the revolt against all endeavours to limit national sovereignty. The deliberate subordination of the individual and of humanity at large to the nation, administrative centralization too, that is to say, the sacrificing of all regionalism to national unity, such, it appears to me, is the fundamental doctrine of philosophic and political nationalism which today dominates and disrupts the world. [12]

This, then, in all its distressing rawness, is the moral climate of modern nationalism.

v

Additional light may be thrown on the notion of economic nationalism by relating this concept to that of "national economic policy". It would seem superfluous to elaborate what surely ought to be clear to all, were it not that symptoms of unexpected confusion occasionally appear in this connection. Thus, to quote from personal

[11] *Ibid.*, Vol. I, pp. 14-15.
[12] William E. Rappard: "Qu'est-ce que le nationalisme économique," in *Introduction à l'étude de Droit comparé*, collection of studies in honour of Edouard Lambert, Paris, 1938, Vol. III, p. 400.

experience, a reviewer discussing a previous book of mine [18] and having reproached me with "never clearly defining" the concept of nationalism, went on as follows:

If we take it [the concept of nationalism] to mean broadly promotion of national interest, it is difficult to square its alleged maleficence with the persuasive argument made for international cooperation as the means of enhancing the selfsame interest. If only the narrow manifestations of nationalism are being attacked and a distinction is inferred between the pursuit of real and illusory selfinterest, the wholesale condemnation must be qualified. Although a policy of co-operation is more prudent than one of isolation, both can be considered nationalistic. [14]

The above is an illuminating instance of how greatly the notions of "nationalism" and "national policy" can become mixed. To resolve the confusion and thereby provide the reader with a further insight into what economic nationalism is, may I be excused for quoting the following observations from an earlier volume of mine; they were written twenty years ago and express the attitude I have maintained throughout my studies of economic nationalism:

In a world divided into a certain number of sovereign States, policies are national. They are national not only when they are independent of policies carried out by other States, but also when national policies of the different States (some or all) are co-ordinated and harmonized with one another. It may seem a commonplace, but it is essential to realize that even policies resulting from an international agreement are national policies. What can be called an "international policy" is a set of co-ordinated national policies, the aims and means of which are combined into an alleged harmonius whole. We can then describe the individual national policies as "internationalism". The difference between that and nationalism is to be found in the fact that the latter subordinates the state of international relations to the realization of purely national objectives. [15]

All policies, then, are national policies [16] — but they can be guided by a nationalistic concept of national interest or by an internationally

---

13 *The Trade of Nations*, New York, 1947.
14 *New York Times Book Review*, June 15, 1947, p. 28.
15 Michael A. Heilperin: *International Monetary Economics*, London, 1939, p. 3.
16 The Social Science Research Council, New York, when appointing in 1934 a commission to study the foreign economic policies of the United States,

inspired concept. A government can adopt policies of autarky, of insulation, of protectionism — or policies of international co-operation or even free trade. The former will be an expression of economic nationalism — not the latter. The relationship between the individual and the state also has a great impact upon the nature of national economic policies directed towards the outside world. The smaller the powers of the government in economic matters, the freer are individuals in their commercial and financial relations, and the less opportunity there exists for practices of economic nationalism. The larger, on the other hand, the government's powers to control and restrict the economic activities of individuals, the more scope there is for nationalistic policies. Indeed, there is a clear connection between *economic internationalism* and *liberalism*, on the one hand, and *economic nationalism* and *collectivism*, on the other. It is these two concepts, *collectivism* and *liberalism*, which I shall endeavour to define, in Chapter II, in their relation to economis nationalism.

VI

The line of thought developed in the previous section of this chapter might lead to a definition of economic nationalism wider than that proposed by Professor Rappard. Thus economic nationalism might be defined as all those national policies which tend to make the economic intercourse between residents of a country and people living beyond its boundaries more difficult than is economic inter-course among people living within the country. Now this definition would include protectionism within the concept of economic national-ism, which thus might appear at first glance to be a distinct advantage. The more restrictive definition, by equating economic nationalism with policies aimed at national self-sufficiency, excludes from its scope policies which *interfere* with international economic relations but *without effectively insulating* a country from the outside world. For a long time my own preference has run to the wider concept, which seemed to me to be "operationally" simpler and more objective than the concept covered by the narrower definition. By degrees,

---

was well inspired when it named this group "Commission of Inquiry into National Policy in International Economic Relations".

however, I have reached the conclusion that the narrower definition is more helpful for the understanding of the modern world. This is so because the major modern phenomenon, that of collectivism, ties in closely with the narrower, but does not necessarily tie in at all with the broader, definition of economic nationalism. The crux of the matter is the interpretation of the nineteenth century brand of protectionism. Is it or is it not to be brought under the definition of economic nationalism?

At first glance the question may surprise or even shock; for was not the long nineteenth century controversy between protectionism and free trade, a controversy between economic nationalism and economic internationalism? In an earlier book [17], I made a distinction between what I called "old-fashioned protectionism" and what I described as "the new economic nationalism". The dividing line between the two I found, historically, to lie in the crisis of economic liberalism in the course of the Great Depression of the thirties. By following that approach to its logical conclusions we are led to a distinction between the nineteenth century type of protectionism, respectful of the free market mechanism, of international interdependence and of private enterprise, and the economic nationalism of an autarkic kind, characteristic of the past three decades and very prevalent today.

It could be objected that Alexander Hamilton, the father of the "infant industries" argument for tariff protection, and Friedrich List, as well as their numerous followers in the nineteenth century, all argued on national and even nationalistic grounds in favour of promoting the industrial development of what would be called to-day "underdeveloped countries", by means of tariff protection. The aim of these writers was to foster industrialization and the diversification of production in the less advanced countries beyond what could be achieved under free trade conditions. Yet not even List — who was by far the greater nationalist of the two — advocated national self-sufficiency. He did not even refer in his writings to Fichte's book *Der geschlossne Handelsstaat* (1800), that early blueprint for the extreme forms of modern economic nationalism (*see below,* Chapter V). Although

---

[17] *The Trade of Nations.*

Professor Jacob Viner described List as "the apostle of economic nationalism" [18], the latter did not advocate any means of economic action more restrictive than customs duties. Specifically, List did not advocate reviving the "direct" controls practiced by mercantilist states, which would interfere with the functioning of the price mechanism, nor, indeed any of the more authoritarian measures favoured by Fichte. Accordingly, while agreeing that List was one of the main apostles of protectionism in the nineteenth century, I hesitate to declare him a forefather of economic nationalism within the more restricted and more recent definition of that term adopted in the present book.

VII

I now turn to what is one of the most important aspects of economic nationalism in the contemporary world, namely, *monetary nationalism*. There is no better way to insulate a national economy from the rest of the world than to cut off its currency from organic links with the currencies of other countries. This can be accomplished either by freely fluctuating exchange rates, or, more expeditiously, by exchange control. It is not my object in the present book to discuss the problem of monetary nationalism in detail [19], but its basic importance in the present context must be emphasized at this point. The monetary systems of the mercantilist era, consisting of, rather than based on, precious metals, did not really lend themselves to policies of national monetary insulation. One cannot but marvel at the intuition and foresight of Fichte, whose blueprint includes (as will presently be shown) the principal tenets of modern monetary nationalism. In brief, national economic planning (for whatever purpose), as widely practised in the modern world, requires the insulation of the national economy from outside influences by means of direct controls on foreign trade and the pursuit of "independent" national monetary policies. Accordingly, there is a basic conflict in our day between, on the one hand, the pursuit of the objectives of

---

[18] Jacob Viner: *The Customs Union Issue*, New York, Carnegie Endowment for International Peace, 1950, p. 94.
[19] See my *International Monetary Economics*, previously cited.

economic nationalism and, on the other, the maintenance of currency convertibility and of membership in an international monetary system based on the gold standard. It is not surprising, therefore, to see that the modern advocates of stimulating by national planning the industrial development of a country, favour monetary nationalism along with other measures, indeed as a condition for effective national planning. More about this in Chapter VII.

To conclude this long discussion of the concept of economic nationalism, the following definition may be proposed: *economic nationalism is a body of economic policies aimed at the loosening of the organic links between economic processes taking place within the boundaries of a country and those taking place beyond these boundaries.* This definition involves the notion of *insulating* — though not necessarily *isolating* — a country from the rest of the world. It involves the notion of a country's seeking more "autonomy" in its economic life than it would have in a well-knit system of economic internationalism. Even though self-sufficiency, in the fullest implications of that term, is not within the reach of most countries (if of any country at all!), a movement in the direction of greater self-sufficiency is possible for any country if it accepts the loss of living standards which such a policy entails. In other words, whereas self-sufficiency is largely unattainable, a quest for self-sufficiency is always possible. This is what is meant by "insulation" as distinct from "isolation". The aims of such policy may, as has been noted above, be military, or they may be peaceable. In the former case the objectives are those of preparing for a war of aggression while remaining able to withstand enemy blockade; or of being in a better position to resist foreign aggression of which one is the victim; or of maintaining one's position in a war to which one is not a party. In the latter case the policy may be determined by objectives of economic development or of full employment or any other aims that national economic planning may have. Whatever their purpose, policies of economic nationalism are most effectively carried out behind the screen of monetary controls, such as exchange restrictions, or of direct controls over a country's external trade. Tariffs are a relatively inefficient method of insulating a national economy and play only a subsidiary role in countries which have embarked on the path of all-out economic nationalism.

CHAPTER II

ECONOMIC NATIONALISM,
COLLECTIVISM AND LIBERALISM

1

Collectivism, as has been stressed above, is at the very roots of economic nationalism in the more restricted sense of that term. But what exactly is collectivism? To define it and its opposite, liberalism, and to examine their respective relations to economic nationalism is the next task before us. Since the terms involved are typically among the "dynamite words" referred to at the beginning of Chapter I, definitions are clearly essential. The need, as will presently be seen, is greater than the ready-made means of satisfying it. Let us begin with *collectivism* and turn first of all to standard dictionaries.

Thus, by consulting *The Shorter Oxford Dictionary* (1936 edition), we find that "collectivism" is a word that goes back to 1880 and is of French origin. (The main body of the 1877 edition of Littré's *Dictionnaire de la Langue Française* has no entry for "collectivisme"; it appears, however in the *Supplément*, as dating back to 1876.) We then learn that it is "the theory that land and the means of production should be owned by the community for the benefit of the people as a whole." This definition is couched in terms of property relations alons, a method that is too narrow today, although it was probably justified in the last quarter of the nineteenth century. But, then as now, the definition raised far more questions than it answered. What, for example, is "the benefit of the people as a whole", how is it de,-fined, by whom, and by what criteria? If we now turn to the compendious *Webster's New International Dictionary* (second edition, 1939 printing), we discover that whoever wrote the relevant entry must have been in a whimsical frame of mind: collectivism is here defined as the "theory of the collectivists", also as "a system based on that theory". To save us from utter frustration the lexicographer adds helpfully: "It is practically equivalent to socialism" (a term which is discussed in *Webster's* at considerably greater length but largely in terms of property relations). Before giving up our quest we turn to the word "collectivist" and find him identified as a "non-revolutionary socialist", a definition for which there is surprisingly little justification either in the literature of the subject or in current usage. From dictionaries let us move on to encyclopaedias. *The Encyclopaedia Britannica* (14th edition) follows, broadly speaking, the brief definition of *The Shorter Oxford Dictionary*, and defines collectivism as the theory that "society and industry should be based upon the collective, or national ownership of land and capital, *i.e.* of the means of production, distribution and exchange. Under such a system, the private ownership of capital would be abolished". Again the definition is limited to the issue between private and public ownership, while questions of economic policy are left out of consideration. None of the definitions quoted so far refers to the relationship of the individual to society, which, it would seem, is the key to the whole problem. It is fair to add that the student consulting the *Britannica* is advised to turn from the article on collectivism to that on socialism, the latter being substantially more complete. "Socialism", we might quote, "is essentially a doctrine and a movement aiming at the collective organisation of the community in the interests of the mass of the people by means of the common ownership and collective control of the means of production and exchange."

Let us look up one more source to which the social scientist (or the inquisitive layman) is likely to turn for enlightenment. The *Encyclopedia of the Social Sciences*, that invaluable compendium published in fifteen volumes in the early thirties, has on the subject of collectivism a thought ful article from the pen of Walton H. Hamilton, a leading social scientist of his day, from which the following is quoted:

> Collectivism is the imposing word to be set over against individualism. It is, broadly, a term for a trend in social development, a program of economic reform, a theory of general welfare and a utopian order of mankind; technically a general label for comprehensive schemes of authoritative control such as socialism,

communism, syndicalism and bolshevism; and, specifically, a name for the trend away from the extreme *laissez faire* of the nineteenth century. [1]

While the other definitions mentioned here were too narrow, this, on the contrary, is far too inclusive. It is also essentially negative. Collectivism is not merely a reaction against something; it is a positive concept of society. It is not enough to say that collectivism is "a word to be set over against individualism"; actually, it is the exact opposite of liberalism. In historical perspective, collectivism is a post-democratic reversion to what in other ages and under the reign of different philosophies was called "absolutism" or "despotism". It is liberalism, individualism, and *laissez faire*, which are, each with its own emphasis, a reaction against the subordination of the human individual to the state and its government.

II

Let us now propose a definition of our own. Throughout this book *collectivism* will be treated as a concept of society which places the collectivity at the head of all social values and subordinates to it all the individuals it comprises. Hence, this concept is favourable to authoritarian as against libertarian forms of political organisation. Louis XIV dramatized his claim to absolute power by identifying himself with the state (*l'Etat, c'est moi*). In our day, the state is being identified with the government in power in societies which are thoroughly collectivized. Such a government — even if originally elected by democratic processes — keeps itself in power by force, after it has lost the consent of the public and so long as it disposes of military and police force. (The public consent might, of course, not have been given to it in the first place.) Collectivism can take many forms: from the relatively mild "Fabian" socialism (and the practices of the post-war Labour government) in Great Britain all the way to the "dictatorship of the proletariat" and the totalitarianism of the Soviet socialist republics. There is one thing in common to all concepts and forms of collectivism, however great the differences

---

[1] *Encyclopedia of the Social Sciences*, New York, 1930, Vol. III, p. 633.

between them may otherwise be: the notion that the individual as such is subordinated to the community at large and to the state.

The dictionary definitions quoted above are mostly based upon the opposition of public to private ownership of the means of production. Public ownership is advocated on the ground that productive resources should be owned by the community for the benefit of the people as a whole, and attention has already been directed to the ambiguity of that phrase. When a community owns something, *who* owns its? Actually, nobody in particular ; and when public ownership is established one soon discovers that, instead of everybody owning the nationalized property, nobody *owns* it. It is *controlled* by those who are the spokesmen of the community as a whole, i.e. the government. When we, anyone of us, own a garden, we can arrange it pretty well to suit our ideas as to what a garden should look like, but in a public park we can neither touch or change anything, nor in any way exercise the right of ownership that, *in theory*, we enjoy as a part of the community. [2]

Public ownership, then, means in practice governmental operations. It is because the theorists of socialism never bothered with "operational" definitions and because there was no socialism in action in their day that they could engage in long disquisitions on public ownership of the means of production without ever finding out what, once established, it would exactly mean in practice. At present, enriched by experience, we know that in the hands of a weak government public ownership means inefficiency, while in the hands of a strong government it means authoritarian rule. But, the reader may well ask, is all this necessarily so? Obviously, some further comments are needed. If all industry (or a good deal of it) and all natural resources (or a good many of them) are publicly owned, this means that the market mechanism, which is a distinctive feature of a liberal economy, can no longer operate freely and becomes entirely frustrated over a large sector of the economy. But in a liberal society, it is the market system which distributes resources among their various uses

---

[2] The above-cited "Supplement" to Littré's *Dictionnaire*, containes the following shrewd comment quoted from the French *Journal Officiel*, November 19, 1876, p. 8423: "Quand chacun connaîtra la part qui lui appartient dans le patrimoine commun, il se rencontrera bientôt quelque individualité peu satisfaite du collectivisme."

and finished products among the various users. If it cannot operate any longer, there arises a need for some alternative system. This alternative is provided by *centralized economic planning*, which, rather than "public ownership", is the most important feature of collectivism. We have seen in Fascist Italy and in Nazi Germany totalitarian governments impose a collectivist pattern upon the peoples of those countries without taking any major measures of nationalization, proving thereby that collectivism can exist without public ownership of the means of production, *provided* the government fully controls the activities of private owners.

The following observations by Sir Alexander Gray (formerly of the University of Manchester), author of one of the best short histories of socialism, will complete our discussion on this point:

> Collectivism had gradually come to denote that type of socialism which concentrates attention on the side of production... By the nationalisation of industry all enterprise is ultimately vested in the State. The private capitalist goes; the critics suggest that State capitalism arrives. All, or nearly all, would ultimately become employees of the State, which, as the unquestioned monopolist in every industry, would be exalted to a place of peculiar power. [3]

> The difficulties of the completely collectivist State are enormous... The State being everything, there would be nothing outside the State... In a world of State capitalism, where there would not even be the satisfaction of changing one's boss, life might be even less pleasant than at present [4].

> The present mania for planning has its dangers, and it may indeed be doubted whether "planning" as understood by the zealous, is consistent with our freedom and our liberties. It may indeed be a short cut to a dictatorship. Let no one delude himself that it is possible to have an economic plan in an isolated chamber, kept rigidly apart from the political life of the country. If we agree to adopt a plan, then either we may not criticise the plan, once it is adopted, in which case the plan becomes our dictator during its currency; or we may reserve the right to criticise and modify the plan, in which case the plan ceases to be a plan as now understood in many quarters. [5]

One more comment before moving on. Collectivism can have its origin in one of two basic types of social movement. It can be the

---

[3] Sir Alexander Gray: *The Socialist Tradition*, London, 1946, p. 495.
[4] *Ibid.*, p. 506.
[5] *Ibid.*, p. 511.

result of a ground-swell of discontent, a reaction against excesses of *laissez faire*, with popular leaders organizing the support of discontented masses for a new form of government and society. But collectivism can also be the result of introducing statism (*étatisme*) into a society, from the top down as it were, the government taking over function after function and power after power, often imperceptibly and without raising any fundamental political and doctrinal issues (as in the case of "planistic" measures adopted during a depression).

Explaining the origins of socialism, Elie Halévy, the great French historian, best known to the English speaking public through his *History of the English People*, makes the following striking comments:

> At the origins of the industrial age, socialists justified their criticisms by the spectacle offered at that time by the industrial part of the north of England. Machinism, which multiplies production, was to increase *the greatest happiness of the greatest number* ; well-being or semi-well-being was to appear in all families. Hours of labour were to be reduced, the machines working faster and faster. Quite on the contrary, one could see a few wealthy people as against thousands of paupers; the hours of work increased (ten, twelve, fourteen, sometimes sixteen hours a day); intensive production, ill-thought-out, brought about overproduction, unemployment, economic crisis. [6]

It is worth while to reflect on how the conditions which gave rise to the birth of socialism were altered in the course of the century or more that followed. And it is worth noting, too, that the widest spread both of stock-ownership (i.e. ownership of means of production) and of the fruits of industrial production, the greatest improvement in the standards of living of the masses, the most substantial reduction in hours of work, in brief, the most widespread distribution of the fruits of technological progress has taken place in the United States, a country which, so far at least, has hardly known an organized socialist movement of major proportions, and where, so far at least, the progress of collectivism has been much less pronounced than anywhere else.

---

[6] Elie Halévy: *Histoire du socialisme*, Paris, 1948, pp. 20-21.

III

Before examining the relationships which exist between collectivism and economic nationalism, let us deal briefly with liberalism,
which, as has been noted, must be regarded as the exact opposite of
collectivism. The entire recorded history of mankind could be written
in terms of the oscillating relationship between the individual and
the state. Or, to put it in another way, in terms of man's perennial
quest for *both* individual freedom *and* a "good society". Benedetto
Croce entitled one of his principal works *History as the Story of
Liberty* [7] — and this title is a terse statement of a very challenging
philosophy of history.

Man, said Aristotle, is a political animal, that is to say, he lives
in society and not in isolation. On the other hand, man has shown
throughout history a great deal of concern over his independence as
an individual and has revolted again and again against political
systems which curtail his freedom to the point of degradation of all
that consittutes human personality. We may, then, define *liberalism*
as a concept of society which is based on a full recognition of the
dignity and the rights of the human person. Liberalism is also an
aggregate of policies which aim at achieving the greatest possible
freedom of the individual that is compatible with life in society, and
which afford the greatest opportunity to men and women, adults and
children, for development and for achievement. Further, liberalism
is an economic system which, respectful of individual freedom and
individual opportunity, promotes the widest spread of material prosperity. Finally, liberalism is the system which, in the industrial age,
best furthers the division of labour, domestically and internationally [8],

---

[7] New York, 1941.

[8] "... un économiste est d'autant plus libéral qu'il a plus de foi dans les
vertus du marché animé et actionné par la concurrence des agents qui s'y
rencontrent, et d'autant plus de méfiance à l'égard des interventions, même
tutélaires dans leur intention professée, de la collectivité organisée. Ainsi,
un économiste libéral aura, en matière de commerce international, un pré-
jugé favorable à tout ce qui le développe, et hostile à toute mesure protection-
niste dont l'effet, comme d'ailleurs le but, ne peut être que de le limiter."
William E. Rappard: "Pourquoi le cas de M. Ludwig Erhard est-il si rare?",
in *Wirtschaftsfragen der Freien Welt*, Frankfurt-am-Mein, [1957].

aims at improving the distribution of income and wealth among all members of society, fights attempts on the part of the more powerful people or groups to reduce the freedom of others by the use of their political or economic strength, and promotes good international relations, economic, political and cultural. [9]

What is the connection between liberalism so defined, on the one hand, and individualism and *laissez faire,* on the other? To the extent to which the human individual is the principal concern of liberalism, one might consider the terms liberalism and individualism as synonymous. The latter, however, tends to place rather too much emphasis on the individual and too little on society; it could, accordingly, lead to an anarchistic concept of society, i.e. to the very negation of society. A liberal society, for all its liberalism, represents a *social order.* [10] It recognizes the need for a government and is generally favourable to (although not necessarily synonymous with) democracy. Although it emphasizes the individual's fundamental right to freedom and is concerned about his enjoyment of the material "good things" in life, a liberal society is not oblivious to the fact that a free individual also has duties towards the community of which he is a part. These are, in the first place, *moral* duties — and it is not an accident that the great liberal philosophers of the eighteenth and early nineteenth centuries were deeply concerned about problems of individual and social morality. [11] Then there are the *legal* obligations, largely revolving round the notion that everybody's enjoyment of his own freedom depends on his respect for the freedom of others. Since equality is not of this world, inequality must not be allowed to destroy the rights and the freedom of the weaker members of society for the benefit of the stronger. Equality of opportunity is a part of the liberal creed. Where moral force does not suffice, the organs of the state must step in and back it up.

This, roughly, is the liberal concept of society and it involves, as can readily be seen, a certain amount of restraint upon pure indivi-

---

[9] Cf. Michael A. Heilperin: *Economic Policy and Democracy,* Public Policy Pamphlet No. 37, University of Chicago Press, Chicago, 1943.
[10] See Jacques Rueff: "L'Ordre dans la nature et dans la société", in *Diogène,* Paris, No. 10, April 1955.
[11] E.g., Adam Smith: "*The Theory of Moral Sentimens*", London, 1759 (i.e., seventeen years before his *Wealth of Nations*).

dualism. Nor must liberalism, so defined, be confused with *laissez faire*. The latter was a reaction against the mercantilist state and its innumerable interferences with the life and the economic activities of individuals. Being a reaction — and formulated as it was by men with strong moral feelings — the *laissez faire* philosophy postulated a well-nigh complete abstention from government interference in the life of society. The concept of the state as a policeman and night watchman had a good deal of vogue in the mid-nineteenth century. In practice, however, it proved rather less than satisfactory since the stronger members of society were far less guided, in practice, by moral laws than had been assumed by the *laissez faire* philosophers. The functions of the state were, in reality, far greater than those of a night watchman even in the mid-nineteenth century, and the liberalism of the twentieth century can never lose sight of that fact. Liberalism, therefore, gives considerably more scope to public policy than does the "pure" *laissez faire* concept of society. [12]

IV

One point in what precedes calls for fuller elaboration. We have noted that the liberalism of the eighteenth and the early nineteenth centuries was a reaction against the all-too-powerful state. It went to the extremes of *laissez faire,* and this, in due course, resulted in a counter-reaction. The reaction against the excesses of *laissez faire* was made on behalf of the weaker elements in society which, left to their own devices, could not hope to hold their own. The immediate result of the Industrial Revolution in England and elsewhere was (as has been noted above) the lengthening of hours of work, the expanding employment of women and children, and the growth rather than the reduction of poverty. Let it be noted, however, that child labour was also favoured by the mercantilists. According to Professor Eli F. Heckscher, one of the greatest authorities on mercantilism, no child was too young in the mercantilist view to go into industry. He quotes

---

[12] As a corrective to the widely held, yet mistaken, view that economists of the "classical school" were all addicted to *laissez faire,* see the excellent study by Lionel Robbins: *The Theory of Economic Policy in English Classical Political Economy,* London, 1952.

Colbert to the effect that "experience has always certainly shown that idleness in the first years of a child's life is a real source of all the disorders in later life", and refers to Colbert's edicts, which in fact amounted to forced labour for children in certain districts of France. Children were also employed, even in the sixteenth century, in the English clothing industry and writers of that century and the next were quite lyrical in their comments on little children earning their own upkeep. "The belief that child labour, whether in fact or as an ideal, was a creation of the industrial revolution is a gross fallacy" — is Hekscher's conclusion. [18]

It is the liberalism of the late eighteenth and early nineteenth centuries which started the protest against inhuman working conditions. Up to a point, early socialism was an extension of liberalism with the object of promoting and protecting individual welfare and human rights. It is one of the misfortunes of history that what might be termed "orthodox liberalism" moved in the mid-nineteenth century in the direction of *laissez faire* whilst early socialism turned towards collectivism.

As already indicated, this unhappy turn of events was due, among liberals, to a failure to realize that the state had positive functions to fulfil even in a society which attached supreme importance to the rights of the individual. The turn taken by early socialism, on the other hand, was due to a failure to recognize that, whereas it was proper for the state to protect the weak, an excessive growth of its prerogatives could not but destroy, in the end, the rights and prerogatives of the individual. The transition from early socialism to statism, can also be attributed to the hold exercised by certain attractive clichés over the minds of socialist writers. The idea that when a collectivity jointly owns land and the means of production, each member of the collectivity owns them, is a notion appealing to the "have-nots"; the truth of the matter is less pleasing, however, for, in practice, it is the government that runs things "on behalf of the community". And when a government runs things "on behalf of the

---

[18] Eli F. Heckscher: *Mercantilism*, authorised translation by Michael Shapiro, London, 1935, Vol. II, pp. 155*sq.*

community", it has an irresistible tendency to become arbitrary and oppressive.

It is beyond the scope of the present study to explain how and by what intermediate stages humanitarian socialism turned eventually into despotic collectivism. Attention must be directed, however, to what strikes me as a basic trend running through developments of the nineteenth and twentieth centuries. It involves a notion that the state has to protect the individual and that it must adopt policies of economic control in order to ensure individual welfare. From there to overestimating the role of the state and to underestimating that of free individual endeavour is only one step, and the social iniquities of the nineteenth century made it an easy step to take. Movement in that direction was inspired in England by humanitarian considerations; in Germany it was also conditioned by the mystical philosophy of the state which, propounded by Hegel and Fichte, has found many followers during the past century and a half. Marx's moral indignation led him to the concept of the "dictatorship of the proletariat", peculiar in theory and dangerous in practical application where it leads to outright despotism. Marxism was to influence and to warp socialist theory and the socialist movement from then on. German socialism developed into a brand of statism with authoritarian overtones, differing therein from the Anglo-Saxon theories of evolutionary or "Fabian" socialism, which were more respectful of democratic principles. British socialism goes back to the Fabian Society, the basic influence behind the Labour Party. Its ideas are refreshingly free from the sinister Marxist doctrines of social revolution and the "dictatorship of the proletariat". They centre around the idea of public ownership of the means of production, an appealing idea so long as its implications are not fully grasped. Once they are fully worked out, however, it appears quite clearly that public ownership cannot be introduced without leading to more advanced forms of statism, i.e. to the centralized direction by the state of the economic activities of society.

Thus, regardless of the road by which it gets there, the socialist concept of society inevitably leads to the supremacy of the state and the subordination of the individual. The institution of private property is so limited as to become well-nigh meaningless (as in

Fabian socialism). Whether state control is established through the nationalization of land and industry or through strict government regulation of the activities of private owners is, on the whole, of secondary importance. The former is the creed of "democratic socialists" (and, in its extremist forms, of totalitarian communists), the latter was the practical policy of the Fascists and Nazis. In either case the individual's loss of direct access to the means of production involves his loss of political rights and prerogatives. That this must be so should really be quite obvious; the following comments by D.W. Brogan bring the point home with particular clarity:

> Czarist Russia was a police state, a censorship-ridden state, a spy-ridden state, but ... there were possibilities of independent thought, action, and information in Czarist Russia that do not exist in Stalin's Russia. There were feeble but genuine organs of independent political activity ...; there was in the last years of the regime a feeble parliament. ... The press, heavily censored as it was, was not entirely controlled and owned by the government. There was a constant movement in and out of Russia of dissident Russians ... And inside Russia there was a large number of people whose immediate livelihood did not depend on keeping on the good side of the government. The opposition, *including the Bolshevik Party,* could get funds from sympathizers because the government did not own all the means of production, distribution and exchange. A Russian millionaire could decide whether to spend his roubles on Cézannes or on Bolsheviks or a mixture of the two. There were in Czarist Russia thousands of men and women with a knowledge of the outside world, with means of leaving and entering Russia, with incomes fairly safe from complete annihilation if they kept out of direct revolutionary activity. These people could and did talk and write. They gave the outside world its main impression of Russia. ... In modern Russia there are no people whom the rulers need fear, whose property or livelihood they need respect. There is a monopoly of the press and of paper and printing facilities. [14]

One could, of course, multiply examples of state control of economic activity interfering with the freedom of individual citizens. Among instruments of policy which, even without nationalizations, effectively limit the scope of individual action, mention should be made of restrictions on foreign payments (exchange control, quanti-

---

[14] D. W. Brogan: *Is Innocence Enough?*, London, 1941, pp. 77-79. Italics in text.

tative trade restrictions) and the widespread use of permits and licences, including what Keynes has called the "socialization of investments".

VI

Although the interference of the government in economic life is as old as recorded history, there has never been anything more inclusive and more sweeping in the past than the type of economic planning and control practised in our own day by the collectivist state. Soviet five-year plans were the pracitcal manifestations of this tendency to plan from a central point the entire economic life of a country. Throughout the twenties there developed a vast literature on centralized economic planning. It was advocated on the grounds of rationality, of equity or of efficiency, always without reference to the effects of planning on the lives of individual members of the planned society. By contrast, opponents of centralized economic planning have repeatedly emphasized the losses in efficiency, cumulative effects of mistakes, and social consequences (including the curtailment of personal freedom) which such a system would entail.

Practical attempts at economic planning which were carried out during the thirties as a means of fighting the depression invariably failed to produce the expected results. [15] This, claimed the advocates of planning, was due to the timidity and half-heartedness of the planners. Less timidity, however, would have produced a more authoritarian rule! Since the end of World War II new opportunities have appeared for collectivist experiments; they all tend to highlight and confirm *the connection between economic planning and economic nationalism*. So long as independent states exist, economic planning must be an essentially national pursuit. How to reconcile the requirements of a well-knit world economy with those of independent national plans is among the most difficult problems that the collectivists of today have to solve. So far, they have found no way out of this

---

[15] Instead, they undermined the workings of a free economy and became, in certain countries, such as Nazi Germany and Fascist Italy, an excuse for introducing political despotism Cf. F.A. Hayek: *The Road to Serfdom*, London, 1944, and the abundant literature to which its publication gave rise.

difficulty and have invariably fallen back upon the practices of economic nationalism.

Having placed the authority of the state above the prerogatives of the individual, collectivists have also placed national planning ahead of the requirements of international order. This conflict was early and very clearly diagnosed by Professor Robbins of the London School of Economics in a book significantly entitled *Economic Planning and International Order*. [16] And the longer the record of practical experience becomes, the more evident it is that in a world of national states, collectivism leads to a great exacerbation of economic nationalism and creates new and well-nigh unlimited opportuities for international dissensions and friction.

VII

But, some readers may object, socialism is an essentially international movement; how, then, can it be considered a source of economic nationalism? This objection cannot be met by saying that we have been discussing collectivism and not socialism, since it is quite clear that socialism is one of the most important manifestations of collectivism. But *is* socialism an internationally-minded movement as well as an international one? It seems to me that here, as so often in the field of social relations, we have been the victims of verbal confusion. There can be no doubt about the international character of the socialist *movement*. Not only have socialist thinkers of the various countries influenced each other and cross-fertilized each other's thinking, but the socialist labour movements of the various western European countries organized the "First International" in 1864 and the "Second International" in 1891. But these ventures were not, in fact, expressions of an international spirit. They were, one might say, attempts at arriving at an international organization of the "underdogs" for the purpose of encouraging each other in the fight they conducted, *each in his own country*, against the "ruling classes".

---

[16] London, 1937. This important book is an expanded version of a series of lectures Professor Robbins originally delivered in the summer of 1935 at the Graduate Institute of International Studies.

The notion of an international solidarity of workers, widely accepted by the socialist movement, was based on several premises, however, all of which have since proved to be fallacious:

(1) the idea that the interests of all workers are solidary within one and the same country;

(2) the idea that the workers' interests are solidary as between the various countries;

(3) the idea that class warfare is a fundamental reality far more important than the internal cohesion of nations or international strife between them.

As regards the first and the second of these three questionable assumptions, one could not improve on the following observations by Sir Alexander Gray:

The assumed solidarity of interest uniting all workers, an essential condition of a class war, is a mere delusion. In a given industry there may be a conflict of interest between the different grades. Station-masters, signalmen, engine-drivers and ticket-collectors may have certain interests in common, springing from their common employment; but equally, and for the same reason, they may have divergent interests. If the station-masters are overpaid, the ticket-collectors may have to do without. Strippers, brushers and on-cost workers may be divided by jealousy as well as united by love. It is equally and glaringly true that workers in different industries may have sharply contrasted interests. A coal strike which successfully raises the wages of miners may lead to dearer coal, hampering employment in countless dependent industries. ... When we approach the assumed solidarity of workers in different countries, the whole argument lamentably collapses ... Competition between countries is reflected in competition between the workers of different countries, and employers and workers have a joint interest in manipulating the tariff (and in doing other things) so that they may keep what they have at the expense of others. Nor is it any answer to say that these things should not be so, and that if the workers were better educated to a higher stage of class consciousness, they would behave otherwise. The point is that the class war is represented as something that is now raging, and has been raging as far back as the memory of man runneth; but the class war postulates solidarity of interests among the workers, and at this moment such solidarity of interests does not exist. [17]

---

[17] *The Socialist Tradition, op. cit.,* p. 500-501.

As for the third assumption, it has been refuted in two different ways. The social history of the United States has demonstrated that a class war is by no means an inevitable feature of an advanced industrial society; and World War I proved that the workers' national feelings are far stronger than their "class consciousness".

Let us look at this matter from another angle. Is it not instructive to note that neither free trade nor any of the other policies aimed at increasing the international economic cohesion of the world has received much support from socialist writers or from trade unions? On the contrary, both writers and unions have frequently supported policies of protectionism as well as restrictions on immigration; they have also favoured the "insulation" of national economies against the rest of the world, as a means of safeguarding national central planning for "full employment" or "economic development". Fichte, who is rightly considered an early forerunner of German socialism, is also one of the leading prophets of autarky. And it is really quite logical that this should be so.

The fact that a number of socialist writers have been favourable, in more recent times, to the League of Nations and to the United Nations must not obscure the other fact that their internationalism has been emotional and political but has not extended to economic policy as such. It is not an accident, either, that the League of Nations, which did all in its power to promote the revival of freer trade and payments and of stable currency relations between nations, was inspired by the philosophy of liberalism, not that of collectivism, while the United Nations, of which the opposite is largely true, has so far proved singularly ineffective in helping rebuild a workable international economy.

It is because collectivism calls for statism and central planning that, in the age of sovereign national states, it has become the major driving force behind economic nationalism. And this force is very strong indeed nowadays over the major part of the planet, and it is extraordinarily dangerous to the peace and the freedom, as well as to the welfare, of all men.

CHAPTER III

ECONOMIC NATIONALISM THROUGH THE AGES

I

The present chapter serves a modest yet important purpose: that of placing the phenomenon of economic nationalism in its historical setting; for thus only, I believe, it is possible fully to measure its significance in our own day.

As the bird's eye view that follows will clearly, albeit very sketchily, show, economic nationalism — or policies similar to it — extends back in time as far as the recorded history of mankind. And its defence is as ancient as political theory. Nor is this very surprising. There would be no barriers to international trade in one of two conceivable cases. One is that of a world organised into one single state, when there would only exist inter-regional and inter-individual, but not international, trade. The other is that of a world divided into many separate and sovereign states — as ours has always been — but in which governments would deliberately abstain, all of them, from interfering with business transactions carried out across national boundary lines by inhabitants of the various countries. In the latter case, free trade would develop as a matter of course, political boundaries in no way affecting the economic relations between people living on either side. Of these hypothetical alternatives, the former has never actually existed, although it has caused rivers of ink to flow, and also rivers of blood. The other was approached, over a short period of time — and only over a part of the world's surface — in the nineteenth century, but so far has only been a mere historical interlude, highly advantageous in material and moral terms to all parties concerned, not sufficiently resilient, however, to survive the manifold storms of the twentieth century.

"Sovereign" constituted governments, whatever their form of organization, their underlying philosophy, their political aims, and the size of the territory and population over which they exercise control, have nearly always been known to interfere with international trade and finance. It is well that this should be realized from the outset, for the goals of economic internationalism, of free trade, of a "well-knit" world economy represent, in historical perspective, a novel and highly revolutionary principle, comparable only to (and intimately connected with) the defence and promotion of individual freedom. It is no accident that the reaction against the highly controlled economic systems of the mercantilist period (sixteenth to eighteenth centuries) coincided with the rise of libertarian philosophies and movements. Nor is it an accident, as will presently be shown, that the reaction against economic internationalism has coincided, in our day, with movements aiming anew at the subordination of the individual to the state.

II

In the pages that follow there is, of course, no claim to provide a history of economic nationalism — a history which, may it incidentally be stressed, sorely needs writing. The development of economic nationalism will merely be illustrated here by some of its highlights. Though we could go further back into the past, let us begin with ancient Greece, where we find not only institutional arrangements but also political doctrines favouring economic nationalism. [1]

Self-sufficiency (which, as shown in Chapter I, is the prime objective of economic nationalism) enjoyed in theory and in practice considerable favour in ancient Greece. Aristotle regarded "political and economic self-sufficiency as a basic prerequisite of the ideal state". Thus, in Book I of his *Politics*, we read:

When several villages are united in a single complete community, large enough to be nearly or quite self-sufficing, the state comes

---

[1] The reader may be referred, however, to the excellent works on prehistory by V. Gordon Childe: *New Light on the most Ancient East*, London, 1958; *What Happened in History*, London, 1952; *The Dawn of European Civilization*, London, 1957, and his chapter on "Barbarian Europe till Roman Times" in *The Cambridge Economic History of Europe*, Cambridge, 1952, Vol. II, pp. 1-32.

into existence, originating in the bare needs of life, and continuing in existence for the sake of a good life. And therefore, if the earlier forms of society are natural so is the state, for it is the end of them, and the nature of a thing is its end. For what each thing is when fully developed, we call its nature, whether we are speaking of a man, a horse, or a family. Besides, the final cause and end of a thing is the best, and to be self-sufficing is the end and the best. [2]

This concern with self-sufficiency runs all through Aristotle's work, and what he has in mind becomes more apparent in Book VII. Having reached the conclusion that the ideal size of the State is for it to be large enough to be self-sufficient but otherwise as small as possible ("the best limit of the population of a state is the largest number which suffices for the purpose of life, and can be taken in at a single view" [3]), he continues:

Much the same principle will apply to the territory of the state. every one would agree in praising the state which is most entirely self-sufficing; and that must be the state which is all-producing, for to have all things and to want nothing is sufficiency. In size and extent it should be such as may enable the inhabitants to live at once temperately and liberally in the enjoyment of leisure. [4]

Self-sufficiency, then, for Aristotle, represents a complete lack of dependency on the outside world, combined with the ability to live a "good life" within the confines of the state. [5] Over twenty-one centuries later this notion was to be taken up, albeit with a very different philosophy behind it, by the German philosopher Fichte, of whom more will be said in Chapter V. Fichte, it should be noted, coupled self-sufficiency with territorial expansion, whereas Aris-

---

[2] Aristotle: *Politica*, translated by Benjamin Jowett, Oxford, 1921, Book I, Ch. 2.

[3] *Ibid.*, Book VII, Ch. 4.

[4] *Ibid.*, Book VII, Ch. 5,

[5] It must be noted, however, that the opposite point of view was also present in the Greek (and Athenian) tradition. Thus we read Pericles' famous "Funeral Oration", as reported in Thucydides' *Peloponnesian War:* "We throw open our city to the world, and never by alien acts exclude foreigners from any opportunity of learning or observing, although the eyes of an enemy may occasionally profit by our liberality; trusting less in system and policy than to the native spirit of our citizens ..." (Ch. II, par. 39, in the Crawley translation). While there is no reference in the "Oration" to commercial policies, we have here a terse statement of the philosophy of an "open society", contrasting with Aristotle's concept of a "closed society" developed in the following century.

totle linked it with his recommendation that the size of the community should be the smallest practically possible. (This is why Fichte, rather than Aristotle, was to inspire, in our own times, Hitler's "geopoliticians".

In turning from political theory to the political and economic practices of ancient Greece, I can do no better than to quote a highly illuminating passage from Sir Alfred Zimmern's authoritative and brilliant work, *The Greek Commonwealth:*

> It was a tradition and a boast of Greek cities to be sovereign States wholly independent of foreign claims. Their fierce love of independence had been nourished by centuries of isolation, and was, as we have seen, one of the strongest forces in the national life. But we shall be merely following the bad example of so many nineteenth century traders and pioneers if we interpret this sentiment in a strictly political sense. If was in origin and essence, in Greece as elsewhere, every whit as much economic as political: for politics and economics, State government and State housekeeping, are to simple people (as they should be to us) merely two aspects of the same thing. So it provided what was for centuries the bedrock of Greek economic policy. If a State was to be independent it must not only govern itself in its own way, but also feed and clothe itself in its own way. It must not only manage its own affairs but supply its own needs. Home rule and self-sufficiency are, in the traditional Greek view, almost convertible terms. How strong was the tradition may be seen by the way it lingered on, years after Greek traders had begun pouring in goods from east and west, in the political economy of the philosophers. [6]

The self-sufficiency idea spread through the Hellenistic world of the Near and Middle East during the third and second centuries B.C. The Hellenistic monarchies in Egypt and Asia Minor, the results of Alexander's conquests and of the disintegration of his short-lived empire, represented a superimposition of Greek political ideas upon a number of very ancient states, each with an old and varied history. One of the Greek influences lay in envisaging self-sufficiensy as the basis of political strength. In fact, the evolution was from "self-sufficiency" to state-controlled trade, and, finally, to commercial hegemony. The impact of these ideas upon the history of the

---

[6] Sir Alfred Zimmern: *The Greek Commonwealth,* 5th edition, Oxford, 1931, pp. 286-7.

Hellenistic monarchies is a fascinating story, told with a great deal of illuminating detail by Professor M. Rostovtzeff in his *Social and Economic History of the Hellenistic World,* to which the present writer is indebted for all that follows on this subject. To obtain the greatest possible measure of economic self-sufficiency Hellinistic monarchies

> strove to develop to the utmost the resources of their kingdoms, mobilizing and organizing all the creative forces of their people and adding thereto new forces, those of Greek or Hellenized immigrants. For the produce of their countries they sought to secure the largest possible market by establishing commercial connections as widely as they could, which meant opening their countries to the rest of the world and putting an end to their economic isolation. The easiest way of achieving this was to control important commercial routes by sea or land and so secure for themselves some measure of economic hegemony as a complement of political hegemony. [7]

It is noteworthy that the principle of self-sufficiency as applied in practice by large states brought, as a corollary, policies aimed at the development of power, not only economic and political, but also military. Among the Hellenistic monarchies it was Egypt which went furthest in the direction of economic nationalism and — this being of particular interest to the modern student — of internal economic planning. As a result, it was the Egypt of the Ptolemies that adopted measures of monetary policy to which the name of "monetary nationalism" can well be applied and which Rostovtzeff describes as the pursuance by the Ptolemies of "their own monetary policy regardless of what happened in this respect in the rest of the world".

He also observes — and this, too, cannot fail to impress the modern student of international economic relations — that "it is very probable that a concomitant of this monopoly of currency was the exclusion of foreign capital from the Egyptian money market". Rostovtzeff further describes how the monetary nationalism of the Ptolemies divided the Hellenistic world into two monetary areas, Egypt and the rest of the said world, and how the isolation of Egypt, so damaging to that country's future prosperity, followed from its policies of monetary and economic nationalism. [8] Internally Egypt

---

[7] M. Rostovtzeff: *The Social and Economic History of the Hellenistic World,* Oxford, 1953, Vol. I, p. 249.
[8] *Op. cit.,* Vol. II, pp. 1294 and *passim.*

adopted, in that period, comprehensive measures of economic planning. The system that emerged bears some striking resemblance to modern totalitarianism. To quote Professor Rostovtzeff once more:

The Ptolemaic reform almost entirely ignored the essence of the Greek economic system: private property, recognized and protected by the State as the basis of society, and the free play of economic forces and economic initiative, with which the State very seldom interfered. These could not be suppressed altogether, for they were among the factors that helped the Ptolemies to achieve their second object, the improvement of technical devices and the development of the natural resources of the country, but they were limited and curtailed in order to bring them into harmony with the general Ptolemaic scheme of centralized State control. Restricted and curtailed as they were, these features never disappeared from the economic system of Egypt, and by the mere fact of their existence they created within it a kind of antinomy of which the Ptolemies were never able to get rid, but which, on the contrary, became more and more apparent as time went on. [9]

This opposition between strict regimentation, on the one hand, and economic progress, on the other, has not been resolved by any country in the two thousand years and more which have elapsed since the downfall of the Ptolemaic regime in Egypt. But in our own day more than one country is becoming involved in the same conflict of objectives that is diagnosed by Rostovtzeff in the above passage. Commenting on Rostovtzeff's findings from the vantage point of 1950, Professor Luigi Einaudi, the great Italian scholar — and the first economist ever to become President of his country — makes the following very pertinent and profound comments:

There is, in the Ptolemaic system of planned economy an essential characteristic, to which great importance should be attached... In the Greek town, the fear of war, of piracy, of revolutions, of confiscations, of liturgies, of forced public services and reduction to slavery weighed like an incubus on the members of the middle class during the last three centuries B.C. ... The system of controlled economy was peculiar to Egypt, or at least was applied there in its complete form; and there it supplemented the other factors of insecurity which were plentiful in the Hellenistic world. At first sight this statement sounds paradoxical. Regulation, programme, plan

---

9 *Ibid.*, Vol. I, p. 273.

of cultivation, are they not beyond the scope of doubt, are they not the opposite of insecurity? ... The insecurity derived from the system of planned economy, in Ptolemaic Egypt, was synonymous with arbitrary power. [10]

And this, says Einaudi "is the worst form of insecurity, worse than the fear of war, revolution and famine and piracy, because instead of the inscrutable will of the gods, it must be attributed to the evil will of Man".

Thus, from the theoretical speculations about self-sufficiency of the Greek philosophers to the exercise of power for the sake of self-sufficiency by Hollenistic rulers, and thence to the establishment of internal conditions of ruthless and arbitrary power, such was the development in the ancient world of the causal relationship between economic nationalism and individual insecurity. This development is not without profound significance for our own day.

III

The economic nationalism of the ancient world did not, of course, destroy international trade; what it did was to substitute state-controlled trade for private trade, with all the consequences such a substitution entails in terms of economic advantage and individual choice. Under certain circumstances, economic nationalism, by enhancing autarky, reduces the absolute volume of international trade; but under other circumstances it merely interferes with its structure and influences its growth along lines which would not be considered sound on purely economic principles. (The case of Nazi Germany shows that totalitarian trade may even be expanding trade — though there the expansion was due to political and military motives; but it obviously was not the kind of trade which would have been developed by the market economy acting freely and concerned with the welfare of the individual rather than with the power of the state.)

It would exceed the scope of this chapter — of necessarily limited length — to discuss the experience of the Roman Empire in terms of

---

[10] Luigi Einandi: *Greatness and Decline of Planned Economy in the Hellenistic World*, Berne, 1950, p. 47.

economic nationalism.[11] Nor is it possible to do full justice to the long, intricate and fascinating developments that took place during the thousand-year span of the Middle Ages. [12] I can hardly do better than quote several passages from the *Economic and Social History of Medieval Europe* by Henri Pirenne, the great Belgian historian who was in his lifetime and remains today the leading authority on this subject:

> Hampered as was all traffic by the multiplication of internal tolls, some compensation at least was to be found in the absence of all obstacles on the political frontiers. It was not until the fifteenth century that the first symptoms of protection began to reveal themselves. Before that, there is no evidence of the slightest desire to favour national trade by protecting it from foreign competition. In this respect, the internationalism which characterised medieval civilisation right into the thirteenth century was manifested with particular clarity in the conduct of the states. ...
>
> The princes of the Middle Ages were still without the slightest tinge of mercantilism, with the exception, perhaps, of Frederic II and his Angevin successors in the Kingdom of Naples. Here, indeed, under the influence of Byzantium and the Moslems in Sicily and Africa, we may detect at least the beginnings of State intervention in the economic system. (p. 91.)

It is the rise of the towns which resulted, according to Pirenne, in the development of "urban protectionism". This took place in the course of the fourteenth century. "Henceforth", Pirenne notes, "the consumer was completely sacrified to the producer" (page 206). The following further comments are of great interest:

> Urban particularism led the towns to hamper large-scale commerce in exactly the same way that they hampered large-scale industry. The decline of fairs in the course of the fourteenth cen-

---

[11] The reader may be interested, however, in turning to Professor Rostovtzeff's *The Social and Economic History of the Roman Empire*, Oxford, 1957. See also the short but well-documented book by H.J. Haskell: *The New Deal in Old Rome*, New York, 1947; and Jules Toutain: *The Economic Life of the Ancient World*, London, 1951.

[12] Cf. *Histoire du Moyen Age*, by Henri Pirenne, Gustave Cohen, Henri Focillon, Vol. VIII: "La Civilisation occidentale au moyen âge du XI° au milieu du XV° siècle", Paris, 1933. Pirenne's chapters (pp. 7-189) were published in 1936 in an English translation entitled: *Economic and Social History of Medieval Europe*. The passages quoted below are from the "Harvest Book" reprint, New York, n.d. See also: *Cambridge Economic History of Europe*, Cambridge, 1952, Vol. II.

tury is not unconnected with the dislike of the artisans for an institution so incompatible with their violent protectionism. ...

But is was in vain that the towns pursued their policy of taxing and exploiting large-scale commerce; they could not escape it, nor indeed did they desire to do so, for the richer, the more active and the more populous a city was, the more was commerce indispensable to it. After all, it provided the townspeople with a great part of their food supply and the crafts with almost all their raw materials. (pp. 209-11.)

But history was not to stand still. "The same fourteenth century which saw urban particularism at its height, also saw the advent of the royal power in the sphere of economic history. Hitherto [royal power] ... had left the economic activity of its subjects to themselves. Only the towns made laws and regulations for them. But their particularism caused them to be continually in opposition to each other ... The princes alone were capable of conceiving a territorial economy, which would comprise and control the urban economies." And so, at the end of the Middle Ages, "whenever it had the power, the State was moving in the direction of mercantilism" (pp. 216-17). Our last quotation from this source shows how the final transition to mercantilism was made:

Obviously the word [mercantilism] can only be used within strict limitations, but, alien as the conception of a national economy still was to the governments of the late fourteenth and early fifteenth centuries, it is plain from their conduct that they desired to protect the industry and commerce of their subjects against foreign competition, and even, here and there, to introduce new forms of activity into their countries. ... It was the beginning of a process which in the long run was destined to throw aside medieval internationalism, and to imbue the relations of states with each other with a particularism every whit as exclusive as that of the towns had been for centuries. (p. 217.)

IV

We now move to a period which, from the point of view of the present inquiry, is of particularly great importance. It extends over roughly three hundred years, the sixteenth, seventeenth and eighteenth centuries, and involves the birth and consolidation of the modern concept of the national state. The economics of that period, in particular the regulation by the state of external trade an behalf of national power, are known as "the mercantile system" or "mercantilism".

Countries which adopted the economic policies of mercantilism had, at least to begin with, authoritarian and powerful governments, absolute monarchies having developed upon the disintegration of the decentralized feudal systems. The rulers of that period had far-reaching powers over the activities of their subjets, while individual liberties were largely submerged. The eventual revolt against mercantilism was associated with the promotion of democratic principles. In England the democratic revolution started in the last quarter of the seventeenth century; in France a hundred years later. The internal policies of mercantilism varied greatly, therefore, as between France (and other continental countries), on the one hand, and England, on the other. There was more similarity in respect of foreign economic policies, i.e. the impact of the state upon the conduct of foreign trade and finance. A separate chapter is devoted below to a more detailed examination of those mercantilist doctrines which have a particular bearing on the national economic policies of modern states.

For the present, suffice it to say that mercantilism evolved for the first time in history a more or less consistent body of doctrines [18] explaining and justifying state action to regulate, control, and restrict various elements of international economic relations. These doctrines, as will be shown later, are inspired by a primary concern for national power and a secondary concern for national well-being. In the nineteenth century, the world having moved very far in the direction of free trade and of economic *inter*nationalism, the mercantilist tradition seemed to be relegated to the historians' domain, while the economic doctrines of mercantilism were looked upon as discredited and discarded curiosities from the past. Since then, instead of moving further ahead in the direction of world order, we have made, through a maze of detours, a turn around ourselves and we seem to be right back where we were two hundred and fifty years ago! Thus Professor Philip W. Buck, a careful student of mercantilism, could write in

---

[18] Although there is no such thing as a *single* mercantilist doctrine.

November 1941 in the preface to his *Politics of Mercantilism* [14] that "modern totalitarianism — an awkward word used in this book to include the Soviet, Facist, and Nazi states and their policies — is in many ways a revival of the ideas and practices of the mercantile system".

Actually, as will presently be shown, the new economic nationalism of the mid-twentieth century stems from two different sources, not from one source alone: one of these is, obviously, mercantilism, the other is the doctrine of "national insulation" which, leaving aside the ancient claims of Aristotle, goes back to Fichte (1800). Of these two sources, the latter, though the less acknowledged and the less known, is certainly the more important. [15]

The mercantilist tradition included certain elements which are not found again in the contemporary world, such as colonialism; and other elements which are very prominent in present-day society, such as concern for balances of payments and for full employment. What is, therefore, particularly important to us today is not so much the entire mercantilist tradition as some special parts of it. These can be described as our mercantilist heritage, and they are discussed in Chapter IV below.

V

The end of mercantilism was due to many causes. Because mercantilism was so intimately related with the state, with state structure and powers, its practical manifestations varied from country to country — as did its eventual contradictions and difficulties. French mercantilism disintegrated with the disintegration of the absolute monarchy. British mercantilism, closely linked with Britain's "old colonial system" (as distinct from the nineteenth century "new" colonial empire, that which was to evolve eventually into the British Commonwealth of Nations), was brought to an end largely by the American Revolution. The Industrial Revolution of the end of the eighteenth century and early nineteenth was another factor instrumental in the liquidation of controls and restrictions characteristic of

---

[14] New York, 1942.
[15] See below, Chapter V.

the mercantilist system. Free trade, heralded by Adam Smith in the year of American Independence, became a reality of British politics about seventy years later, in the age of Cobden and Peel.

When Great Britain decided to give up its agriculture in favour of its industry, it also decided to accept international economic interdependence as a basic fact of life. Such an acceptance could only be made on the assumption of durable peace, an assumption which seemed reasonable during the century when "Britannia ruled the waves" (instead, as a recent wit remarked, of "waiving the rules"). International insecurity produces, of course, economic nationalism. This was undoubtedly a factor in the mercantilist period, as it is again a factor in our own day. Cobden — whose overriding passion was the establishment of durable peace in the world — believed that free trade could make peace secure; we may be somewhat sceptical about this today, but even our own experience tells us that the fear of war or the preparation for war tends to stimulate economic nationalism, while political security is a prerequisite (or at least a concomitant) of economic internationalism. It may also be said (and this anticipates later chapters of the present book) that economic nationalism tends to make peace more precarious and conflict more likely.

Upon the ruins of mercantilism, and notwithstanding the increasing prestige of Adam Smith, new forms of economic nationalism soon began to grow. These took, however, all through the nineteenth century, the form of "liberal protectionism" and not of what we defined in Chapter I as "economic nationalism" in the restricted sense of the term. Although, in one of its aspects at least, the American Revolution was a reaction against mercantilism, as early a builder of the republic as Alexander Hamilton laid the intellectual and practical foundations for a new cause of economic nationalism in his *Report on the Subject of Manufactures,* [16] published in 1791. This report represents one of the most important early reactions against the free trade doctrines of Adam Smith's *Wealth of Nations.* Also — and therein lies its importance — it is the cornerstone of American protectionism. Alexander Hamilton was as fascinated in his day as statesmen from the so-called underdeveloped countries are today by

---

[16] See *The Works of Alexander Hamilton,* New York, 1910.

the sight of a wealthy industrial nation. In Hamilton's time that nation was England and its industrial advance was an attractive and stimulating model for the young republic to follow.

In 1791, it will be recalled, mercantilism was breaking down but free trade existed only on paper. State interference in foreign trade was still the rule even in England. Hamilton advocated the adoption of governmental measures for the encouragement of domestic industries, not because of any concern for foreign trade and balances of payments (he does not seem to have been influenced by mercantilist considerations) but because of his interest in the development of the domestic economy of the United States. This is made quite clear in the following observations in his report:

It is now proper... to enumerate the principal circumstances from which it may be inferred that manufacturing establishments not only occasion a positive augmentation of the produce and revenue of the society, but that they contribute essentially to rendering them greater than they could possibly be without such establishments. These circumstances are :

1. The division of labour.

2. An extension of the use of machinery.

3. Additional employment to classes of the community not ordinarily engaged in the business.

4. The promoting of emigration from foreign countries.

5. The furnishing greater scope for the diversity of talents and dispositions, which discriminate men from each other.

6. The affording a more ample and various field for enterprise.

7. The creating, in some instances, a new, and securing, in all, a more certain and steady demand for the surplus produce of the soil. [17]

It might be noted, by the way, that Hamilton proposed to use government subsidies or bounties to stimulate the development of domestic manufacturers quite as much as — and even in preference

---

[17] Quoted from Louis M. Hacker: *The Shaping of the American Tradition,* New York, 1947, p. 301. See, however, Alexander Hamilton: *Papers on Public Credit, Commerce and Finance,* edited by Samuel McKee, Jr. New York, 1934. Also see Richard B. Morris: *Alexander Hamilton and the Founding of the Nation,* New York, 1957.

to — tariffs to reduce the competition of foreign-made goods. Concerning the latter, he had the following comments to make:

> It shall be taken for granted ... that manufacturing pursuits are susceptible, in a greater degree, of the application of machinery, than those of agriculture. If so, all the difference is lost to a community which, instead of manufacturing for itself, procures the fabrics requisite to its supply from other countries. The substitution of foreign for domestic manufactures is a transfer to foreign nations of the advantages accruing from the employment of machinery, in the modes in which it is capable of being employed with most utility and to the greatest extent. [18]

Although Hamilton had textile industries in mind, his proposition is susceptible of broader application.

There comes a time when the question must be asked whether a fully developed new domestic industry can produce goods as cheaply as they can be imported from abroad, and in as good a quality; and the issue between protection and free trade was ultimately argued on that basis. Hamilton's concern was, however, most of all for the creation of new industries on the assumption that they would be entirely viable when they reached their full bloom. His argument, further developed by later economists, especially by Friedrich List, has come to be known as the "infant industries" argument for protection. To apply it to fully developed industries is actually an abuse of the argument. Although Alexander Hamilton can be considered the father of American protectionism during the first half or two-thirds of the nineteenth century, he surely must *not* be burdened with that responsibility for the protectionnism of the late nineteenth and the twentieh centuries. His arguments (but not his name) are today widely used by spokesmen of the so-called underdeveloped countries, in combination with other much less defensible arguments and policies. [19]

The artificial stimulation of new industries can be defended on economic grounds only if these industries are to receive no further state support once they are fully grown. The argument for increasing the diversity of occupations and skills within the nation can, of course,

---

[18] *Loc. cit.,* p. 302.
[19] See below, Chapter VII.

be defended with the greatest of ease on grounds other than economic. On economic grounds, one must inquire into the consequences of such diversification in terms of the higher prices the man in the street has to pay for what he buys; this is the sole basis on which an economically valid decision can be made. [20]

Although his primary interest was directed towards the development of new industries, Alexander Hamilton regarded his proposals as very advantageous to agriculture as well. He drew attention to the consequences for American agricultural producers of the uncertainties resulting from fluctuations in foreign demand, and he noted that a growth of industry combined with immigration would increase the domestic market for agricultural products. It was Hamilton's opinion that "a domestic market is greatly to be preferred to a foreign one, because it is, in the nature of things, far more to be relied upon". Reverting to that subject on a later page of his report, "there appear", he says, "strong reasons to regard the foreign demand for that surplus [products of the soil] as too uncertain a reliance, and to desire a *substitute* for it in an extensive domestic market. To secure such a market there is no other expedient than to *promote* manufacturing establishments" [21] (my italics).

The "infant industries" argument was further developed, indeed brought to its most perfect formulation by the German economist, Friedrich List, whose major work, *The National System of Political*

---

[20] Alexander Hamilton enjoys great favour today with the American protectionists and many a labour leader. They will (or should) be interested in point 4 of the statement quoted above in which he expresses himself in favour of increased "emigration" from foreign countries to the United States, an objective not very popular with Hamilton's modern admirers. On the other hand, those members of the labour movement who favour economic development through protectionist measures or the maintenance of employment through such measures, may be interested, in the following observations, also quoted from Hamilton's report (where he appears to be partial to one, at least, of the mercantilist predilections):

"It is worthy of particular remark that, in general, women and children are rendered more useful, and the latter more early useful, by manufacturing establishments, than they would otherwise be. Of the number of persons employed in the cotton manufactories of Great Britain, it is computed that four-sevenths nearly are women and children, of whom the greatest proportion are children, and many of them of a tender age."

[21] A point of view shared by the contemporary advocates of national economic planning and of "insulation".

Economy, appeared in 1840. Note the title of that work and compare it with Adam Smith's *An Inquiry Into the Nature and Causes of the Wealth of Nations*: the contrast is most illuminating! Actually, it would be very misleading to place Hamilton and List into one and the same doctrinal "compartment": the differences between them exceed the similarities. There was nothing aggressive towards the outside world in Alexander Hamilton's protectionism; List, however, is very much concerned with considerations of power. Economic policy in his eyes is for the state a means of achieving its full bloom. He envisages the acquisition of a "well-rounded" territory [22], a large population, and a well-balanced economic structure. He also emphasizes that a nation must possess adequate military power to protect its political independence and its trade routes. Unlike Hamilton, List is interested in outlets for surplus population and emphasizes the need for colonies.

The next observation which shows the contrast between the philosophy of List and that of Alexander Hamilton has been brought out by William E. Rappard in his essay on *The Common Menace of Economic and Military Armaments.* [23] Rappard notes that according to List industrial protection "is not the artificial product of political speculation, as the school erroneously teaches. History shows that trade restrictions are born either of the natural efforts of the nation to attain well-being, independence, and power, or of wars and hostile commercial measures on the part of the dominating manufacturing nations." Wars, then, are regarded by List as a frequent source of protectionist policies, and Rappard draws attention to List's conclusions that "a war which promotes the transition from the purely agricultural to the mixed agricultural-manufacturing State is therefore a blessing for a nation ... whereas a peace which throws back into a purely agricultural condition a State destined to become industrialised, is a course incomparably more harmful than a war." [24] Here economic nationalism rears its very ugly (and often hidden) head: far from being a mere adjunct of political nationalism, it

---

[22] Which is highly reminiscent of Fichte (whom List does not quote).
[23] The Eighth Richard Cobden Lecture, given in London on 25 May, 1936, London, Cobden-Sanderson, 1936, pp. 21 and 22.
[24] *Ibid.,* p. 22.

appears as a policy which even welcomes war as a means of attaining certain economic ends.

VII

Once American industry came of age and once German industry became powerful, the arguments of Hamilton and List ought no longer to have been invoked in their countries (although they still were available for the new underdeveloped areas and indeed were to be frequently used by their statesmen). But the protected industrial "infants" continued to cling to the state's apron-strings — or purse-strings — and would insist that protection of infant industries should become the protection of — increasingly powerful — vested interests. It is these interests which are largely responsible for the upsurge of protectionism in western Europe in the last quarter of the nineteenth century and the early part of the twentieth, and for the persistence of protectionism in the United States.

However motivated, nineteenth century protectionism was a considerably milder instrument of state interference with economic life than were the quantitative trade restrictions (coupled with tariffs) practiced in the preceding centuries. Tariffs did not stultify the price mechanism, nor did they disrupt the intricate interrelationships of world markets. They affected the distribution of resources and of industries throughout the world; the "liberal" mechanism of markets and prices continued to function undisturbed. The protectionism of the nineteenth century operated in the environment of a liberal society and at a time when the economic powers of the state were, throughout the western world, at a low ebb. There was in those days a good deal of interest everywhere in an expanding world economy. The growth of trade, the smooth functioning of the gold standard, the sustained flow of capital from country to country, not to forget the easy migrations, all were expressions of the same favourable attitude towards the world economy. Political nationalism, to be sure, was unabated, but liberal democracy was making increasing inroads on authoritarianism, such as the liberalization of the Czarist regime in Russia after 1905. The world economy was in a state of continuous growth and expansion. The clash of powerful nationalisms culminating in World War I took place in what was, for all the growth of protectionism, a reasonably close approximation to a well-integrated world economy.

To say this is not in the least to deny that the widely spread protectionist miasma had very dangerous implications for the future of international relations. World War I disrupted world economic processes and, in conformity with List's prevision, considerably stepped up economic nationalism. It is interesting to speculate on the possible course of events if there had been no war. Would American, German and Russian protectionism have continued to grow and would Great Britain have succumbed to the blandishments of the followere of Joseph Chamberlain and given up free trade? No one can tell, of course, but there is no doubt that even in the absence of World War I free trade would have needed new enthusiastic, forceful, and persuasive champions in the twentieth century in order to continue its course towards complete world economic integration, rather than be eroded by a rising tide of protectionism.

VIII

Trade and war do not mix well. A war on a world scale, a war taxing all the resources of the belligerents, could not but disrupt international economic relations. The international gold standard broke down under the strain, trade and payment controls were widely adopted, trade routes were disrupted, war needs acquired a veto power over the decisions of the price mechanism. Economic nationalism was the real victor of World War I, just as collectivism was to be the real victor of World War II.

We now come to events which are familiar to the older readers of this book, although they are already remote to the younger. The reconstruction that took place after 1918, largely under League of Nations auspices, proved very precarious, owing to the contradictory tendencies prevailing in the world of the twenties. Monetary reconstruction was carried out as the first item on the post-war international agenda; there was a large expansion of international capital movements, especially out of the United States; trade routes were reestablished fairly rapidly. Nevertheless, the foundation of that reconstruction was very tenuous. The monetary reconstruction was superficial and proved to be largely spurious. [25] The revived capital movements were more the product of the bond salesmen's zeal than of the banks' shrewd appraisal of the economic outlook in borrowing countries. Many of these investments carried with them the seeds of default. The combination of erratic foreign investments with the technical faults of the "new gold standard" promoted an inflationary wave, worldwide in scope, with the most devastating depression of modern times following in its wake.

The financial internationalism of the twenties, such as it was, stood in contrast to the increasingly protectionist commercial policies of the period and to the spread of monetary nationalism (of mild expression). True, exchange controls and quantitative import restrictions which sprang up during World War I disappeared again a few years later, but economic nationalism was very strong and growing, both in the old-established countries and in those which either regained their independence or were newly formed at the Paris Peace Conference of 1919. The "new" countries were largely inspired by the "infant industries" argument; the older countries by the protection of vested interests. In Great Britain the increase of protectonist tendencies was a symptom of economic decline; in the United States it was consequence of the failure of Congress, government, and the public to understand the effects of the country's drastically changed position in world affairs. From a fast-growing adolescent, the United States became the new leader of the world economy. It inherited from its elders responsibilities which they, crippled by war, were no longer able to discharge. These were, however, responsibilities which the United States was not yet mature enough to carry out wisely. Hence the twenties with their orgy of indiscriminate foreign lending and simultaneously rising tariffs. Hence, also, the failure to realize that a creditor country must move towards free trade, and not away from it, if it is not to suffer great losses itself while upsetting the international economic balance.

---

[25] Through the substitution of the gold exchange standard for the gold standard, with the "rules of the game" of the former largely ignored and with the price of gold at an unreasonably low level. Cf. Michael A. Heilperin: *International Monetary Economics, op. cit.* Chapter IX.

The *decade of unreason* (as it might well be called) culminated in the most spectacular economic crisis of modern times and socially the most upsetting. It ushered in the destructive depression of the thirties — a complex economic process with internationally interlocking causal connections which still awaits careful, complete, and penetrating study. It has led to a great expansion of collectivist creeds and collectivist practices throughout the world, including the West, and to at least a temporary decline of economic liberalism and internationalism. Economic nationalism reappeared after over a century of decline, first in the form of neo-mercantilism, later in the more extreme forms advocated in 1800 by Johann Gottlieb Fichte. The views of Fichte on national self-sufficiency were rediscovered, or, rather, re-invented, by John Maynard Keynes in 1933. Easily the most influential economic thinker of this century, Keynes at this crucial time placed his immense gifts, intellectual as well as literary, and his great powers of persuasion at the service of economic nationalism (*see* Chapter VI below).

It was, however, not a thinker but a man of action who was to apply the Fichtean blueprint in practice: Dr. Hjalmar Schacht of Germany, the architect of the Nazi economic policies. In the mid-thirties "Schachtian" policies were instrumental in promoting Germany's self-sufficiency, or *autarky,* through totalitarian trade methods which included "peaceful conquests" of several neighbours of Germany in the Danubian basin, a necessary prelude to her military march into Austria (in 1938) and Prague (Spring 1939) and to the wars of aggression started on September 1, 1939. Thus Fichte's blueprint was put into effect one hundred and thirty-odd years after its publication! The "Schachtian" concept of economic nationalism was also instrumental, at least implicitly so, in shaping the foreign economic policies of the Soviet Union, today the greatest outpost in the world of ruthless economic nationalism.

After the end of World War II economic nationalism remained the prevalent tendency of most countries of the world. Although its most extreme forms, those which hark back to Fichte, were limited to the Soviet bloc, many other countries continued to practice strict trade and payments controls in order to insulate from outside influences their national plans for economic development or full employment or, in the mercantilist tradition, to "protect" their balances

PART II

**PROPONENTS OF ECONOMIC NATIONALISM,
PAST AND PRESENT**

SECTION I

THE INHERITANCE FROM THE PAST

CHAPTER IV

THE MERCANTILIST HERITAGE

I

Two major revolutions against mercantilism took place in the last quarter of the eighteenth century. One of them, highlighted by the Boston Tea-Party of December 16, 1773, led to the formation of the United States of America. The other, heralded by the publication by Adam Smith on March 9, 1776, of *An Inquiry Into the Nature and Causes of the Wealth of Nations,* was to lead to the adoption of free trade by England as a national policy some three quarters of a century later. The death of mercantilism seemed as definitive as anything could possibly be. In the doctrinal field it was superseded by *laissez faire,* in the practical field by economic liberalism. Both were checked in due course by the growth of collectivist movements in the nineteenth century and their prevalence in the twentieth. Of mercantilism Proessor Eli Heckscher, its most authoritative modern student, wrote that, once superseded by *laissez faire,* it "has never been able to raise its head again and, indeed, ... no one has tried to revive it." This, he says of mercantilism *as a form of society;* individual ideas of mercantilism have proved to have a far greater vitality than that, and among them "the idea of protection ... has undoubtedly been the most vital of all." [1]

---

[1] *Mercantilism, op. cit.,* Vol. II, p. 335.

The "mercantile system" was the name given by Adam Smith to a conglomerate of economic ideas and policies which, prevalent in his day, he regarded as wrong intellectually and harmful in practice. At the hands of nineteenth century writers the "mercantile system" was contracted into "mercantilism" and became a standard term in the economist's vocabulary. Thus "mercantilism" is a name given, after the fact, to a long period of economic thought and practice. Chronologically, mercantilism covers three centuries, the sixteenth, seventeenth and eighteenth; geographically, its scope includes England and the continental countries of western Europe. It was a system of great complexity. Its manifestations and expressions varied not inconsiderably in time and in space. It may even be questioned whether a single concept can cover so much territory. Professor Heckscher was led by his studies to the conclusion that mercantilism had enough of a "fundamental outlook, uniform in essence, which was expressed in all [its] measures". A uniformity, he found, "does exist, though certainly never without inconsistencies and not always clear even to the people involved". He concluded that mercantilism must be treated "as a uniform, coherent system and not merely as a chronologically determined period". [2] As far as I am able to ascertain, this is the view of the principal contemporary students of mercantilism and it is in this spirit that the discussion that follows is conducted.

But what *is* mercantilism? In the popular mind, it is most closely associated with the determination of a country to accumulate gold and silver by means of a "favourable" balance of trade, this favourable balance to be sought by means of trade restrictions of various kinds. It is because this represents the popular concept of mercantilism that its revival was so generally heralded during the decade of the thirties, when countries — all of them — competed for an export surplus, or in our own days, when many of them are so greatly concerned about the acquisition of gold-convertible dollars.

We shall presently see that there was more to mercantilism than this; there is no doubt, however, that the popular view is largely justified in its belief, for these were the features of mercatilism which contributed most to the intellectual and political reactions against it.

---

[2] *Ibid.,* Vol. I, p. 21.

As good a way as any to explain what mercantilism was is to quote the criticism levied against it by Adam Smith. His attack was directed against those features of the system which he considered to be intellectually absurd or politically dangerous. Considering that he lived at a time when mercantilism was still the ruling system, that he took part in many of the intellectual debates of his day, and that he had a very keen perception of practical realities, the judgement of Adam Smith deserves to be heard wherever mercantilism is discussed in our own times:

The two principles being established, ... that wealth consisted in gold and silver, and that those metals could be brought into a country which had no mines only by the balance of trade, or by exporting to a greater value than it imported; it necessarily became the great object of political economy to diminish as much as possible the importation of foreign goods for home consumption, and to increase as much as possible the exportation of the produce of domestic industry Its two great engines for enriching the country, therefore, were restraints upon importation, and encouragements to exportation.

The restraints upon importation were of two kinds.

First, restraints upon the importation of such foreign goods for home consumption as could be produced at home, from whatever country they were imported.

Secondly, restraints upon the importation of goods of almost all kinds from those particular countries with which the balance of trade was supposed to be disadvantageous.

These different restraints consisted sometimes in high duties, and sometimes in absolute prohibitions.

Exportation was encouraged sometimes by drawbacks, sometimes by bounties, sometimes by advantageous treaties of commerce with foreign states, and sometimes by the establishment of colonies in distant countries.

Drawbacks were given upon two different occasions. When the home-manufactures were subject to any duty or excise, either the whole or a part of it was frequently drawn back upon their exportation; and when foreign goods liable to a duty were imported in order to be exported again, either the whole or a part of this duty was sometimes given back upon such exportation.

Bounties were given for the encouragement either of some beginning manufactures, or of such sorts of industry of other kinds as were supposed to deserve particular favour.

By advantageous treaties of commerce, particular privileges were procured in some foreign state for the goods and merchants of the country, beyond what were granted to those of other countries.

By the establishment of colonies in distant countries, not only particular privileges, but a monopoly was frequently procured for the goods and merchants of the country which established them.

The two sorts of restraints upon importation above-mentioned, together with these four encouragments to exportation, constitute the six principal means by which the commercial system proposes to increase the quantity of gold and silver in any country by turning the balance of trade in its favour. [8]

II

This was Adam Smith's view of the system against which he launched his devastating, and eventually successful, attack. It might be noted, in passing, that it were the colonial policies of mercantilism and the monopoly power they conferred upon British merchants that aroused the greatest resentments and were instrumental in the advent of the American Revolution. Paradoxically, as has already been stressed in Chapter III, the new American republic did not embrace the free trade doctrines of Adam Smith; it may even be doubted that the connection between the two reactions against mercantilism, noted at the beginning of the present chapter, were even perceived by the fathers of the republic.

"Wee must ever observe this rule; to sell more to strangers yearly than wee consume of theirs in value." Such was, in the words of Thomas Mun, the quintessence of the mercantilist policy. [4] "It would be too ridiculous to go about seriously to prove that wealth does not consist in money, or in gold and silver; but in what money purchases, and is valuable only for purchasing." This is the reply of Adam Smith. [5]

The first contrast, therefore, between the mercantilist conceptions and those of later times relates to the notion of wealth. Mercan-

---

[8] Adam Smith: *The Wealth of Nations*, Cannan edition, London, 1930, Vol. I. pp. 416-17.
[4] Thomas Mun: *England's Treasure by Forraign Trade*, written about 1628, published in 1664. Oxford reprint, 1949, p. 5.
[5] *The Wealth of Nations, op. cit.*, Vol. I, p. 404.

tilists associated wealth with the possession of precious metals. Their successors regarded as wealth the goods and services which people consume and the means of producing them.

Because mercantilists attached such importance to the importation of precious metals into the country, they aimed at an excess of exports over imports as a means of achieving the inflow of gold and silver. Since, however, movements of precious metals could take place only if one country were to lose some of its stock to the benefit of another, it was considered by the mercantilists that what was one country's advantage in trade had to be another country's disadvantage. The notion of mutually beneficial trade can arise only out of a realization that what matters in trade is the exchange of goods and not the acquisition of cash. The following few lines from *The Wealth of Nations* point out the contrast between the mercantilist concepts and those of Adam Smith. Similar views can be found in the writings of David Hume, the great philosopher, predecessor and friend of Adam Smith.

> It is not by the importation of gold and silver, that the discovery of America has enriched Europe. ... By opening a new and inexhaustible market to all the commodities of Europe, it gave occasion to new divisions of labour and improvements of art, which, in the narrow circle of the ancient commerce, could never have taken place for want of a market to take off the greater part of their produce. ... The commodities of Europe were almost all new to America, and many of those of America were new to Europe. A new set of exchanges, therefore, began to take place which had never been thought of before, and which should naturally have proved as advantageous to the new, as it certainly did to the old continent. [6]

Because mercantilists believed that a country's gain in trade must be matched by another country's loss, trade itself became an abundant source of friction and conflict. But the three centuries of mercantilism were also the period in which modern states were being formed on the ruins of feudalism, and this formation of states had also as its counterpart instability and conflict. In order better to understand the economic ideas of mercantilism, it is necessary to place it against the background of the history of these three hundred years, and this is what is done by its most prominent students.

---

[6] *The Wealth of Nations, op. cit.*, Vol. I, pp. 413-14.

III

It is only fair to note that the late Professor Edwin Cannan of the University of London, the editor of the best modern edition of *The Wealth of Nations*, protested against a broadening of the concept of mercantilism:

> ... the "mercantile theory" should be the doctrine that States must not leave the balance of trade to take care of itself, but must encourage exportation and discourage importation, and "mercantilism" should be [according to the context] either this theory or the practice which it recommends. This is quite a convenient sense for the term and I fail to see any convenience whatever in the sense which some German writers and English writers following them have given to mercantilism by treating it as equivalent to economic nationalism inspired by military consideration. [7]

Whatever the convenience of the more restrictive interpretations of the term, there are great benefits to be derived from the broader interpretation when trying to establish the exact impact of the mercantilist heritage upon our own doctrines and practices.

This broader definition mercantilism in terms of the national state seeking by methods of economic control to secure its own unity and power underlies Professor Heckscher's monumental work on the subject [8], which must be regarded as the most important guide to this long and intricate period in the history of economic thought and practice. Professor Heckscher defines mercantilism in five different and concurrent ways. Mercantilism is, in the first place, a system of internal national unification [9]; it is, second, a system of power; third, a system of protection; fourth, a monetary system; and finally, a conception of society. It would go far beyond the scope of the present chapter to elaborate on all these aspects of mercantilism; it is important, however, to realize that elements of the mercantilist doctrines which are of special concern to us in the present context are an integral part of a larger and more inclusive system. Indeed, there are vagaries of mercantilism which could not be understood

---

[7] Edwin Cannan: *A Review of Economic Theory*, London, 1930, p. 13.
[8] *Mercantilism, op. cit.*
[9] This he regards as so important an aspect of the system that the entire first volume of his work is devoted to it.

otherwise; or, more correctly, there are mercantilist doctrines which are reasonable enough as parts of the entire system, but which, taken out of it, acquire all the qualities of the absurd.

Thus it must be realized that in their quest to establish unified national states, mercantilist statesmen were fighting *both* against the universalist traditions inherited by the Middle Ages from the old Roman Empire *and* against the excessive particularism that followed upon the disintegration of feudalism. The reaction against universalism was very general in the sixteenth and seventeenty centuries, especially in the religious field, and it had political concomitants. To assert itself against rivals in the quest for territory and power, the modern national state had to be consolidated and strong within. To achieve that unity was one of the main objectives of statescraft in the mercantilist period. It is interesting to note, with Professor Heckscher, that mercantilism "had to leave much of its work of unification for its successors to complete". [10]

As a policy of power, mercantilism "followed two different methods; the first consisted in deflecting economic activity directly towards the particular ends demanded by political, and more especially military, power; the second in creating a kind of reservoir of economic resources generally, from which the policy of power could draw what it required". [11] The first method involved the use of comprehensive economic controls throughout the national economy. In contrast with what was to follow in the age of liberalism and *laissez faire,* although not so much in contrast with what came before, mercantilism involved comprehensive government regulation of economic life. The second method let to what was one of mercantilism's most important features: its concept of colonialism.

Colonies "opened up the possibility of providing a system of supply within a self-contained empire". [12] Here, as we might have expected, entered the self-sufficiency aspect of mercantilism. This aspect never became its dominant feature, but it has resulted in the desire of metropolitan countries to acquire and control outlying territories. On that aspect, our guide Heckscher has an interesting

---

[10] *Mercantilism, op. cit.,* Vol. I, p. 456.
[11] *Ibid.,* Vol. II, p. 31.
[12] *Ibid.,* Vol. I, p. 40.

comment to offer; the policy of self-sufficiency had the function of preventing the colonies "from so developing their potentialities that they would be able to stand on their own feet and become politically independent". [18]

Although this explains the resentments which were to lead to revolutions and wars of independence, it is not one on which we need to dwell at great length in this book. Having noted it, we must turn to the mercantilist conceptions of money and of foreign trade. That mercantilism never quite succumbed to the temptation to seek national self-sufficiency was presumably due to the importance attached to precious metals. To obtain these — not only symbols of wealth but wealth itself — foreign trade was indispensable. This is an important point to note, for the self-sufficiency ideal would rule out foreign trade as essentially undesirable, whereas mercantilism regarded foreign trade as an important method of acquiring wealth (on condition, of course, that it produced an export surplus and thereby an influx of precious metals). There was more agreement between the mercantilists and Adam Smith on the importance of foreign trade than between them and the advocates of national self-sufficiency, such as Fichte. The contrast is important to note, for in the period of neo-mercantilism in the 1930's the idea that, as a matter of sound national policy, foreign trade should be kept at the lowest possible level was widely accepted in intellectually influential circles.

The attraction of gold and silver is not a very easy one to understand otherwise than in relation to military power in the anticipated international strife. A country which wanted to command resources lying outside its boundaries needed precious metals with which to make payments, especially at a time when the credit mechanism was in its infancy. In an age of professional armies gold and silver were also the only means by which a ruler could acquire and hold the services of mercenaries. Hence precious metals were important, in power terms, as a war chest. This argument in favour of acquiring gold and silver is very persuasive and it is all the more interesting to read in the studies of Professor Jacob Viner, another leading authority on mercantilist literature, that in England at least "there

---

[18] *Ibid.,* Vol. II, p. 41.

is little mention of state treasure in the mercantilist literature and its use as an argument for a favourable balance of trade is extremely rare". [14] This, however, should not by itself lead to discard the explanation, the less so as Professor Viner himself observes that "there are... passages in the mercantilist literature which may have state treasure in mind, even though they do not explicitly refer to it. Such perhaps are the frequent references to money as the 'sinews of war', and especially to its importance in diplomacy and in conducting war in foreign territory with mercenary troops". [15]

It is all very well to attribute the mercantilist policies to a confusion between money and wealth; it is very difficult to suppose that for three hundred years or so economic policies would be conducted in a certain fashion *solely* because of such a misconception. The relationship between the possession of precious metals in those days and the country's power in war is too important to be easily brushed aside. It stands to reason that should, at another point in time, governments again be concerned with power and anticipate conflict, they would so direct their economic and commercial policies as to acquire either gold or other resources of military significance. Although the mercantilist literature did not apparently refer to such "other resources", they are included in the foregoing sentences as a means of bringing mercantilism, as it were, up to date on that particular point. Given the motivation, manifestations may vary in detail but not in essence.

IV

We now come to another aspect of mercantilism which has considerable bearing upon our own times, namely, its views on protection and employment. It appears from the studies carried out by Heckscher and others that the acquisition of precious metals was not the only reason for the protectionist policies of the mercantile system. Actually, and this is a point to which scholars like Heckscher attach a great deal of importance, mercantilists were animated by a "fear

---

[14] Jacob Viner: *Studies in the Theory of International Trade*, New York, 1937, p. 23.
[15] *Ibid.*, p. 25.

of goods". This notion he explains as follows: "People were ... influenced simply by a naive fear of buying and an equally naive eagerness for selling. The most extreme formulation of this attitude is, perhaps, to be found in the writings of Johann Joachim Becher, the most famous of German mercantilist authors. The third of his 'mercantilist rules and axioms' was 'that it is always better to sell goods to others than to buy goods from others, for the former brings a certain advantage and the latter inevitable damage'." And Heckscher adds not unreasonably: "It was hardly possible to push the argument any further than that." [16]

To state this argument in its extreme form is to reveal its utter absurdity. It is less absurd, however, for a country to try to expand its exports by subsidy, exchange depreciation and other devices, while at the same time erecting higher and more insuperable barriers to imports? Yet, wasn't this exactly what most countries were doing during the depression of the thirties? "Export", notes Heckscher, "was an end in itself." [17] A strange delusion, surely. And yet how much effort has to be spent *in our own times* in the United States on trying to persuade politicians and the public that trade is a two-way street and that a country cannot sell abroad and be paid unless it buys too. It seems that some elements, at least, of the mercantilist heritage — and not the most sensible ones at that — are still with us today.

The next comment by our guide through the mercantilist jungle is of particularly great interest: "The mercantilist 'fear of goods' was nourished, among other things, by the idea of creating work at home and of taking measures against unemployment." [18] The mercantilist concern about unemployment had led to further measures against imports, since imported goods might displace home produce and reduce employment. This concern seems to go back very far in modern history, for Heckscher quotes an English Act of Parliament of 1455 placing the blame for unemployment in the silk industry on

---

[16] *Mercantilism, op. cit.,* Vol. II, p. 116.
[17] *Ibid.,* Vol. II, p. 118. Heckscher also quotes a saying which he frequently finds in the French mercantilist literature, to the effect that "one should unburden the kingdom of its goods" (*décharger le royaume de ses marchandises*), p. 116.
[18] *Ibid.,* Vol. II, p. 121.

foreign competition, while a later Act, of 1463, stated that "all workers in the silk industry, both men and women, are impoverished by the lack of occupations" due to imports. [19] Keeping out foreign goods for the sake of creating employment at home seems to have been a frequently recurring argument in the mercantilist literature. Although the attitude of mercantilist to labour was at great variance with the contemporary view — they generally believed in low wages and child labour — the connection in their doctrines between trade restrictions and the furtherance of employment has a very modern ring to it.

Reference has already been made to the mercantilist notion that in trade transactions there must always be a loser and a winner. "*Within* the State", Heckscher remarks, "mercantilism pursued thoroughgoing dynamic ends. But the important thing is that this was bound up with a static conception of the total economic resources in the world; for this it was that created that fundamental disharmony which sustained the endless commercial wars. Both elements together implied that the position of a particular country could change and was capable of progress, but that this could only happen through acquisitions from other countries. This was the tragedy of mercantilism. Both the Middle Ages with their universal static ideal and *laissez faire* with its universal dynamic ideal avoided this consequence. Without grasping this it is impossible to understand mercantilism either in theory or practice." [20]

It was the mercantilist insistence on a gold influx as the main object of trade which led to the doctrine of one-sided trade advantage and to the practice of trade wars. Adam Smith — and David Hume before him — exposed this fallacy of the mercantilists. The following passage from Hume's essay "The Jealousy of Trade" is a brilliant refutation of one of the most unfortunate mercantilist doctrines:

> The increase of domestic industry lays the foundation of foreign commerce. Where a great number of commodities are raised and perfected for the home market, there will always be found some which can be exported with advantage. But if our neighbours have

---

[19] *Ibid.*, Vol. II, p. 122.
[20] *Ibid.*, Vol. II, p. 25.

no art or cultivation, they cannot take them; because they will have nothing to give in exchange. ...

Nor need any State entertain apprehensions, that their neighbours will improve to such a degree in every art and manufacture, as to have no demand from them. Nature, by giving a diversity of geniuses, climates, and soils to different nations, has secured their mutual intercourse and commerce, as long as they all remain industrious and civilized. Nay, the more the arts increase in any State, the more will be its demands from its industrious neighbours. The inhabitants, having become opulent and skilful, desire to have every commodity in the utmost perfection; and as they have plenty of commodities to give in exchange, they make large importations from every foreign country. The industry of nations from whom they import receives encouragement; their own is also increased, by the sale of the commodities which they give in exchange. [21]

It is a token of the prevalence of the mercanlist concepts in our own midst that the above passage still does not strike us today as a commonplace, and that all of us who stand for freer trade have to use similar arguments in the controversies in which we become engaged. David Hume was by no means a free trader; he was in point of fact a moderate protectionist himself. What he objected to was the fear of mercantilist governments at seeing the growth of the prosperity and welfare of other countries. The conclusion of his essay, in all its forcefulness and eloquence is one of the classic pages of economic literature:

Were our narrow and malignant politics to meet with success, we should reduce all our neighbouring nations to the same state of sloth and ignorance that prevails in Morocco and the coast of Barbary. But what would be the consequences? They could send us no commodities; they could take none from us: our domestic commerce itself would languish for want of emulation, example, and instruction: and we ourselves should soon fall into the same abject condition to which we had reduced them. I shall therefore venture to acknowledge that, not only as a man, but as a British subject, I pray for the flourishing commerce of Germany, Spain, Italy, and even France itself. I am at least certain that Great Britain, and all those nations, would flourish more, did their sovereigns and ministers adopt such enlarged and benevolent sentiments towards each other. [22]

---

[21] David Hume: *Essays,* London, The New Universal Library edition, p. 238.
[22] *Ibid.,* p. 240.

Because a favourable attitude towards free trade is often confused with a lack of patriotism, the concluding lines are particularly worth quoting, and the reader will note, in Chapter VI, the contrast between Hume's final sentences and Keynes' opinions expressed in his *General Theory,* which put the blame for wars on trade, a curious mercantilist throwback. Adam Smith, as usual, has the clinching phrase, the *mot juste,* on this subject:

> The wealth of a neighbouring nation..., though dangerous in war and politics, is certainly advantageous in trade. [28]

Adam Smith also observes, very much in Hume's vein, that "a nation that would enrich itself by foreign trade, is certainly most likely to do so when its neighbours are all rich, industrious, and commercial nations. ... The modern [i.e., mercantilist] maxims of foreign commerce, by aiming at the impoverishment of all our neighbours, so far as they are capable of producing their intended effect, tend to render that very commerce insignificant and contemptible." [24]

In the field of foreign trade policy, there is another mercantilist concept which must be mentioned in the present discussion. It is the idea that exports should be made a condition for imports. Heckscher finds the earliest provision of this kind in pre-mercantilist times already, in a treaty between Venice and Ancona of 1264 stipulating that the proceeds of goods sold to Venice be used by Ancona only for purchases in Venice. [25] This is the practice which, since the 1930's, has been called, bilateralism. Adam Smith included it in his indictment, in a passage which remains a classic criticism of a malpractice that, to the great detriment of all concerned, is again very widespread in our days:

> The restraints upon the wine trade in Great Britain ... favour the wine trade of Portugal, and discourage that of France. The Portuguese, it is said, indeed, are better customers for our manufactures than the French, and should therefore be encouraged in preference to them. As they give us their custom, it is presented, we should give them ours. *The sneaking arts of underling tradesmen are thus erected into political maxims for the conduct of a great empire;* for

28 *The Wealth of Nations, op. cit.,* Vol. I, p. 458.
24 *Ibid.,* p. 459.
25 *Mercantilism, op. cit.,* Vol. II, p. 140

it is the most underling tradesmen only who make it a rule to employ chiefly their own customers. A great trader purchases his goods always where they are cheapest and best, without regard to any little interest of this kind. [26]

V

The temptation to speak of other aspects of mercantilism is indeed very great. Since, however, we are primarily interested in the mercantilist heritage for our times rather than in mercantilism *per se*, we have gone far enough in quoting, chapter and verse, the mercantilists themselves, the expert historians who have written about them, and their early influential opponents. What then, exactly, is the mercantilist heritage? Let us begin by saying what it is not. It is not the colonialism of the mercantilist era; that is past history, superseded by other developments. In a sense, free trade paved the way for the downfall of colonialism even though Great Britain built an empire at the very time she was promoting free trade throughout the world. But then Britain's colonial empire developed into the British Commonwealth of Nations, an evolution that is still under way. The break-up of empires and the end of colonialism is a characteristic of our times. Nor is internal unification an object of major concern on the part of governments, at least of the western countries, and in the countries where it remains an objective, such as the Soviet Union or China, totalitarianism has taken the place of mercantilism. The nineteenth century having brought about national unifications, there is no mercantilist heritage to carry forward.

The third and basic concern of mercantilism, over the acquisition of precious metals, although still present — especially in times of crisis — no longer plays the important role it had in days gone by. In the nineteenth century this concern was largely overcome. The function of precious metals was to circulate, not to stand still. Under the rules of the gold standard, a country would regard losses of gold as much a part of the game as gold earnings. The value of trade consisted not in the balance but in the volume. But with the breakdown of monetary internationalism we are partly back where we were in older days. In the thirties there was a great recrudescence of

---

[26] *The Wealth of Nations, op. cit.,* Vol. I, p. 457 (italics added).

mercantilist policies for the purpose of creating or accumulating monetary reserves, and today restrictive trade policies are applied by many countries for the same purpose. [27]

The mercantilist heritage consists, however, primarily of other elements than those already mentioned. They are the following:

(1) The deliberate management of balances of payments, instead of allowing them "to take care of themselves".

(2) The promotion of domestic employment by restricting imports and promoting exports.

(3) Deliberate state action to control the structure and the volume of imports and exports (and of financial operations as well, which played a relatively small role before the nineteenth century).

(4) The manifold practices of protectionism and the remaining vestiges of the idea that it is better for a country to sell abroad than to buy abroad.

(5) The concept that one should buy from one's customers, a relatively minor element in the mercantilist doctrines but one that has blossomed in our day into "bilateralism".

(6) The concept that it is the raison d'état rather than individual decisions which should guide the country's foreign economic relations.

This, then, is our inheritance from mercantilism. That it all adds up to economic nationalism hardly needs saying. What needs very much saying, however, is that although the mercantilist heritage carries with it the notion of the state's superiority over the individual, it would be greatly overstating the case to say that modern collectivism has mercantilist roots. We must look elsewhere for theories which regarded the determination, regulation, and control of every aspect of individual activity and of economic life as proper functions of the state. These we shall find in the writings of Johann Gottlieb Fichte.

---

[27] Instead of gold and silver, as in mercantilist times, we say today dollars and gold but the principle is the same whenever the size of these reserves causes the government of a country deliberately to manipulate its foreign trade.

CHAPTER V

FICHTE'S BLUEPRINT FOR AUTARKY

It is the principal conclusion of the studies underlying the present book that, in our age, collectivism is the mainspring of economic nationalism. While, historically, this link is of relatively recent origin, analytically it goes back over a century and a half. Its blueprint was the child of the fertile mind of Johann Gottlieb Fichte (1762-1814) and appears in a relatively obscure tract, published in 1800 by that famous German philosopher under the intriguing title, *The Closed Commercial State*. [1]

Fichte's fame is that of a philosopher and of a leading champion, in the era of the Napoleonic wars, of German nationalism. His principal works deal with ethics and with the philosophy of science, while his *Speeches to the German Nation* are a classic of German political literature. His excursion into the realm of political economy seems to have been an isolated episode, without any response from his contemporaries. Fichte wrote *The Closed Commercial State* fully realizing that it would get no response from practising statesmen. His thesis was that — in the interest of peace — countries should be completely isolated from one another in all but cultural relations. The means of action he recommended for the achievement of such complete isolation were very drastic and stood in sharp contrast to the liberal trend of the times. It is not surprising, therefore, that his book has remained an obscure curiosity ever since its publication. In Germany, Fichte came eventually to be considered as an early forerunner of state socialism, a verdict confirmed by modern

---

[1] Johann Gottlieb Fichte: *Der Geschlossne Handelsstaat*, Tubingen, 1800. Republished by the Gustav Fischer Verlag in Jena, 1920, with a preface by Professor Heinrich Waentig. The page references that follow are to the latter edition.

historians of socialism, such as Sir Alexander Gray in his book *The Socialist Tradition*. [2] Outside Germany, *The Closed Commercial State* remained largely unknown. It is characteristic that all the space given to Fichte in the compendious and authoritative history of economic doctrines by Gide and Rist is a footnote (albeit a lengthy one) in the chapter on State socialism, where his book is described as "very curious". [3] Quincy Wright's voluminous *Study of War* [4] makes practically no reference to Fichte and does not even mention his *Closed Commercial State*. Noteworthy too is the fact that there seems to exist neither an English nor a French translation of this book, whose ponderous and involved style in its original German provides little inducement for potential readers to come to grips with it.

After over a century of neglect, Fichte began to attract some attention in his own land during World War I, when Germany, her allies, and the territories occupied by her armies, became to all intents and purposes a "closed commercial State" in consequence of the successful Allied blockade. His position as an early prophet of modern policies was not, however, made secure till after 1933, when Hitler's "New Order" and Schacht's economic policies carried into effect the Fichtean blueprint. Attention began to be drawn to some passages, at least, of his book. Professor Rappard, whose writings on economic nationalism were cited in Chapter I, did more than anyone to familiarize the English-speaking world with that aspect of Fichte's economics which was particularly relevant in the circumstances of the late thirties. [5] In spite of these beginnings of interest in Fichte, the full implications of his economic philosophy remain buried in his unavailable prophetic little book.

The reader may well ask why he should concern himself with a tract over a century and a half old which, since it remained largely

---

[2] *Op. cit.*, pp. 109-14.
[3] Charles Rist and Charles Gide: *Histoire des doctrines économiques*, Paris, 1926, pp. 518-19. The seventh edition of that work (Paris, 1947) includes a further brief reference to Fichte, as forerunner of *autarky* (pp. 802-3). See also the English translation: *History of Economic Doctrines*, London, 1953, pp. 436-7; 700-1.
[4] Quincy Wright: *A Study of War*, Chicago, 1942.
[5] See Rappard's paper on "Economic Nationalism" delivered at the Harvard Tercentenary Conference, *op. cit.*, and his Richard Cobden Lecture for 1936, *The Common Menace of Economic and Military Armaments*, London, 1936.

unknown, could not have been really influential? Fichte's book is important not only because it is the *first* analytical description of the international implications of collectivism, but because it remains to this day the *only* such analysis available, ruthless, unadorned, and complete. There is as much self-righteousness in Fichte as there is in the modern protagonists of national planning, as much conviction that he alone has found the key to the truth and that his is the only way leading to a rational organization of society. But, unlike his modern (and unwitting) followers, Fichte accepts *all* the international implications of his social philosophy, indeed he postulates them. Because it is so completely consistent and so entirely candid a blueprint of what seemed in his day to be a peculiar vagary of a philosopher's logic, but has become in the past twenty-five years a political reality at various times and in various places, *The Closed Commercial State* must be carefully read and seriously pondered over by students of international affairs. While it is true that authoritarian policies of national self-sufficiency have not made their appearance as a direct result of Fichte's influence, it is equally true that a good knowledge of Fichte's utopia can greatly help us in understanding some of the most perplexing aspects of the modern forms of economic nationalism. [6]   *Habent sua fata libelli!*

II

From beginning to end, Fichte's short treatise attributes to the state powers of regulating the country's economy as well as the lives of its inhabitants: "It is the purpose of the state to give everyone what is his, to set him up in his property, and then to protect him in it." A concept which occurs time and again throughout the book is that everybody in the state should live as pleasantly as possible. We can leave out from the present context Fichte's version of the philosophy of the social compact, so fashionable in his day as a

---

[6] Because an English translation of *Der geschlossne Handelsstaat* is not available, I use direct quotation to an extent which in different circumstances would appear excessive. I feel that to get a proper understanding of Fichte, the reader should be exposed to samples of his style and not merely provided with a paraphrased version.

[7] *Der Geschlossne Handelsstaat, op. cit.,* p. 4.

philosophical device. His system starts from a most confusing network of agreements and contracts, one more fictitious than the other, and all quite unnecessary in terms of his later proposals. Fichte's "statism" has an equalitarian tinge to it: "All must first be comfortable and warmly dressed before anyone dresses beautifully." [8] As Sir Alexander Gray paraphrased it: "There must be enough for all before there are superfluities for some." [9]

The national economy, according to Fichte, should be fully planned by the government. It is the government which will determine what is to be produced and in what quantities, how many people will work in each field of endeavour, at what price goods will be sold and by whom, and even who will be the buyers. The following passage is typical:

> It is easy to see, how the government could assure itself that the fixed number of craftsmen will not be exceeded. Everybody who wishes to devote himself exclusively to some particular occupation must register himself with the government... If he registers for a branch of activity where the largest number of employees allowed by law is already engaged, the authorization will be refused and he will be suggested other lines of work in which his talents might be needed. [10]

What becomes of individual freedom under such a system of all-pervasive regulations is another matter and one about which Fichte has little to say; the little he does have to say will be quoted later.

It is impossible, in the space of this chapter, to go into the details of Fichte's planned economy. [11] What is of special interest in the present context are the international repercussions of this approach. "There is hardly any need to prove", says Fichte, "that the maintenance by subjects of relations with foreigners does not fit at all into the proposed commercial system." Why not? Here is the answer:

> The government must be in a position to count upon a certain quantity of goods entering into the commercial network so that the subjects might always be assured of the continued satisfaction of

---

[8] *Ibid.*, p. 14.
[9] *The Socialist Tradition, op. cit.*, p. 111.
[10] *Der geschlossne Handelsstaat, op. cit.*, pp. 14-15.
[11] The reader might usefully consult Sir Alexander Gray's analysis cited above.

their usual needs. But how could the government reliably count upon a foreign contribution to this quantity of goods since this foreign contribution is not subject to its power? The government must determine and guarantee commodity prices. How could it do so in relation to foreign goods when it has no power of determining prices which prevail in the foreigner's own land and at which he has to buy his raw materials? On the other hand, should the government set a price which the foreigner cannot accept, the latter will avoid that country's market and there will develop a shortage of goods with which to satisfy customary needs. The goverment must guarantee to its subjects a market for their products and manufactures and the price at which these can be sold. How can it do so if goods are sold abroad in countries where it has no power either to control or to determine the demand for or the price of the products of its subjects? [12]

Here we have in a nutshell the perennial conflict between national planning and foreign trade. [13] The state can control economic life within the country but not beyond its boundaries; foreign trade brings into the picture uncertainties which are disturbing to the planner. Hence one must choose between "rational" state organization of the national economy and foreign trade. Fichte chooses the former but is careful to qualify as follows: "Then only the government alone should conduct such trade, just as it alone can declare war, make peace, and conclude alliances." [14] One of the much-debated issues in our own times is the opposition between state trading and private trade, the collectivist planners leaning heavily toward the former. "In a rational state (*Vernunftstaat*)", says Fichte,, "the private citizens simply cannot be allowed to trade directly with a citizen of a foreign country." [15]

And so Fichte is led to the notion of economic isolation as a method of establishing an environment in which the state can plan the economic and social life of the country in a "rational" way and without disturbing influences originating abroad.

---

[12] *Der geschlossne Handelsstaat, op. cit.*, p. 26.
[13] See also Chapter VII below.
[14] *Der geschlossne Handelsstaat*, p. 27.
[15] *Ibid.*

III

This point reached, the balance of Fichte's argument falls into two parts. In the first of these he looks into international relations in a world where partial and incomplete measures are taken to promote self-sufficiency. This he finds unsatisfactory because it does not lead to the full achievement of domestic aims and yet results in a great deal of international strife. He concludes, therefore, that national isolation must be complete, and in the last part of his book he examines ways and means by which a state can isolate itself successfully from the rest of the world. Fichte's views along both of these lines will be quoted in the present and next section of this chapter.

First a word concerning Fichte's views on money. They are interesting in themselves and occupy an important position in his argumentation. In his approach to money and to goods, Fichte is very far removed from the mercantilists. He considers that wealth consists in raw materials, food and manufactured goods, not in money. He does not believe that the monetary instrument needs to have, within an isolated economy, any intrinsic value. [16] He writes:

> The closed commercial state whose citizen entertains no direct relations with foreigners can make into money practically anything it wants by declaring that the state itself will only accept payments in that money and in no other. ... Thus, the national currency [Landesgeld] is created, about which there never arises the question of whether it is acceptable abroad, since, for a closed commercial state, foreign countries are as good as non-existent. [17]

So far so good; as far as domestic monetary relations are concerned, the state is absolutely sovereign, but what of foreign trade (since, at this stage of his argument, Fichte analyses conditions which exist in a world from which foreign trade has not yet been fully eliminated)? In a controlled economy, the circulation of money is subject to all the state regulations that govern the production and

---

[16] Fichte is a real precursor of what was to be called in the latter part of the nineteenth century monetary nominalism, associated with the name of the German economist, G.F. Knapp.
[17] *Der geschlossne Handelsstaat*, p. 41.

distribution of goods. In an uncontrolled economy, however, Fichte anticipates a great scramble for money, everybody trying to garner as much of it as possible at the expense of everybody else. It all results, says Fichte, in an endless war of everybody against everybody else, a war between buyers and sellers, a war that grows more violent and more dangerous as the population of the world increases, as production and the crafts improve, and as the number of needs grows and multiplies. The buyer wants to get goods as cheaply as possible and therefore calls for free trade as a means to arrive at increased competition and falling prices — all of which Fichte regards as undesirable and harmful. "People want absolutely to be free to destroy one another," he scornfully remarks. [18] Now, so long as there is international trade — possibly free international trade — things will go this unhappy way, and this must be so since the state can apply the regulation based on reason only within its own boundaries.

Here Fichte turns mercantilist for a while. We have already seen how the mercantilist concept that trade can only be advantageous to one but not to both partners has led to conflict and strife. This notion recurs in Fichte. Indeed, he makes this into the major cause of war [19], which surely is a wild exaggeration even in terms of the mercantilist world picture. We shall note with interest, in the next chapter, what becomes of that notion in the writings of Lord Keynes, follower in that respect both of mercantilism and (probably without realizing it) of Fichte. The doctrines of David Hume and Adam Smith do not seem to have affected Fichte's thinking in any way, although it is hardly conceivable that he could have been ignorant of their writings. His tract, however, is written in a dogmatic, rather than polemic vein, and no reference is made in it to the writings of anyone else.

Having thus established, to his satisfaction at least, that, in an unplanned world, trade leads to conflict and war, Fichte addresses himself to a further examination of the consequences of foreign trade for the welfare of an individual country. The following observations are illuminating:

---

[18] *Ibid.*, pp. 69-70.
[18] *Ibid.*, p. 70.

No state which counts on foreign markets and encourages and directs domestic industry with that expectation in mind, can guarantee to its subjects the continued existence of these markets. Should the neighbouring country turn to the same line of food production, or should it, because of a prohibition by its government, suddenly find itself obliged to renounce the foreign merchandise, then the worker of our country would be left without food and be reduced to poverty. The only consolation which one is given in such a case is that the interruption of the usual trade would not happen suddenly, so that one might find other markets somewhere else, or, should one lose these markets as well, one could move over to other kinds of food, seeing that one cannot be adequately supplied with the former kinds. [20]

Fichte goes on to say that in practice sudden trade prohibitions are adopted and that their consequences are very drastic indeed; hence he regards as very considerable the risks arising from foreign trade.

But these are not, in Fichte's mind, all the consequences that might result from changes in trade channels. The domestic difficulties mentioned in the foregoing excerpt lead to widespread discontent. So will the state control of foreign trade, taxes on imports, and other regulations. People will feel that something is wrong, that they are being deprived of a part of their welfare, and, being uninformed and knowing little or nothing about "the real aims which any rational government has in mind when applying this kind of trade restriction," [21] they will think that they are being deprived of goods merely to enable the government to acquire them for itself. Fichte notes, in passing, that taxes and levies on foreign trade are more resented by the population than any others. And then there is trouble in store for the state:

There arises in the hearts of the subjects a hatred against the government and, with this hatred, a war against it, which is conducted first through subterfuge and then through the use of open violence; there develops contraband trade [22] and an artificial system of defrauding the government. In the opinion of the people, it ceases to be an offence to swindle the government, but indeed this becomes an admitted and even glorious self-defence against the

---

[20] *Ibid.*, pp. 82-3.
[21] *Ibid.*, p. 86.
[22] Or, to use a modern term, black markets.

general enemy. [23] ... To oppose these hostilities on the part of subjects, the government then adopts for its part harsh and hostile counter-measures, which are carried out even more harshly by embittered underlings. [24]

Fichte's conclusion is clear [25]: "Such a system of only partly eliminating foreign trade ... does not bring about the results which it should bring about and creates new evils." [26]

IV

And so we reach the political part of Fichte's book, the closing of the frontiers of the state and the cessation of all foreign economic relations. Now, says Fichte, it must by no means be considered that by closing its boundaries the state simply renounces all the former advantages of foreign trade and declares itself content with whatever the country happens to produce at that time. On the contrary, the state, *before it can close its boundaries*, must reach its "natural boundaries". It must also develop to the utmost all its resources, introduce from abroad new productive techniques, and create, as far as possible, substitutes for hitherto imported goods.

This notion of "natural boundaries" is one that brings with it a great deal of trouble. Let us quote Fichte's somewhat heavy definition of what natural boundaries are:

Certain parts of the surface of the globe including their inhabitants are by nature clearly predestined to form political units. They are separated from the rest of the earth by large rivers, seas and impassable mountains; ... it is to these indications of nature as to what shall remain together and what shall be separated that one refers when, in contemporary political discussion, one speaks of the natural frontiers of empires. This conception is far more important and more serious than is usually thought. It is based not only on well-

---

[23] What happened during the war in occupied countries is a good illustration of the attitudes described by Fichte.
[24] *Der geschlossne Handelsstaat, op. cit.,* pp. 86-7.
[25] *Ibid.,* p. 88.
[26] One can well imagine an extreme British socialist making a similar comment about the semi-socialist system established in that country after the war and drawing the conclusion that one must adopt a complete and rigorous planning of the entire economy.

protected and solid military frontiers, but far more still on productive independence and self-sufficiency. [27]

However, a state may not be and generally is not endowed, to begin with, with its natural boundaries. These have to be acquired. How? By the use of force and at the expense of neighbours unable adequately to protect and defend themselves. And so Fichte's recommendations lead to wars of conquest:

It has always been the privilege of philosophers to sigh over wars. The present author loves them no more than anyone else. But he believes in their inevitability in the present circumstances and deems it uncalled for to complain of the inevitable. In order to abolish war it is necessary to abolish its cause. Every state must receive what it intends to obtain through war and what it alone can reasonably determine, that is, its natural frontiers. When that is accomplished it will have no further claims on any other state, since it will possess what it has sought.

While the state to be closed is seeking its natural frontiers, it should, in Fichte's opinion, continue to engage in foreign trade, but on a state trading basis. The government of the expanding state will have, because of its monetary wealth, the means of arming itself and of attacking for that purpose large foreign resources. It will be so strong "that no resistance can be made to its expansion. Thus, it could carry out its notion [of reaching natural boundaries] without bloodshed and almost without using the sword, and this operation will be far more an armed occupation than a war." [28] When a hundred and thirty-odd years later Dr. Schacht regimented the foreign trade of Germany for the sake of Germany's rearmament and thereby paved the way for Hitler's eventual "armed occupation" (without war) of Austria and Czechoslovakia, he was literally (if perhaps unconsciously) applying Fichte's precepts!

---

[27] This passage is quoted in Professor Rappard's translation in his pamphlet *The Common Menace of Economic and Military Armaments, op. cit.,* p. 16. Owing to Rappard's writings, this passage and that directly following are probably the two paragraphs of Fichte's book best known to the English-speaking public.

[28] *Der geschlossne Handelsstaat, op. cit.,* p. 120.

V

These, then, are the military aspects, as it were, of the closing of the commercial state. [29] The purely economic measures also present the greatest interest. In the first place, "all direct relations of the citizens with any foreigners whatever must be entirely discontinued".[30] In order to be discontinued, they must be rendered impracticable and impossible. How can this best be accomplished? Here is Fichte's recommendation:

> All possibility of world trade depends upon the possession of means of exchange that are accepted throughout the world and upon our ability to accept such means of exchange. ... Hence the real solution of our problem is the following: all world money [Welt-geld] found in the hands of citizens, i.e. all gold and silver, must be taken out of circulation and must be exchanged against a new national currency [Landesgeld], i.e. a currency which is only valid within the country. ... The government must ensure for all eternity the value of the money it issues, i.e. that value in comparison with goods which it is given at the time of its introduction. Hence, with the introduction of national currency, it is also necessary to introduce the fixing of prices which have to be maintained from then on. [31]

In brief, monetary reform associated with price fixing. Next comes the nationalization of foreign trade:

> With the same single move by which it introduces the new internal currency, the state will take over the entire import and export trade of the country. This takes place in the following way: immediately before the introduction of the new internal currency the government will buy all foreign merchandise that is found in the country. ... It is, in part, the purpose of this purchase to ascertain exactly the existing supplies of and current needs for this merchandise, and in part to obtain control over the prices of these goods. ... The government settles with the merchants in the new currency immediately after its introduction. [32]

As the government introduces the "national" currency, Fichte would have it issue a manifesto to all foreign countries inviting them

---

[29] Or, to use modern language, these are the military aspects of isolating a country from the rest of the world.
[30] *Der geschlossne Handelsstaat, op. cit.,* p. 99.
[31] *Ibid.,* pp. 99-100 and 102-3.
[32] *Ibid.,* pp. 111, 112.

to transfer all the deals they might have in progress with the inhabitants of the "closing state" to its government, and that within prescribed time limits. Should they fail to do so, they would be penalized through the loss of their claims. Nationals of the state would be requested to transfer to the government all their claims against foreigners. In addition, foreigners would be warned not to enter into any new business transactions with inhabitants of the "closing state" without specific permission by its government; for the government would refuse responsibility for any "unauthorized" claims acquired by foreigners against nationals of the country after the issuance of that declaration. [38]

In taking over the country's foreign trade the government would aim at gradually reducing its volume until at long last it could be eliminated altogether. This transition should be fully planned. A very "modern" notion of economic planning underlies the entire approach to this "transitional period". As the volume of foreign trade declines, people will have to "disaccustom" themselves from using foreign goods — a process in which they will be assisted by the progressive rise in price of the increasingly scarce foreign goods. At the same time the government will plan the development of manufacture in order to provide substitutes for goods hitherto obtained through foreign trade: foreign goods will be replaced by home produce, according as domestic manufacture, promoted through deliberate planning "and no longer left to blind chance", steadily increases in volume. [34] Exports too will decline, and the productive capacity thus liberated will be used to produce for the domestic market. This entire transition will be planned by the government. Just how these plans will be implemented Fichte does not say.

And so, by degrees, Fichte's state will expand its boundaries, reduce its foreign trade, and introduce increasingly stringent measures of national economic planning.

---

[38] *Ibid.*, pp. 112-3.
[34] *Ibid.*, p. 116.

VI

A few niceties of the Fichtean system remain to be noted. Being a philosopher himself, and a philosopher of science at that, Fichte was well aware of the importance for a country not to stultify itself by keeping aloof from the achievements of science and arts elsewhere in the world. In order to achieve the highest possible living standards of the population, the government of the isolated state should attract from abroad such foreign resources as it might need and, most of all, foreign talent:

> The government will attract from abroad, at any price, great minds in applied science, inventive chemists, physicists, technicians, artists, and manufacturers. It will pay what no other government could afford and so everybody will rush to serve it. It will conclude with these foreigners long-term contracts. During the years they will spend in the country they will bring into it their science and art and they will instruct nationals, and as they go abroad they will receive world currency for the domestic currency in which they will thus far have been paid. Thus, they will go back to their countries enriched with money which is acceptable there, or should they wish to stay and be naturalized, so much the better. Only one must leave them full liberty and choice, and guarantee it to them from the start — one will also buy foreign machinery and imitate it at home. [85]

How reminiscent is the above passage — its last lines not least so — of the practices of the Soviet Union in the 1920's and 1930's.

It is interesting how the logic of a system, once its fundamental assumptions are adopted, carries one, step by step, relentlessly, to almost fully foreseeable conclusions. Our modern economic planner, addicted as he is to exchange control, frowns upon an individual's freedom to travel abroad at will. So does Fichte:

> Only the scholar and the major artist should have a reason to travel out of the closed commercial state; idle curiosity must not be allowed any longer to carry its boredom across all countries. The former travels are for the best advantage of humanity and of the state. Far from interfering with them, the government should even

---

[85] *Der geschlossne Handelsstaat, op. cit.,* pp. 116-17.

encourage them and send scholars and artists abroad at public expense. [86]

But what of people who, during the transitional period, might wish to leave a country in which they might run the risk of being imprisoned? Fichte recognizes this possibility but believes that it can easily be taken care of. (So did Dr. Schacht in the 1930's.) People, if they wish, can leave, but they will only be allowed to take with them what cash they had on hand at the time of the monetary reform. They may not take their possessions along. But let us hear once again Fichte speaking in his own words:

A significant migration might have to be expected at first by people to whom the new order — which alone is the true order — would appear oppressive, depressing, and pedantic. The state loses nothing through the departure of such persons. The amount of money that their departure would take away from the government would not be large in comparison with the total. They can take out as a maximum what cash they had at the time of the monetary reform ... as much real cash as was in their possession, I repeat, because after the monetary reform they will not be allowed to sell commodities or property and exchange the proceeds against world currency. The government would know from its books where such a sale had taken place, and proceeds of such a transaction would not be converted. At the utmost they might receive abroad the interest on such sums for the rest of their life... The principal, as a part of the national wealth, remains in the country and goes to the nearest non-emigrated heirs. [87]

---

[86] *Ibid.*, p. 124.
[87] *Ibid.*, pp. 123-4. In his *Politics of Democratic Socialism* (London, 1940, pp. 284-6), E.F.M. Durbin was faced with a similar problem: what would the consequences be of a hostile attitude towards progressive socialization on the part of certain sectors of the British public? Would they be so great that they might interfere with the entire programme? Fichte notes that, among other things, those displeased with socialization might withdraw their capital from the country, thereby causing a crisis in the foreign exchange markets and maybe an economic depression. This, Durbin considers an exaggerated fear. The danger of a foreign exchange crisis he deems to be very small. "There is not a country in Europe", he observes, "that has not met, fought, and survived this unfavourable development in its economic position. The problems and methods of exchange control are well understood and largely perfected by now. We have already created in this country a powerful agent for the control of precisely this weak point in our financial armoury — the Exchange Equalization Fund — and there is not the slightest reason for supposing that a resolute government could not in a few days, if it wished, bring the foreign exchange market under effective governance, and prevent an organized minority from frustrating the chosen purposes of a majority of the nation." As in the case of Fichte, so also here the ultimate resort is the power of compulsion in the hands of the state.

Fichte makes no bones, throughout his entire treatise, about the state using methods of compulsion to achieve the proposed objectives. He regards this as rational and normal. Indeed, he refers scornfully in the last pages of his book to those who might greatly object to his theories. These remarks are our last quotation from *Der geschlossne Handelsstaat* [38], and they answer the question put earlier in this chapter: what is Fichte's attitude towards individual freedom:

> It is ... a trait of our generation that it wants to play. ... It is very inclined, in order to satisfy this desire, to transform life itself into a game. ... Because of this inclination, people want to do nothing according to rules but would like to achieve everything by chance and luck. Achievement and all human relations are to be like a gamble. ... These people derive more enjoyment from the excitement of the quest than from the security of possession. These are the people who all the time call aloud for freedom of trade and production, freedom from control and police, freedom from all order and morality. To them all that aims at strict regularity and a well-ordered and steady march of events appears to be an infringement of their natural freedom. [39]

Clearly, there is no room for either individual freedom or friendly international relations in the kind of planned society that Fichte regards as the new and only rational order.

So long as all this was a philosopher's daydream, *Der geschlossne Handelsstaat* deserved probably the relative obscurity which was its fate. Now that we are endowed with the questionable blessings of national collectivisms, Fichte's blueprint should be widely known and carefully meditated on.

---

[38] *Op. cit.,* pp. 128-9.

CHAPTER VI

THE ECONOMIC NATIONALISM OF JOHN MAYNARD KEYNES

I

The mercantilist heritage and Fichte's blueprint for an isolated and collectivist state are both greatly honoured in the deeds of the contemporary world. The extent of the impact of these ideas upon the doctrines of our times can best be gauged through the writings of John Maynard (later Lord) Keynes, the most controversial and, beyond any doubt, the most influential political economist of the second quarter of the twentieth century. Soon after the end of World War I, Keynes revolted against the international discipline inherent in the gold standard and set himself up as a defender of national monetary autonomy. He later exerted the leading intellectual influence in Great Britain's departure from the canons of free trade. The next step was his advocacy of national self-sufficiency (from 1933 onward). Having gone far along this line and in the direction of the "bilateralist" practice (meantime developed into a fine art by Nazi Germany's Hjalmar Schacht), he experienced during World War II a progressive change of heart and became in the last and all-too-short phase of his life, an ardent fighter for international economic co-operation, based on Anglo-American partnership.

Keynes' early training was, of course, in the classical economics and he was a worthy heir to the liberal, free trade tradition of British economics. He held strongly to these views as late as January 1923. At that time Keynes was the chief editor of a series of special supplements issued by the *Manchester Guardian* under the title *Reconstruction in Europe*. The first issue of that series appeared on April 20, 1922, and there we can read in Keynes' leading article, devoted to "The Stabilisation of the European Exchanges: a Plan for Genoa", the following views on monetary reconstruction:

> I see no other solution of stabilisation practicable now, except the traditiona solution — namely, a gold standard in as many countries as possible.

The twelfth and last issue of the series, dated January 4, 1923, contained Keynes' moving article entitled "The Underlying Principles" from which I quote the following:

> We must hold to free trade in its widest interpretation, as an inflexible dogma to which no exception is admitted, wherever the decision rests with us. We must hold to this even if we receive no reciprocity of treatment and even in those rare cases where by infringing it we could in fact obtain a direct economic advange. We should hold to free trade as a principle of international morals, and not merely as a doctrine of economic advantage. I include in free trade the abandonment of any attempt to secure for ourselves exclusive supplies of food and materials — in spite of what is said below about the pressure of population on resources. For if pressure of population is to lead to a regime of armed and powerful nations grabbing resources from weak holders, our last state will be worse than it ever can be under any alternative policy.

Keynes' "conversion" to economic nationalism was a slow and gradual process. It was undoubtedly prompted by his sense of disappointment and frustration over the strength of protectionist feelings and policies in the post-war world; the failures of monetary reconstruction during the twenties; the way in which the leading nations of the world entered the Great Depression without having evolved means of coping with such a calamity through co-operation rather than in insulation from one another. There was indeed much to discourage the most enthusiastic liberal and free trader; still it is a matter of historical record that a great many liberals and free traders did not become discouraged but continued the fight for a workable world economy.

Be this as it may, Keynes' work falls, from the point of view of our inquiry, into three periods. The first, the free trade period, to which reference has just been made, ended about 1923 with the publication of the *Tract on Monetary Reform,* a book about which more will be said below. The second, in which Keynes gradually became a partisan of economic insulation, lasted from 1923 until about 1943. The third period started in the middle of the war, in 1943 or thereabout, and lasted until his untimely death in 1946.

Keynes' wartime "conversion" — or, rather, "reconversion" — to international economic cooperation, had on his many followers divergent and conflicting effects. Those who like his biographer, Sir Roy Harrod, followed him in the path of internationalism developed a tendency to regard their master's previous economic nationalism as a temporary aberration which meant but little, and his newly regained faith as the basic, fundamental feature of his personal philosophy. They could claim in favour of their position the fact that the internationalist philosophy of Keynes' last years was in line with the philosophy of the young Keynes as expressed in the *Manchester Guardian's* "Reconstruction Supplements".

The other group of Keynes' disciple, the confirmed economic nationalists, refused to follow him into the new fight he undertook from about 1943 onwards. In their opinion it is the "last phase" which represented an "aberration" brought about by wartime conditions and exigencies; they feel confident that, had he lived, Keynes would have returned to the nationalistic fold along the path of national insulation. This latter group of Keynes' ex-followers can claim to be the "orthodox Keynesiams", since the major writings of their prophet, from the *Tract on Monetary Reform* (1923) to the *General Theory of Employment, Interest and Money* (1936), bear them out; it is the prophet himself who, as I pointed out in an earlier book [1] (written while he was still alive but published after his death), was no longer a "Keynesian" in good standing towards the end of his career. Although his writings espousing economic nationalism are what interest us mostly here, his "conversion" first and "re-conversion", afterwards, have implications that cast a great deal of light upon the problems discussed in this book. More will be said about this later.

---

[1] *The Trade of Nations, op. cit.,* p. 94.

Mine is, of course, not a biographer's interest in the person of Keynes but the student's interest in his doctrines. It so happens, however, that the intellectual portrait of Keynes that results from the present study is considerably at variance with the image drawn for posterity by his official biographer. [2] This makes it all the more necessary for me to document the account that follows by extensive quotations, and to take issue with certain interpretations divergent from and conflicting with my own. The discussion that follows falls into five parts: The *first* deals with Keynes' monetary nationalism; the *second* with his fight for the adoption of a tariff to supplant Britain's traditional policy of free trade; the *third* is devoted to Keyne's advocacy of national self-sufficiency and to his attitudes towards bilateralism; the *fourth* deals with his "re-conversion" to internationalism — its causes and significance; while the *fifth* examines Keynes' attitudes towards liberalism and collectivism.

II

When, in 1923, Keynes published *A Tract on Monetary Reform* [3], he was no newcomer to the literature of money. His *Indian Currency and Finance* had won him in 1913 considerable recognition as well as a seat, notwithstanding his youth, on a royal commission. During World War I and at the Peace Conference that followed he was a Treasury official. By 1923 he was also the celebrated author of *The Economic Consequences of the Peace* [3a], a book which did as much as any single one possibly could to sabotage the Peace Treaty of Versailles. *The Tract on Monetary Reform*, Keynes' first major offensive against the gold standard, was a time-bomb placed on the rails upon which the slow-moving train of international monetary reconstruction was eventually to pass. What that system stood for, namely, international discipline in matters of monetary policy and the subordination of domestic policy objectives to the requirements of a country's international solvency (under a system of stable ex-

---

[2] R.F. Harrod: *The Life of John Maynard Keynes*, London, 1951.
[3] Published in the United States under the title *Monetary Reform*. Page references are to the London edition.
[3a] London, 1919.

change rates), was deeply repellent to Keynes. Independent national economic policy and fluctuating exchange rates — that was what he, personally, now stood for. In varying presentations, this was to remain one of the principal themes of his writing.

To trace the development of Keynes' ideas, let us begin with the *Tract on Monetary Reform*. The argument of that book is twofold. On the theoretical plane, Keynes places national monetary autonomy ahead of the international interdependence of prices and of stable exchange relations between currencies. On the practical plane, he opposes the then growing influence of the United States Federal Reserve System on the functioning of the gold standard. On either plane he favours national monetary autonomy as against monetary internationalism. The following quotation contains the gist of the theoretical argument:

> Since ... the rate of exchange of a country's currency with the currency of the rest of the world (assuming for the sake of simplicity that there is only one external currency) depends on the relation between the internal price level and the external price level, it follows that the exchange cannot be stable unless *both* internal *and* external price levels remain stable. If, therefore, the external price level lies outside our control, we must submit either to our own internal price level or to our exchange being pulled about by external influences. If the external price level is unstable, we cannot keep both our own price level *and* our exchanges stable. And we are compelled to choose. ...
>
> The right choice is not necessarily the same for all countries. It must partly depend on the relative importance of foreign trade in the economic life of the country. Nevertheless, there does seem to be in almost every case a presumption in favour of the stability of prices, if only it can be achieved. Stability of exchange is in the nature of a convenience which adds to the efficiency and prosperity of those who are engaged in foreign trade. Stability of prices, on the other hand, is profoundly important. [4]

Having analysed elsewhere [5] Keynes' argument in greater detail, I shall limit myself here to a few brief observations. The definition of foreign exchange rates in terms of relations between the domestic price levels of the respective countries is a great oversimplification

---

[4] *A Tract on Monetary Reform, op. cit.*, pp. 154-6.
[5] See my *International Monetary Economics, op. cit.*, pp. 228-30.

of the really existing, and far more complex, relationships. [6] In the words of Professor John H. Williams, "the dilemma between the aims of external and internal monetary stability is [probably] more apparent than real, and ... it arises very largely out of a too literal acceptance of the abstractions of gold-standard theory". [7] What is true, however, is that if there are fluctuations of major amplitude in world prices, due, e.g., to the business cycle, a country can either participate in these price movements and maintain exchange stability or it can abandon that stability and seek an autonomous course for its domestic prices. Whatever the reasons may be for choosing the latter as against the former course, it must be realized that the country deciding upon it severs up to a point its organic relations with the world economy. Such a decision represents a first step in the direction of economic insulation. And a first step is, most frequently, followed by others.

"Stability of exchange is in the nature of a convenience which adds to the efficiency and prosperity of those who are engaged in foreign trade", says Keynes in the passage quoted above, displaying a surprising lack of appreciation of the real significance of stable exchange rates between the various currencies. Just as in the past the introduction of a single national monetary unit helped countries to achieve internal economic cohesion, so stable parities are the basis upon which a coherent world economy is built. Stable currencies, freely convertible into one another, are the best approximation we have ever had to a single world currency. They render possible the development of stable and sustained currents of trade; combined with free trade, they bring about real international economic integration. Not only those who are directly engaged in foreign trade benefit from such a state of affairs; benefits are extended to *all* producers, traders, and consumers alike, for their welfare is promoted by the growing international division of labour and by the existence of wide and dependable markets. The future author of the essay on "National Self-Sufficiency" had evidently no appreciation in 1923, of the importance of an international monetary order. What attracted him, on the contrary, was the quest for national monetary autonomy.

---

[6] *Ibid.*, pp. 128-36.
[7] John H. Williams: *The World Monetary Dilemma*, 1934, reprinted in *Postwar Monetary Plans and Other Essays*, New York, 1944, p. 195.

Along with many economists of the early twenties Keynes was all in favour of innovation; a *stable price level,* proclaimed by Irving Fisher to be the only true aim of monetary policy, was then an objective greatly in vogue, and the "bright young economists" looked scornfully upon that prehistoric relic of the unscientific past, the gold standard. Thus Keynes:

In truth, the gold standard is already a barbarous relic. All of us, from the Governor of the Bank of England downwards, are now primarily interested in preserving the stability of business, prices, and employment, and are not likely, when the choice is forced upon us, deliberately to sacrifice these to the outworn dogma, which had its value once, of £3: 17: 10½ per ounce. Advocates of the ancient standard do not observe how remote it now is from the spirit and the requirements of the age. A regulated non-metallic standard has slipped in unnoticed. *It exists.* Whilst the economists dozed, the academic dream of a hundred years, doffing its cap and gown, clad in paper rags, has crept into the real world by means of the bad fairies — always so much more potent than the good — the wicked ministers of finance. [8]

The other — and very important — reason for Keynes' opposition to Britain's return to the gold standard had to do with the emergence of the United States after World War I as a major financial centre:

... I see grave objections to reinstating gold in the pious hope that international co-operation will keep it in order. With the existing distribution of the world's gold, the reinstatement of the gold standard means, inevitably, that we surrender the regulation of our price level and the handling of the credit cycle to the Federal Reserve Board of the United States. Even if the most intimate and cordial co-operation is established between the Board and the Bank of England, the preponderance of power will still belong to the former. The Board will be in a position to disregard the Bank. But if the Bank disregard the Board, it will render itself liable to be flooded with, or depleted of, gold, as the case may be. Moreover, we can be confident beforehand that there will be much suspicion amongst Americans (for that is their disposition) of any supposed attempt on the part of the Bank of England to dictate their policy or to influence American discount rates in the interests of Great Britain. We must also be prepared to incur our share of the vain expense of bottling up the world's redundant gold.

---

[8] *A Tract on Monetary Reform, op. cit.,* pp. 172-3; italics in the text.

It would be rash in the present circumstances to surrender our freedom of action to the Federal Reserve Board of the United States. We do not yet possess sufficient experience of its capacity to act in times of stress with courage and independence. The Federal Reserve Board is striving to free itself from the pressure of sectional interests; but we are not yet certain that it will wholly succeed. It is still liable to be overwhelmed by the impetuosity of a cheap money campaign. A suspicion of British influence would, so far from strengthening the Board, greatly weaken its resistance to popular clamour. Nor is it certain, quite spart from weakness or mistakes, that the simultaneous application of the same policy will always be in the interests of both countries. The development of the credit cycle and the state of business may sometimes be widely different on the two sides of the Atlantic. [9]

That the emergence of the Federal Reserve Board as the world's major central bank raised serious problems, no one would deny. That the gold standard as a "two-headed" system would be more difficult to run than it was in the days when the Bank of England ran it alone, was also a foregone conclusion. But it was essential in the interest of rebuilding a well-knit world economy that co-operation between these two great central banks should be tried. Keynes, instead of examining the implications of such an Anglo-American central banking partnership, and suggesting ways in which it could be made to work, rashly rejected the whole notion and objected *a priori* to any surrender of Britain's "freedom of action". Here was, not very loud yet — but to grow louder in later years — the voice of monetary nationalism.

Keynes' criticism of the return of Great Britain to the gold standard in 1925 is well-known. [10] It should be noted here that it was formulated more in terms of the gold parity adopted for the pound [11] than in those of outright opposition to the gold standard itself. In later years all the economic difficulties of Great Britain were to be blamed all too exclusively on that operation. [12]

---

[9] *Ibid.*, pp. 174-5.
[10] J.M. Keynes: *The Economic Consequences of Mr. Churchill*, London, 1925.
[11] The parity adopted was identical with the pre-1914 price of gold, while *actually* the pound sterling was devalued by 10 per cent in terms of gold.
[12] See, for penetrating comments on other causes of Britain's economic difficulties, André Siegfried: *La Crise britannique au XX° siècle*, Paris, 1931; also English edition.

Thus there were two strands in Keynes' thought and the burden of criticism was placed now on the new gold parity of the pound, now on the gold standard system itself. In 1925, Keynes still saw a way out: an American inflation. As this too will be a recurring tune in his writings, a short quotation may be in order:

When the return to the gold standard was first announced, many authorities agreed that we were gambling on rising prices in the United States. The rise has not taken place, so far.

In my opinion we need not yet abandon the hope that it will take place. The tendency of American prices is upwards, rather than downwards, and it only requires a match to set alight the dormant possibilities of inflation in the United States. This possibility is the one real ground for not being too pessimistic. [13]

Interestingly enough the same hope for an American inflation can be read between the lines of some of Keynes' writings of 1933 and again at the end of World War II. Given a certain dollar-sterling parity relation, a rise of prices in the United States would reduce the competitiveness of American as compared to British goods in third markets. It was not until 1951 that the inflationary effect of an American inflation on raw materials prices began to worry the British economists because of the consequences for Britain's terms of trade. This, however, is in the nature of a digression. Let us return to Keynes' attitudes towards the international monetary system. Next to the *Tract on Monetary Reform,* his most comprehensive treatment of the problem is to be found in the second volume of his *Treatise on Money* (1930). In Chapter 35 of that monumental work [14] he speaks of *auri sacra fames*: "The choice of gold as a standard of value is chiefly based on tradition. ... Dr. Freud relates that there are peculiar reasons deep in our subconscious why gold in particular should satisfy strong instincts and serve as a symbol. ... Of late years the

---

[13] *The Economic Consequences of Mr. Churchill, op. cit.,* p. 27. The second of the paragraphs quoted is the footnote attached by Keynes to the first paragraph. It is not clear from the context whether Keynes has in mind a rise of prices which, under the gold standard, is a normal occurence for a country with a balance-of-payments surplus, or a sustained inflationary movement.

[14] Which some "non-Keynesians" regard as Keynes' best — superior in many ways to his far more famous and influential *General Theory of Employment, Interest and Money.*

auri sacra fames has sought to envelop itself in a garment of respectability as densely respectable as was ever met with, even in the realm of sex and religion. ... Gold has become part of the apparatus of conservatism and is one of the matters we cannot expect to see handled without prejudice." [15]   Because he was an enthusiastic iconoclast, Keynes' prejudice was all against what he had called in 1923 "a barbarous relic". But prejudice it was, not cool reason, which led Keynes to oppose eventually not only the monetary use of gold, but also economic internationalism as such, and to accuse the gold standard and world trade of causing all the ills of the world, including strife and war. In 1930, as in 1923, Keynes was hankering after national monetary autonomy, impatient with the "discipline" of an international monetary standard:

> But is it certain that the ideal standard is an international standard ? It has been usual to assume that the answer is so obviously in the affirmative as to need no argument. I do not know where it has been questioned, except in my own *Tract on Monetary Reform*, Chapter IV. The conveniences and facilities which an international standard offers to foreign trade and foreign investment is thought sufficient to clinch the matter. The lack of an international standard of value is assumed to be just one more of those foolish hindrances to international mobility, such as tariffs, which can only serve to impoverish the whole world in the misguided attempt to benefit some separate part of it. [16]

Keynes' arguments in 1930 were much more sophisticated than those advanced seven years previously had been — but they are equally vulnerable to technical analysis. [17]   What interests us most in the present context is the fact that Keynes regarded the requirements imposed by membership in an international monetary system as unduly limiting the freedom of national economic action. What he was willing to accept, was "the management of the value of gold by a supernational authority" [18] — but just how such an authority would function, he did not say. It is not uncommon for a "planner" to seek an outlet for his idealism in an expression of yearning for

---

[15] J. M. Keynes, *A Treatise on Money*, London, 1930, Vol. II, pp. 289-91.
[16] *Ibid.*, p. 301.
[17] May I refer the reader to the criticism offered in my *International Monetary Economics, op. cit.*, pp. 231-7.
[18] *A Treatise on Money, op. cit.*, p. 338.

supernational planning; what he cannot accept is an "unmanaged" international system.

After the publication of the *Treatise on Money* and under the impact of the depression, Keynes moved rapidly in the direction, first, of protectionism, then, of self-sufficiency. Before we turn to these aspects of his economic nationalism, one final quotation, this from the *General Theory of Employment, Interest and Money* published in 1936, the Master's *magnum opus* and most influential work on economics. [19] Here is the passage in question:

> Never in history was there a method devised of such efficacy for setting each country's advantage at variance with its neighbours' as the international gold (or, formerly, silver) standard. For it made domestic prosperity directly dependent on a competitive pursuit of markets and a competitive appetite for precious metals. [20]

This strange phrase appears in Keynes' discussion (and rehabilitation) of the mercantilists. The phrase is strange because, applicable though it may be to the mercantilist quest for precious metals, it bears no relationship whatsoever to the gold standard of the latter part of the nineteenth and early twentieth centuries. But this is not all:

> The mercantilists were under no illusions as to the nationalistic character of their policies and their tendency to promote war. It was *national* advantage and *relative* strength at which they were admittedly aiming.
>
> We may criticize them for the apparent indifference with which they accepted this inevitable consequence of an international monetary system. But intellectually their realism is much preferable to the confused thinking of contemporary advocates of an international fixed gold standard and *laissez-faire* in international lending, who believe that it is precisely these policies which will best promote peace. [21]

As a matter of historical record, these "contemporary advocates" were entirely justified in their beliefs — far more so than Keynes was in his disbelief.

---

[19] Comparable in terms of influence to the *political* impact of *The Economic Consequences of the Peace, op. cit.*

[20] J.M. Keynes: *Genearl Theory of Employment, Interest and Money*, London, 1936, p. 349.

[21] *Ibid.*, p. 348.

III

From monetary nationalism — advocacy of autonomous national monetary policies as against the "discipline" of an international system — Keynes moved to protectionism. As already indicated, this phase in the evolution of his ideas did not start till 1931. Until then he managed to reconcile (in his own mind, at least) the demands for monetary "autonomy" with a traditionalist attachment to the principles of free trade. Eventually, the iconoclast [22] got the better of the traditionalist, all the more so as intellectually Keynes was on the march in the direction of "national self-sufficiency". The immediate occasion, however, for the formulation of his protectionist proposals was the depression and the aggravation of unemployment. The vindicator of mercantilism could readily see the connection between trade restrictions and the creation of employment. On March 7, 1931, there appeared in the *New Statesman and Nation* Keynes' article on "Proposals for A Revenue Tariff", the initial thrust in a campaign that was to end — in the following year — in the abandonment of free trade as Great Britain's official policy [28]:

> ... the main decision which seems to me today to be absolutely forced on any wise Chancellor of the Exchequer, whatever his beliefs about protection, is the introduction of a substantial revenue tariff. ... Compared with any alternative which is open to us, this measure is unique in that it would at the same time relieve the pressing problems of the budget and restore business confidence. I do not believe that a wise and prudent budget can be framed today without recourse to a revenue tariff. But this is not its only advantage. In so far as it leads to the substitution of home produced goods for goods previously imported, it will increase employment in this country.

As was to be expected, this proposal met with a storm of protest. Professor Robbins answered in the very next issue of the *New*

---

[22] Keynes' biographer, Sir Roy Harrod, remarks on this turnabout of his hero: "Was he [Keynes] a little too ready to be an iconoclast? ... This piece of iconoclasm ... represented a move towards something less good in itself, for hte sake of temporary expediency." (*The Life of John Maynard Keynes*, *op. cit.*, p. 428.) Here Harrod is somewhat less than fair to his biographee — for Keynes was in fact moving into economic nationalism as a *policy*, not as an *expedient*.

[28] Albeit already weakened by exceptions inherited from World War I.

Statesman and Nation. Two passages from Keynes' retort, appearing in the same weekly on March 21, 1931, are worth quoting for they throw a good deal of light on his frame of mind. In the first place, he attributes to the then prevailing fall in prices the revived interest in protection. He then proceeds as follows:

... If prices rise to their former level, and if unqualified free trade turns out to be as much in the interests of this country in the conditions of the twentieth century as it certainly was in the conditions of the nineteenth century, then I believe that the tariff will be taken off again. But if I look into the bottom of my own heart, the feeling which I find there is, rather, that a tariff is a crude departure from *laissez-faire,* which we have to adopt because we have at present no better weapon in our hands, but that it will be superseded in time, not by a return to *laissez faire,* but by some more comprehensive scheme of national planning.

Now this is a very interesting statement, revealing as it does Keynes' preoccupation with the eventual introduction of "some more comprehensive scheme of national planning" to take the place of free trade. It is so important a pronouncement, in fact, in relation to Keynes' intellectual evolution, that I am surprised that his biographer, although he quotes another passage of this article, passes it over in silence. The second passage which needs to be quoted here follows:

Professor Robbins taunts me in conclusion with abandoning 'the service of high and worthy ideals in international relations' for 'the service of the mean and petty devices of economic nationalism'. I know that he sincerely feels this, and that for him, as for many others, free trade stands as a banner and as a symbol of fundamental reason and decency between nations. Free trade unbesmirched invokes old loyalties, and recalls one of the greatest triumphs of reason in politics which adorn our history. It is a poor retort, perhaps, to this, to say that one must not let one's sense of the past grow stronger than one's sense of the present and of the future, or sacrifice the substance to the symbol.

Keynes' "sense of the present and of the future" was taking him deeper and deeper into the morass of economic nationalism. From a deliberate defender of the mercantilists he was now to become an unwitting rediscoverer of Fichte's economic isolationism. On the road from monetary "autonomy" to "national self-suffciciency" he also embraced, not unnaturally, "comprehensive national planning".

In the same year, 1931, there appeared the celebrated Macmillan Report. [24] Keynes was a member of the Committee on Finance and Industry and one of the principal authors of the report. He was also — and from the point of view of our present inquiry, more significantly — one of the signers of the important Addendum I to the report. This addendum, described by Sir Roy Harrod in his biography as "a supplementary report in favour of a public works programme", contains an interesting section entitled: "Control of Imports and Aids to Exports", of which the following passages are the most striking:

> Proposals under this heading raise political and social issues which extend far beyond the necessities of the present emergency. ... We shall confine ourselves ... to considering briefly the uses of tariffs or Import Boards, etc., and subsidies on articles of foreign trade regarded as an expedient to meet a situation in which a country has a large unemployed surplus of labour and of plant which it is unable to bring into use in the conditions imposed on it by its economic relations, arising out of relative rates of interest and money-costs, with the rest of the world. ... (Paragraph 39.)

> It appears to us ... that, if imports were to be controlled, whether by a tariff with compensation for exports, or by Import Boards, or in some other way and home produced goods substituted for them, there is a presumption, so long as present circumstances last, that this would mean a net increase of employment and of national productivity. ... (Paragraph 41.)

> Since many of the arguments in favour of a restriction of imports apply equally in favour of schemes of assistance to exports, some system of restricting imports, accompanied by a policy of giving advantages to the export industries, would seem to be the most practical plan of action. (Paragraph 43.)

Now, these proposals go far beyond a revenue tarif. They foreshadow the use of import quotas (the cryptic reference to Import Boards) and they include export subsidies. The armoury of mercantilism was speedily being re-established!

---

[24] *Report of the Committee on Finance and Industry*, London, H. M. Stationery Office, 1931, Cmd. 3897.

IV

Having, in his first world-famous book [25], done as much as one man could do to undermine the peace treaty of Versailles, having later placed an intellectual time-bomb under the international gold standard, having produced the ammunition which decisively helped in the destruction of the last vestiges of Great Britain's free trade policy, Keynes was next led to giving his personal version of the gospel of national self-suciciency. It appeared in two instalments in the *New Statesman and Nation*, on July 8 and 15, 1933, as well as in the Summer 1933 issue of the *Yale Review*. Entitled "National Self-Sufficiency", this is one of Keynes' most brilliant and most wrong-headed essays, displaying to an exceptional extent the qualities of persuasiveness, drama, self-assurance, and that mixture of genuine "strong feelings" and intellectual irresponsibility which were characteristic of so many of the writings of this extraordinary man. [26] This essay, which is not readily available outside the periodicals where it appeared, can well be regarded, for all its brevity, as one of Keynes' most significant writings. Because of its importance and because it is not easily accessible, there are several passages that must be quoted in full.

Keynes starts with a reference to his past beliefs on the question of free trade:

> I was brought up, like most Englishmen, to respect free trade not only as an economic doctrine which a rational and instructed person could not doubt, but almost as a part of the moral law. I regarded ordinary departures from it as being at the same time an imbecility and an outrage. I thought England's unshakable free trade convictions, maintained for nearly a hundred years, to be both the explanation before man and the justification before heaven of her economic supremacy. As lately as 1923 I was writing that free trade was based on fundamental truths "which, stated with their

---

[25] *The Economic Consequences of the Peace, op. cit.*
[26] Especially *The Economic Consequences of the Peace, A Tract on Monetary Reform,* parts of the *General Theory,* and much of his journalistic output.

due qualifications, no one can dispute who is capable of understanding the meaning of the words". [27]

Looking again today at the statements of these fundamental truths which I then gave, I do not find myself disputing them. Yet the orientation of my mind is changed; and I share this change of mind with many others. Partly, indeed my background of economic theory is modified... But mainly I attribute my change of outlook to something else — to my hopes and fears and preoccupations, along with those of many or most, I believe, of this generation throughout the world, being different from what they were. [28]

Keynes then proceeds to examine the relation between world trade and peace, and his views are the exact opposite of those that were advanced by Richard Cobden in the middle of the previous century:

We are pacifist today with so much strength of conviction that, if the economic internationalist could win this point, he would soon recapture our support. But it does not now seem obvious that a great concentration of national effort on the capture of foreign trade ... and that a close dependence of our own economic life on the fluctuating economic policies of foreign countries are safeguards and assurances of international peace. It is easier, in the light of experience and foresight, to argue quite the contrary. ...

I sympathize, therefore, with those who would minimize, rather than with those who would maximize, economic entanglement among nations. Ideas, knowledge, science, hospitality, travel — these are the things which should of their nature be international. But let goods be homespun whenever it is reasonably and conveniently possible, and, above all, let finance be primarily national. ...

For these strong reasons, therefore, I am inclined to the belief that, after the transition is accomplished, a greater measure of national self-sufficiency and economic isolation among countries than existed in 1914 may tend to serve the cause of peace, rather than otherwise. [29]

---

[27] Yet, at that time, Keynes, as has been brought out before, was already advocating national monetary autonomy as against an international monetary system, thus taking the first decisive step in the direction of economic nationalism.

[28] J.M. Keynes: "National Sel-Sufficiency" in *Yale Review*, 1933, p. 755.

[29] *Ibid.*, pp. 757-8 (italics added). In the very next sentence Keynes says: "At any rate, the age of economic internationalism was not particularly successful in avoiding war..." A curious statement if one considers that the century that elapsed between the end of the Napoleonic Wars and the outbreak of World War I was the century of the greatest expansion of economic liberalism

That economic isolation among countries would serve the cause of peace is precisely the doctrine of Fichte — who also claimed to be a devotee of peace. But Fichte, in examining the conditions under which a country could envisage self-sufficiency, was led to the inescapable conclusion that it first had to conquer enough of the world's surface to have the resources it needed to live self-sufficiently in well-being and in comfort. This is why Fichte's celebrated "pacifism" was, in the first instance, a theory justifying aggressive warfare. Keynes' approach is free from such disturbing overtones. The reason is simple: he does not go into the question of whether self-sufficiency is a goal that *can* be achieved without a major surrender of well-being. In this he is intensely British. He takes the British Empire and Commonwealth links for granted and, with one exception (or possibly two), is not concerned with the rest of the world. To these exceptions I shall presently revert. But first a few additional quotations will be useful to provide the reader with a full appreciation of the scope of Keynes' position:

> ... I am not persuaded that the economic advantages of the international division of labour today are at all comparable with what they were. ... A considerable degree of international specialization is necessary in a rational world in all cases where it is dictated by wide differences of climate, natural resources, native aptitudes, level of culture and density of population. But over an increasingly wide range of industrial products ... I have become doubful whether the economic loss of national self-sufficiency is great enough to outweigh the other advantages of gradually bringing the product and the consumer within the ambit of the same national economic and financial organization. ... National self-sufficiency, in short, *though it costs something, may be becoming a luxury which we can afford, if we happen to want it.* (pp. 759-60, italics added.)

Having gone so far, Keynes asks a very pertinent question — a question which is at the heart of this entire issue. Are there sufficiently good reasons, he queries, why we may happen to want it? Indeed *why* should we want self-sufficiency? What has it to offer us that is worth even the smallest price which it would cost? If it were to carry the promise of peace, then, indeed, it would be worth almost

---

and of free trade, and that early in this century, when the evil seeds of World War I were being sown, a strong reaction against free trade was setting in in many parts of the western world. Keynes had a very personal way of reading history and here is a good example of it.

any price, short of actual distress; but Keynes' affirmations notwithstanding, the weight of historical evidence is surely to the contrary. Nor does Keynes rest his case on the "pacifism" which he claims for his proposal. No, he rests his case on what he regards as the wholesome and desirable right of a country to carry out within its boundaries any economic and social experiments in which it may wish to engage. But let us hear this in his own words:

> Each year it becomes more obvious that the world is embarking on a variety of politico-economic experiments, and that different types of experiment appeal to different national temperaments and historical environment. The nineteenth century free trader's economic internationalism assumed that the whole world was, or would be, organised on a basis of private competitive capitalism and of the freedom of private contract inviolably protected by the sanctions of law...
>
> But today one country after another abandons these presumptions. Russia is still alone in her particular experiment, but no longer alone in her abandonment of the old presumptions. Italy, Ireland, Germany have cast their eyes, or are casting them, towards new modes of political economy. Many more countries after them I predict, will seek, one by one, after new ecoonomic gods. ... [80]
>
> But the point for my present discussion is this. We each have our own fancy. Not believing that we are saved already, we each should like to have a try at working out our own salvation. *We do not wish*, therefore, *to be at the mercy of world forces* working out, or trying to work out, some uniform equilibrium according to the ideal principles, if they can be called such, of *laissez faire* capitalism. There are still those who cling to the old ideas, but in no country of the world today can they be reckoned as a serious force. *We wish* — for the time at least and so long as the present transitional, experimental phase endures — *to be our own masters, and to be as free as we can make ourselves from the interferences of the outside world.* (pp. 761-62; italics added.)

This, then, is the ultimate motivation of Keynes' advocacy of national self-sufficiency. In a later section of this chapter it will be

---

[80] The fact that the "new economic gods" of Russia, Italy and Germany were totalitarian despotic gods, destructive of human dignity and human rights did not, it seems, appear, worthy of note. They were experimenting — that was the wonderful thing about it! Indeed Keynes is very open-minded on the subect. "No one can tell", he says later in the same paragraph, "which of the new systems will prove itself best." Best by what standards? *That Keynes does not say.*

shown that Keynes' philosophy must be regarded as a peculiar mixture of collectivism and liberalism. The above quotation has much bearing on this matter. Who are the "we" of the last paragraph quoted? "We" who have our own fancies, "we" who do not wish to be at the mercy of world forces, "we" who wish to be our own masters — who are "we"? Is it each of the individuals who compose the British (or any other) society — or is it the British nation as distinct from any nation, or any nation as distinct from all other nations? Much evidently depends on the answer to that question: the human individual had the greatest opportunity to work out *his* destiny in accordance with *his* wishes, *his* fancies, and *his* desires for freedom from interferences under the system that Keynes decries as the "*laissez faire* capitalism" of days gone by. He enjoyed similar opportunities neither before the advent of that system nor since its partial disappearance in the thirthies (under the impact of the Great Depression). But if Keynes means the right of nations to be "free from the interferences of the outside world", this is another story altogether, for such "national independence" can only be achieved at the expense of the freedom of the individual citizen and of the requirements of world order. There cannot be much doubt that it is the latter interpretation of "we", i.e. *we, the community,* that Keynes has in mind.

Having thus taken us very far into the dangerous world of nationalism and collectivism, Keynes ends his essay with a forceful plea for "bold, free, and remorseless criticism" and sharply critizes Stalin because he "has eliminated every independent, critical mind" and "has produced an environment in which the processes of mind are atrophied". "The bleat of propaganda", says Keynes in a final bouquet of verbal fireworks, "bores even the birds and the beasts of the field into stupefaction. Let Stalin be a terrifying example to all who seek to make experiments."

These are fine words, and had Keynes but reflected on the connection that exists between collectivist planning and intolerance of criticism, he might have decided not to publish his essay after all. As it is, having given a tremendous amount of encouragement to all the budding collectivist experimenters, he opened for himself a little avenue of retreat. Should Stalin's "terrifying example" not be heeded, "I, at any rate," he says, "will soon be back again in my old nineteenth century ideals." As a matter of fact, while Keynes moved impenitently for another decade along the path of nationalism, he seems to have made at least a beginning along the road back in the last years of his life. [31]

Keynes never reverted again, at any length, to the subjectmatter of the essay just discussed; there are sufficient grounds to believe, though, that it represented far more than a passing mood. I have previously referred to some of the views formulated in his *General Theory of Employment, Interest and Money.* In the final passage of that influential book he takes up again the problem of the economic causes of war:

> War has several causes. Dictators and others such, to whom war offers, in expectation at least, a pleasurable excitement, find it easy to work on the natural bellicosity of their peoples. But, over and above this, facilitating their task of fanning the popular flame, are the economic causes of war, namely, the pressure of population and the competitive struggle for markets. It is the second factor, which probably played a predominant part in the nineteenth century, and might again, that is germane to this discussion.
>
> I have pointed out ... that, under the system of domestic *laissez faire* and an international gold standard such as was orthodox in the latter half of the nineteenth century, there was no means open

---

[31] Sir Roy Harrod underestimates, it seems to me, the essay on "National Self-Sufficiency" in his *Life of Keynes.* He only devotes to it one page, makes no reference to its having appeared in a leading American publication along with its publication in England, and does not elaborate on what cannot but be regarded as one of Keynes' foremost pronouncements on international economic relations. One comment which Harrod makes, however, should be quoted:
> "There is no doubt that what he mainly had in mind was that he wanted Britain, sooner or later, to make a bold experiment in achieving full employment by the methods that he advocated; in order that the experiment should be successful, British dependence on foreign conditions should be limited. The International Conference made it abundantly clear ... that the world was *not ripe for Keynesian experiments.* So let us cultivate our own garden; it was the best we could do. ..." (*Op. cit.,* p. 446; italics added.)

One may wonder whether the publication of this essay in the United States was not prompted by Keynes' desire to convert the United States to the "Keynesian doctrines". However that may be, his influence in the States became very considerable for a time. It may also be noted — although this might be pure coincidence — that the United States did embark upon an isolationist course of domestic policy in pursuit of an expansionist programme just about the time when Keynes' essay appeared.

to a government whereby to mitigate economic distress at home except through the competitive struggle for markets. For all measures helpful to a state of chronic or intermittent underemployment were ruled out, except measures to improve the balance of trade on income account. [32]

But this is precisely where Keynes' interpretation of history has no foundation in recorded facts. Except for minor conflicts, most of them colonial, and for the Franco-Prussian War, the nineteenth century was a century of peace — the most peaceful century indeed in many hundreds of years. The Franco-Prussian War itself was not due to economic reasons but to Bismarck's need for a foreign war which would speed up the consolidation of a German empire. Nor was there, as far as I know, any recorded instance in the liberal countries of the nineteenth century of governments adopting aggressive economic policies to improve "the balance of trade" as a cure for underemployment. The very concept of *laissez faire* precluded the adoption of such policies. Actually, there was no visible concern at that time over cures for chronic "underemployment" (should such a condition have then existed for any length of time, which also is subject to doubt).

This evident misinterpretation of history serves a purpose, however, for Keynes goes on as follows — in a vein reminiscent both of his earlier essay and of the views of Fichte:

> But if nations can learn to provide themselves with full employment by their domestic policy ... there need be no important economic forces calculated to set the interest of one country against that of its neighbours. There would still be room for the international division of labour and for international lending in appropriate conditions. But there would no longer be a pressing motive why one country need force its wares on another or repulse the offering of its neighbour... with the express object of upsetting the equilibrium of payments so as to develop a balance of trade in its own favour. International trade would cease to be what it is, namely, a desperate expedient to maintain employment at home by forcing sales on foreign markets and restricting purchases,... but a willing and unimpeded exchange of goods and services in conditions of mutual advantage.

---

[32] *General Theory*, pp. 381-2.
[33] *Ibid.*, pp. 382-3.

The type of international trade that Keynes describes and rejects is precisely trade dominated by the mercantilist creed. It had ceased to be that in the age of free trade, from the middle of the ninetheenth century up to World War I. It reverted to the old pattern once again when national planning and a revival of mercantilism resulted in attempts to regulate imports and exports for nationalistic purposes and without due regard for the welfare of people living in the various trading nations. Keynes' concern with measures to fight unemployment in the deep depression of the thirties was very honourable. His scorn for what has been called "beggar-my-neighbour policies" in international commerce is also highly understandable and commendable. But the judgment he passes on liberal international trade as a whole and the references he makes, in the passages quoted, to nineteenth century conditions, can only be regarded as a misrepresentation of history. It is almost an intellectual tragedy when a man of Keynes' stature and of Keynes' mind stoops to such methods in support of questionable policy recommendations!

Following the line of his intellectual development, it is not surprising to find Keynes entering eventually upon the path of bilateralism. "Keynes is believed to have had a mild flirtation with bilateralistic ideas at some time in the late thirties or early forties," wrote an American student of his works, "but if this is true, there are no traces of it in his published writings." [34] Actually, although it would appear that Keynes did not express his views on this subject in print, his "flirtation" with bilateralism is confirmed by a number of people who knew him during the early years of World War II. It is also confirmed by his biographer, Sir Roy Harrod. [35] Having gone thus far, Keynes was faced with new situations and it is at that point, somewhere between 1941 and 1943, that his famous "conversion" back to internationalism took place.

V

There can be no doubt that in the course of the early years of the war Keynes' approach to international economic relations under-

[34] Ragnar Nurkse: "Domestic and International Equilibrium", in the volume *The New Economics*, edited by Seymour E. Harris, New York, 1947, p. 290.
[35] *The Life of John Maynard Keynes, op. cit.*, p. 513.

went a profound change, that he abandoned the path of narrow economic nationalism which, for a time, had led him to the notion that England should adopt bilateralist policies in its future relations with the rest of the world, and became, in the last years of his life, an eloquent and convinced champion of an Anglo-American partnership for the restoration of multilateral world trade. Just what brought about such a change of heart is a fascinating question and it appears not to be an insoluble one.

As noted at the beginning of this chapter, one can consider this "conversion" as Keynes' return to "his earlier internationalism", to which Professor Robbins refers in his refutation of the essay on "National Self-Sufficiency". [86] In view of that we must regard it as a "re-conversion" rather than a "conversion", Keynes' first conversion having been from his early internationalism to, first, monetary and, then, economic nationalism. But such a "re-conversion" — from economic internationalism to economic nationalism and back again, some twenty years later — is a very rare occurrence indeed, especially when a man of the intellectual calibre and of the immense influence of John Maynard Keynes is involved! And it is a matter of very great interest to find out what brought about this change of attitude. Although Harrod, because he does not admit Keynes' economic nationalism to have been deep-rooted and consistent for about twenty years prior to the period we are investigating, does not deal with this problem in the particular way outlined here, he nevertheless furnishes us, I believe, with the most important elements of an explanation.

Harrod recalls the negotiations that took place in 1941 for the Master Lend-Lease Agreement, Article VII of which included provisions of great importance for the future Anglo-American partnership for the revival of multilateral trade. According to Harrod's account, Keynes reacted unfavourably to the original American proposals, which went far in the direction of eliminating, after the war, discriminatory trade practices and quantitative restrictions on trade and payments. "He, too," Harrod recounts, "had had the idea that the lend-lease commitments might somehow be tied up with a big programme of collaboration in world reconstruction. What he

---

[86] *Economic Planning and International Order, op. cit.,* p. 321.

had in mind was the application with American assistance of *Keynesian remedies* for unemployment and trade depression on a world scale. ... He had also in the forefront of his mind the appalling problems that Britain would face after the war in the matter of her own trade balance." [37] He was averse, therefore, to the non-discrimination provisions of the American draft. From there on Harrod's account must be quoted in full [38], for here, I believe, we find the key to the drastic change that took place in Keynes' views on post-war Anglo-American co-operation and thereby on the nature of the future world economy:

The word was passed around in certain British official quarters that Keynes had created an unhappy impression in the United States by insisting that after the war Britain would have to adopt bilateral methods in her trade policy. When the matter came to his ears, he strongly denied that he had advocated such a policy. He had in fact only had one talk about such matters in the State Department. In this he had taken the line that Britain would be driven willy-nilly to such a policy, unless there was a determined effort to reconstruct world trade and finance after the war, an effort which presupposed generous support from the United States. This single talk had been interrupted in the midst by the other engagements of his interlocutors. It was quite monstrous to charge him with having spread the doctrine of bilateralism on the strength of it.

Mr. Harry Hawkins recalls the occasion; he had been the spokesman of the State Department. Keynes had indeed warned his audience that Britain would have to employ all the weapons of Dr. Schacht, unless there was a large joint Anglo-American effort to restore equilibrium of trade and thus make such devices unnecessary. Mr. Hawkins had not come briefed to make any adequate reply, and they had been pressed for time. He had confined himself to giving a counter-warning. Should Britain indeed feel compelled to adopt such measures, the United States would be driven, not out of ill-will, but by the inevitable logic of events, to adopt a similar policy herself. She would have to do so to protect and enforce the just claims of her own citizens. In this economic warfare, he pointed out, it was only too probable that the United States would be the victor. If Britain was hard driven and seriously attempted to employ Schachtian tactics, she must remember that she would not gain the benefits of a Power who did this alone, but

---

[37] *The Life of John Maynard Keynes, op. cit.,* p. 512 (italics added).
[38] *Ibid.,* p. 513.

would lead all others, including the United States, to similar ways, and the law of the jungle would rule in foreign trade. Weighty words!

It follows from the above passage that Keynes was induced by his American conversations to proceed to a far-reaching re-examination of his views on Britain's post-war economic policy. [39] Obviously these conversations could only have given the original impetus, or maybe they precipitated a process of "agonizing reappraisal" which had already started in his mind. It is well-known that Keynes' closest circle during the war included people who were thoroughly convinced, all along, of the need for Britain to engage in the closest co-operation with the United States, not only during but also after the war. These people, who certainly did not underestimate — as some of Keynes' American connections might have done — the scope of post-war readjustment that it would be necessary for Britain to undertake, were convinced that only within the framework of revived multilateral world trade and only in closest partnership with the United States could Britain's problem be resolved. Be that as it may, there is evidence that these conservations in Washington played a role in bringing about a change in Keynes' general attitude to British foreign economic policy. In 1923 and in 1933, Keynes evidently believed that Anglo-American co-operation was neither urgent nor essential and, possibly, he even doubted whether it was possible. By 1943 he must have come to the conclusion that it was henceforth not

---

[39] When I read Harrod's biography of Keynes I found the statement quoted above so important that I sought, for my own enlightenment, to obtain Mr. Hawkins' personal recollections. He indeed, "vividly recalled" the conversation which took place in 1941 and gave me the account he had given previously to Harrod, when the latter was engaged in his biographer's job. I also might mention a conversation with my regretted friend Leo Pasvolsky, who all through the war occupied an important State Department position as Special Assistant to the Secretary of State, and who had conversations with Keynes along the same lines during 1943. Pasvolsky told me how he related to Keynes a discussion he had had with Dr. Schacht some time before the war: "How can you hope", Pasvolsky inquired of Schacht, "to hold your own, even using all your economic tactics against the very large population of the democratic world, once the democracies will have decided to oppose you actively throughout the world by economic counter-measures?" Dr. Schacht's answer was quick to come and entirely precise: "Should it ever come to that", he told Pasvolsky, "we shall just have to abandon our present policies." This story, Leo Pasvolsky told me, appeared to make a considerable impression on Keynes.

only possible but indeed indispensable. Once this was admitted, there was no further scope for economic nationalism.

This would seem to me to be the true explanaiton of Keynes' "re-conversion". [40] Having reached the conclusion that co-operation with America was indispensable for Great Britain, Keynes devoted the remaining (and all too few) years of his life to promoting and cementing this partnership. There is little published material from these strenuous years and Keynes' last great speech delivered in the House of Lords, on December 18, 1945 [41], must be regarded as the most important declaration of his new faith. In that speech, from which key pasages are quoted below, he made an unequivocal stand in favour of multilateral trade:

> The object of the multilateral system is to enable us to pay the United States by exporting to any part of the world and it is partly for that very reason that the Americans have felt the multilateral system was the only sound basis for any arrangement of this kind.

Referring to the kind of policy the United States and Great Britain could agree upon and foreshadowing the conversations that were about to begin concerning the establishment of an International Trade Organization, Keynes went on as follows:

> ... much of these policies seem to me to be in the prime interest of our country, little though we may like some parts of them. They are calculated to help us regain a full measure of prosperity and prestige in the world's commerce. They aim, above all, at the restoration of *multilateral trade, which is a system upon which British commerce essentially depends.* [42] You can draw your supplies from any source that suits you and sell your goods in any market where they can be sold to advantage. The bias of the policies before you is against bilateral barter and every kind of discriminatory practice. The separate economic blocs and all the friction

---

[40] Harrod contributes another, which strikes me as far less convincing: so long as England alone was willing to translate his doctrines into policies Keynes was all in favour of economic isolation. But when the United States and many of the other countries of the world turned Keynesian, international co-operation became, in his view, a possibility (*op. cit.,* pp. 525-6).

[41] *Parliamentary Debates* (Hansard), House of Lords, Vol. 138, No. 41. The subject of the speech was the Anglo-American financial arrangements of which Keynes had been the principal negotiator and which had been concluded earlier that month.

[42] Italics added.

and loss of friendship they must bring with them are expedients to which one may be driven in a hostile world, where trade has ceased over wide areas to be co-operative and peaceful and where are forgotten the healthy rules of mutual advantage and equal treatment. But it is surely crazy to prefer that. Above all, this determination to make trade truly international and to avoid the establishment of economic blocs which limit and restrict commercial intercourse outside them, is plainly an essential condition of the world's best hope, an Anglo-American understanding, which brings us and others together in international institutions which may be in the long run the first step towards something more comprehensive. Some of us, in the tasks of war and more lately in those of peace, have learnt by experience that our two countries can work together. Yet it would be only too easy for us to walk apart. I beg those who look askance at these plans to ponder deeply and responsibly where it is they think they want to go.

It is impressive to see how far Keynes had travelled since the days of 1933 and of 1936. Although we can trace his change of heart and its probable causes, it is difficult to say how deep his "reconversion" actually was. There are strong indications that he would have continued to travel the new road. In June 1946 the *Economic Journal,* of which Keynes had been Editor for many years, published posthumously his last article. Its subject is: "The Balance of Payments of the United States". In that article, between the lines of which one can read Keynes' recurring hope for an American inflation (a hope discreetly voiced in the House of Lords speech as well), he seems to be turning away from some of his other inter-war conceptions. "I find myself moved, not for the first time," he writes, "to remind contemporary economists that the classical teaching embodied some permanent truths of great significance, which we are liable today to overlook because we associate them with other doctrines which we cannot now accept without much qualification. There are in these matters deep undercurrents at work, natural forces, one can call them, or even the invisible hand, which are operating towards equilibrium. If it were not so, we could not have got on even so well as we have for many decades past. ... I must not be misunderstood. I do not suppose that the classical medicine will work by itself or that we can depend on it. We need quicker and less painful aids, of which exchange variation and overall import control are the most important. But in the long run these expedients will work better, and we shall need them less, if the classical medicine is also at work. And if we reject the medicine from our system altogether, we may just drift on from expedient to expedient and never get really fit again." [48]

It is impossible to be certain about the direction in which Keynes would have gone on from there. Would he have come to reject import quotas and exchange controls or would he have maintained his adherence to these mercantilist controls? No one can say, and the different schools of his disciples are entirely at odds when it comes to this question. Fortunately, this is not a matter on which it is necessary to express an opinion here. The important thing to note in the present context is the fact that Keynes reached the end of the road of economic nationalism and found it to be a blind alley, and that findig it to be a blind alley he retraced his steps and entered the highway of international co-operation for the re-establishment of multilateral trade. What is one man's intellectual and moral experience is, of course, of primary interest to his biographer and many will regret that Sir Roy Harrod did not tell us much more about this phase of Keynes' life, upon which he should be in a unique position to enlighten his readers. But the fact that circumstances of the real world forced so enthusiastic an iconoclast and so influential an advocate of economic nationalism as Keynes to revise and reverse his views is not *just* one man's experience; it is an experience which sheds much light upon the nature of economic nationalism itself. What this experience reveals is the essential sterility of the nationalistic and isolationist approach to a country's major economic problems. This is why an account of Keynes' "reconversion" to internationalism had to find a prominent place in the present book.

VI

Our main theme in this inquiry is the connection between economic nationalism and collectivism. Was Keynes, then, a liberal or a collectivist? This question calls for careful consideration.

---

[48] Lord Keynes: "The Balance of Payments of the United States" in *The Econamic Journal*, London, Vol. LVI, No. 222, June, 1946, pp. 185-6.

As everybody familiar with his work will readily concede, Keynes was not the kind of man on whom it would be easy to pin a label. We find troughout Keynes' writings a great many statements upholding a liberal outlook on life and on individual prerogatives and liberties. It would be easy to compose an impressive anthology of such statements in which practically every single major work of Keynes would be represented. Keynes considered himself to be a liberal and yet even in his writings on the subject of liberalism he expresses views which only a collectivist could hold. In an earlier book, *The Trade of Nations,* I myself described Keynes as having been "fundamentally a liberal". [44] Since then I have re-read and pondered over practically everything Keynes has written. It is my conclusion now that Keynes never took a *clear-cut* stand in the controversy between liberalism and collectivism. He never found it necessary to make a choice. He seems not to have been impressed by anything contradictory between sets of divergent views which he would almost simultaneously express and which would strike almost anyone else as inconsistent. There is, however, one criterion that could be usefully applied in this connection. It is this: what are his actual policy recommendations? And here the general impression is that Keynes was fascinated by collectivism, even while he would say kind and beautiful things about liberalism and even though he was a foe of totalitarianism. Although Keynes very frequently expressed sentiments favourable to individual liberty and to political freedom, his *policy recommendations* invariably go the other way. If he was a liberal, then he was that extraordinary kind of liberal whose practical recommendations consistently promote collectivism.

I have already commented on the clearly collectivist implications of Keynes' essay on "National Self-Sufficiency". But let us go further back. In 1926 Keynes wrote a small book entitled *The End of Laissez-Faire,* a part of which he included in his *Essays in Persuasion* published in 1931. From this I quote the following: [45]

> I believe that some co-ordinated act of intelligent judgment is required as to the scale on which it is desirable that the community as a whole should save, the scale on which these savings should go

---

[44] *Op. cit.,* p. 94.
[45] J.M. Keynes: *Essays in Persuasion,* London, 1931, pp. 318-19.

abroad in the form of foreign investments, and whether the present organisation of the investment market distributes savings along the most nationally productive channels. I do not think that these matters should be left entirely to the chances of private judgment and private profits, as they are at present.

Now, this is a collectivist recommendation, involving the determination by the state of matters which, in a liberal society, are left to individual decisions. In his *General Theory*, Keynes takes up this idea in much greater detail. "I expect to see the State", he says, "taking an ever greater responsibility for directly organizing investment"; and again: "I conceive ... that a somewhat comprehensive socialisation of investment will prove the only means of securing an approximation to full employment ... ." It is true that he goes on to say that "beyond this no obvious case is made out for a system of State socialism which would embrace most of the economic life of the community" [46], thereby lending support to those who claim that he was not a socialist. Unfortunately, having never examined the practical consequences of a "somewhat comprehensive socialisation of investment", he had no opportunity to say whether he would accept these consequences or abandon his socialization proposal, for it is hard to see how an economic system could long remain liberal in which all investment decisions would have to be taken by the state. It is precisely because Keynes frequently failed to follow his suggestions to their logical end that his doctrinal position is, in many cases, far from clear.

Let us turn once more to the *The End of Laissez-Faire*:

The time has already come when each country needs a considered national policy about what size of Population, whether larger or smaller than at present or the same, is most expedient. And having settled this policy, we must take steps to carry it into operation. The time may arrive a little later when the community as a whole must pay attention to the innate quality as well as to the mere numbers of its future members. [47]

Now, any careful reader of these lines will perceive how alien they are to the liberal concept of society. What Keynes is actually

---

[46] *General Theory, op. cit.,* pp. 164, 378.
[47] *Essays in Persuasion, op. cit.,* p. 319.

advocating is government regulation not only of the size of the population but also of the qualitative aspects of that population — and that opens the door to very unwholesome speculations indeed. Again, Keynes does not spell out his thought in full and we are merely left with an uneasy feeling that there is a good deal of the collectivist in him. [48]

Examples could be multiplied, but the above quotations coupled with Keynes' views on "national self-sufficiensy" and his views — already cited — on the need for comprehensive economic planning, all lead to the same conclusion. Even though Keynes was not a consistent doctrinal collectivist, his practical recommendations would allow collectivism to infiltrate the social system and, very likely, to

---

[48] The puzzling episode of Keynes' preface to the German translation of the *General Theory* is an indelible blot on his record as a liberal. It is to be noted (with regret) that Harrod's biography, instead of explaining this episode, ignores it altogether. The German translation appeared in the same year as the English original, i.e. in 1936, three and a half years after Hitler came to power and after many scholars had been summarily dismissed form German universities and others, including my colleague and friend, Wilhelm Röpke, had left voluntarily in protest against the Nazi tyranny. Yet Keynes saw no objection to publishing a German translation, indeed wrote a special preface to commend his book to the German readers. Leaving aside the moral climate of this, let me just quote an important passage from the preface. I quote it in German since Keynes' original text is not available. The gist of it is this: while the book (*General Theory*) is adressed primarily to an Anglo-Saxon public, it may constitute a contribution, however modest, to the "full meal" prepared by German economists in view of conditions prevailing in their country — such is, at least, Keynes' hope. And he draws the atention of the German readers to the fact that the theory of global output, the principal contents of his book, fits much better the conditions prevailing in a totalitarian State than does a theory of production and distribution based on free competition and a large measure of *laissez faire*. The German text follows:

"Und wenn ich einige einzelne Brocken beitragen kann zu einem von deutschen Ökonomen zubereiteten vollen Mahl, eigens auf deutsche Verhältnisse abgestellt, werde ich zufrieden sein. Denn ich gestehe, dass vieles in dem folgenden Buche hauptsächlich mit Bezug auf die Verhältnisse in den angelsächsischen Ländern erläutert und dargelegt worden ist. Trotzdem kann die Theorie der Produktion als Ganzes, die den Zweck des folgenden Buches bildet, viel leichter den Verhältnissen eines totalen Staates angepasst werden, als die Theorie der Erzeugung und Verteilung einer gegebenen, unter Bedingungen des freien Wettbewerbes und eines grossen Masses von *laissez-faire* erstellten Produktion." (*Allgemeine Theorie der Beschäftigung, des Zinses und des Geldes*, Berlin, Duncker & Humblot, 1936).

Keynes' Preface is dated 7 September 1936 and it has been maintained in the recent printings of the book (such as the 1955 printing from which my quotation is taken).

conquer it. In that, as in his views on monetary autonomy and economic insulation, Keynes is truly a child of his age, and that age is full of confusion and is a very dangerous one for the freedom of man.

Far be it from my intention to pass an overall judgment here on Keynes' economic and political work. His influence has been immense and has stemmed from the books and other writings analysed in the preceding pages, as well as from his personal qualities. In summing up, I feel I can do no better than quote the following passages from Professor Jacob Viner's review of Harrod's *Life*:

> Keynes probably contributed more than any other one person to the abandonment by England of its most important legacies from the classical tradition: the belief in the gold standard, in free trade, in free competition, in private and public frugality and thrift, and in a moderately cosmopolitan approach to international economic problems. ... I am not convinced ... that the final result of Keynes' application of his unequalled power of advocacy to the overturn of the classical tradition in economics will be to make this a better or safer world to live in. Keynes was a great man but he was also at a number of critical moments in recent history — from 1919 to 1939 — a greatly wrong man. [49]

[49] *Saturday Review of Literature*, New York, March 24, 1951.

CHAPTER VII

ECONOMIC NATIONALISM SINCE WORLD WAR II:
COLLECTIVIST PLANNING AND ECONOMIC NATIONALISM

I

At this final stage of our discussion a further short excursion into semantics appears indicated as a supplement to the analysis of basic concepts proposed in Chapters I and II. I use in the title of the present chapter the term "collectivist planning", rather than "economic planning", in order to forestall a possible misunderstanding. Advocates of planned economies often hope to confound their opponents by pointing out that every purposeful action, whether private or public, requires planning and that there is nothing very special about taking cognizance of that fact in the field of economics. Professor Gunnar Myrdal suggested in an essay on "The Trend towards Economic Planning" [2] that "the term 'economic planning' and perhaps still more bluntly 'planned economy' contains a tautology. ... The word 'economy' by itself implies, of course, a co-ordination of activities, directed towards a purpose. It implies a subject, a will, a plan, and a rational adaptation of means towards an end or a goal. To add 'planned' in order to indicate that this co-ordination of

---

[1] The scope of the present chapter is limited in the two following ways: in the first place, only the late war and early postwar (World War II) economic literature is considered, for it is there that we find the best guide to the intellectual "climate" of the economic nationalism of the past fifteen years. In the second place, as regards the motivation of national planning, I have concentrated on full employment planning as example, rather than on economic development planning. The implications for international economic relations are the same, or sufficiently so, I think, to justify this limitation (without which the present chapter could easily have become as long as the six chapters that precede, taken jointly).

[2] *Manchester School of Economic and Social Studies*, Vol. XIX, No. 1, January, 1951, pp. 1-42.

activities has a purpose, does not make much sense or cannot, anyhow, be good usage." Nevertheless, he finds it necessary to use that terminology throughout the balance of his essay. Clearly, when we speak of economic planning, we mean something else than the fact of a rational juxtaposition of ends and means. By giving the word "planned" too comprehensive a meaning we would render it useless for the purpose of intellectual clarification. In order to be useful, it has to be defined in a more restrictive sense and in opposition to something else. Myrdal perceives that, for he quickly knocks down his own man of straw and opposes planned economies to liberal economies.

It is to avoid this kind of confusion, at times unwitting and at times deliberate, that I propose to use here the term "collectivist planning" to describe a form of economic organization where the government, acting on behalf of the community (as the phrase goes), determines by authority the distribution of resources between various uses and of end-products between various users. The liberal economy, by contrast, leaves such determination to the operation of the price system and of the mechanism of free markets. Collectivist planning is, then, a notion opposed not only to *laissez faire* (an opposition particularly dear to the proponents of collectivist planning, as it greatly facilitates their arguments) but also to economic liberalism, which, unlike *laissez faire,* involves important elements of deliberate policy on the part of the public authorities. Now the line between a liberal economy, as distinct from *laissez faire,* and a planned economy (in the collectivist sense) is not always an easy one to draw. Yet, as already pointed out in Chapter I, it is an important distinction to make. Liberal economic policies will always be designed in such a way as to protect and supplement the price system rather than interfere with it or substitute something else for it. Just when public policy starts interfering with the operation of the price mechanism may be difficult to establish in marginal cases; nevertheless, with the use of a modicum of "horse sense" (without which one cannot get very far in the realm of social sciences and in the realm of human relations generally), one cannot fail to distinguish between policies which are truly liberal and those which stultify the market economy and constitute a prelude to collectivist planning.

Let us add, in passing, that certain concepts wich have been introduced rather recently into economic analysis favour a collectivist approach to economic policy-making. These are the "global" or "aggregative" concepts, such as aggregate demand, gross national product, net national income, and many others. These concepts are very useful tools of knowledge but their use by policy-makers is not devoid of risk. They provide a strong temptation for the policy-maker to try to influence these magnitudes directly, whereas, in a liberal society, changes in these magnitudes are always the indirect outcome of a very large number of individual decisions, freely taken. There is one exception to that rule and it is to be found in the field of monetary relations. Under central banking the total amount of money in circulation not only *can* but *must* be determined by a central monetary authority. It is a characteristic feature of a liberal economy that the amount of money in circulation should be controlled while everything else is left to the operation of the market (with some correctives and supplements as need arises). Actually, the concept of "aggregate demand" for goods and services has become the most important single tool used by the collectivist planner in western societies.

The mercantilists were, in one respect at least, forerunners of the collectivist planners of today. They regarded the desired condition of the trade balance (i.e. an export surplus) as something to be striven for by deliberate policy, rather than left to spontaneous economic processes. The adoption of a number of authoritarian economic controls was the result of that attitude. The concept of a centralized plan covering all the various aspects of the national economy was, however, alien to the mercantilists. The real precursor of collectivist planning is, of course, Fichte. Unlike free trade, collectivist planning has not been, by and large, the result of doctrinal influence but rather an outgrowth of empirical situations, rationalized *ex post facto*. As Professor Myrdal rightly points out in the essay cited above, economic planning is not a marxist concept and there is no reference to planning in the works of Marx. It is a concept, however, which inevitably had to grow out of the doctrines which deprecated private property and the market system. As pointed out in Chapter II, the advocates of public ownership of the means of production did not come to grips with the problem of centralized planning as long as their schemes were proposals on paper only. As soon as these were adopted in practice, the question had to arise of how the nationalized means of production were to be operated and co-ordinated — and then the gates were thrown open to collectivist planning.

What would have happened to socialism in that respect if it had not been for the Bolshevik Revolution of 1917 is an idle, albeit a very intriguing, speculation. By suppressing private property almost overnight and by nationalizing all the means of production — and all this in the midst of external war and internal revolution — the Soviet regime could not have avoided centralized planning even if it had wanted to. We have since learned that a war economy must, to a large extent, be a centrally planned economy, and in newly sovietized Russia war was compounded with revolution, while the entire "class" of private entrepreneurs was quickly and by no means bloodlessly "liquidated".

After a few years many western socialists began to look to the Soviet system as a model, indignant maybe at its oppressive features but fascinated by its economic "plan". That the connection, in that system, between planning and oppression was far from fortuitous, these early enthusiasts of economic planning have curiously failed to see. As recently as 1937, Professor G. D. H. Cole of Oxford extolled the virtues of "socialist planning" in the U.S.S.R. [3] A vast "planistic" literature developed on both sides of the Atlantic in the twenties and thirties; in the latter decade the economic depression greatly stimulated its growth. Nevertheless, there is no single modern writer who could possibly be singled out as a leading exponent of economic planning. If one considers the degree of wishful thinking which permeates the literature on economic planning of the western world when matters such as its impact on individual freedom or its impact on international relations are concerned, one can find no better antidote than old Fichte, whose logic was relentless and who spent no time paying lip service to victims of his system.

---

[3] G.D.H. Cole: *Practical Economics*, London, 1937, a small book especially written for the popular series of "Penguin Books". The following remark is typical of the general tone of this book: "The planned system of the Soviet Union begets not only maximum production but also within the bounds of practical ability maximum welfare." A highly questionable statement, to say the least!

Keynes, in all fairness, cannot be regarded as a "prophet" of collectivist planning, although most of his practical proposals actually stimulated collectivism and did much damage to liberal economic policies. Keynes' contrast with Fichte is very interesting. Fichte deliberately promoted a system which in our day would have been described as collectivist, but his practical influence in that direction was nil; Keynes, on the other hand, never endorsed the collectivist creed, but had a very strong influence on the rising collectivists who were in search of a prophet more urbane and more up to date than Marx. All in all, however, there is no *single* individual writer in our day who might be regarded as *the* authoritative spokesman for the collectivist position. Because of that, it will be necessary in this chapter to quote from the writings of several members of this school of thought in order to illustrate those phases of the collectivist doctrine which are particularly relevant to the present inquiry.

II

"We are all aware nowadays of the strong case for State planning and control", says Professor James E. Meade in the opening pages of his *Planning and the Price Mechanism* [4] (the word "all" is one with which one might pick a quarrel, but let us ignore it for the present). This he attributes largely to "welfare considerations", three in number. The first is "the inter-war experience of mass unemployment. By the end of the 1930's there was widespread, in fact practically general, [5] agreement that the State should at least intervene to control the total demand for goods and services." The second consideration is "a growing realization of the shocking inequalities of income and property which *laissez faire* had produced." He notes that during the inter-war years "there was developing a school of thought which held the view that an effective remedy could be found only through so extensive a system of State control of the

---

[4] London, 1948. This quotation and those immediately following are from pp. 2 and 3 of that book.
[5] Here again Professor Meade is exaggerating the extent to which these views were accepted in the thirties or are accepted now. This very exaggeration, however, is typical of the school of thought to which he belongs.

community's resources as to make possible a centrally planned distribution of the product of industry." The third condideration Professor Meade finds in "a growing consciousness of those wastes of competition which result when there is, for one reason or another, a divergence between the private and the social interest in an economic act." [6] He gives certain examples of waste more in the nature of abuses than of typical features of the competitive economy and adds that these abuses "convinced many persons that it would be wise to replace the profit motive which could have such ugly results by planned production for the common good." [7]

To the pre-war arguments in favour of planning, Meade adds "a special post-war argument" applying to the transitional period. Now, no one would, of course, deny that the great destruction caused by war would require special remedial measures involving a similar degree of centralized planning as that incident to the conduct of war. A liberal economist would add that such a transitional period should be as short as possible and that the centralized planning should give way, at the earliest possible time, to the free operation of the market economy. This, however, does not seem to be Professor Meade's conclusion, and it certainly is not the conclusion of the school of economists who favour collectivist economic planning *per se,* as intrinsically superior to a free economy. As regards these economists, the three reasons for collectivist planning put forward by Meade seem to be a very good explanation of their point of view.

Having accepted planning, Professor Meade examines two methods of carrying it out: one without the use of the price mechanism, the other with. To the former he rightly objects and, considering how favourable to state planning his general outlook is, these objections are worth quoting in his own word:

---

[6] Professor Meade does not say, and here again his omission is typical, just who is to determine "the social interest in an economic act" and its divergence from the private interest. To present the case in that language is to beg the question, for a determination by government is presupposed in the very argument that is to lead to the conclusion that such an interference is necessary.

[7] Among the abuses mentioned we find "the exploitation of consumers and workers by monopolistic concerns." How the evil would be cured by substituting for private monopolies government sponsored monopolies is not explained.

In the first place, the method of direct controls contains a threat to personal freedom. It is not merely that it threatens our freedom of choice as consumers, important though this is. ... But the most dangerous threat to freedom arises from the problem of allocating labour as a factor of production among its various alternative employments. ...

In the second place, a system of direct quantitative controls is the breeding ground for spivery and corruption. It is the father of black markets and carries with it an insidious threat to public morality. ...

Thirdly, such a system of planning through direct controls involves the use of much manpower and other economic resources merely in working the controls. [8] ...

Fourthly, the method of control by the quantitative allocation of resources ... is bound to be clumsy, inefficient and wasteful as compared with a properly functioning price system. [9]

There can be no quarrel with any of these statements. Nor can one take issue with Professor Meade when he declares that "money and the pricing system are among the greatest social inventions of mankind." [10]

And so we are in a dilemma if the objectives of state planning as formulated by Meade are accepted (as he accepts them and I do not); and if one objects to the methods of direct planning by government decree (as both he and I do), then what is one to do? Professor Meade speaks for the entire school of what one might call the "urbane" collectivists (in contradistinction to the "bull in the china shop" collectivists) when he looks to the so-called "indirect" controls for a solution. These he describes as making "a controlled and planned use of money and pricing systems." [11] He continues as follows:

Such a solution would combine as much as possible of the decentralized freedoms and peculiar efficiencies of the price mechanism with that large extension of the field for State planning and control over total money demand, over the distribution of income and property, and over private monopoly which is necessary to avoid the chief evils of the inter-war system. And a controlled use of in-

---

[8] Interestingly enough, this is the point on which Fichte too had made a pertinent comment.
[9] *Op. cit.*, pp. 6-7.
[10] *Ibid.*, p. 9.
[11] *Ibid.*, p. 10.

ducements, through the mechanism of the money and price system, although, for reasons already examined, it could scarcely be relied upon alone to accomplish the rapid and large structural changes which are needed, might do much to influence the adjustments required in the present transitional period.

Professor Meade describes his own proposals as "an efficient middle way" between Soviet communism and American capitalism. He calls this "the liberal-socialist solution" — a rather contradictory and confusing use of words — and formulates as follows the three fundamental conditions of its success:

> First, that the total monetary demand for goods and services is neither too great nor too small in relation to the total supply of goods and services that can be made available for the purchase; secondly, that there is a tolerably equitable distribution of money income and property so that no individual can command more than his fair share of the community's resources; and, thirdly, that no private person or body of persons should be allowed to remain uncontrolled in a sufficiently powerful position to rig the market for his own selfish ends. [12]

The vagueness of these three conditions is apparent as soon as one tries to search beyond the sound of the words for their meaning: how does one establish the proper relationship between the total of money measured in monetary units and a heterogeneous aggregate of goods and services? What is "a tolerably equitable distribution of money income"? Who is to tell what is an individual's "fair share" of the community's resources? How is the control over excessive private economic power to be made fully effective? No workable system can be built on such vague precepts. The "practical proposals" which form the substance of Professor Meade's book are made, on the whole, of the same materials as the three "fundamental conditions" quoted above.

In practice, the middle course, in so far as it has been experimented with, has been far more successful in reducing the efficiency of the free economy than in providing the advantages of planning which its proponents seek to achieve. When the "middle course"

---

[12] *Ibid.*, p. 11.

doesn't succeed, advocates of planning have an easy enough excuse for its failure; it is not comprehensive and far-reaching enough. And so the drift towards more collectivism goes on until complete state control over economic life becomes a reality. Looked upon as a series of expedients, the "middle course" obviously exists; but as a consistent body or doctrine, there is no room for it. Intellectual consistency — and practical stability — can only be achieved by either a liberal economic system, in which the state does not attempt to do the architect's work in relation to the economic system, or by a collectivist system, where the state undertakes to be architect, administrator, and judge, all in one. Some British socialist writers, like G. D. H. Cole, saw this very clearly when, as already noted, they declared in the thirties that the Soviet system was the only true case of socialist planning then in existence. On the other hand, the failure of the Labour government in Great Britain to achieve any success in planning over the six years of its career is an indication that the "middle of the road" schemes are far better on paper than in reality. To plan more effectively the British government would have had to turn away more and more from democratic principles and to disregard increasingly those freedoms which may survive under a system of "monetary controls" but which must surely perish under "direct" methods of centralized planning.

III

We must not stray, however, from the main line of our inquiry. Having briefly surveyed the various approaches to collectivist planning and formulated some critical comments concerning the "urbane" collectivist position, let us now examine the international consequences of collectivist planning. To a collectivist, foreign trade is, of course, a very inconvenient factor, liable to upset his most careful calculations through some accidental occurences in the external world. If only all countries had planned economies and thereby (let us hope) were to become rational and foreseeable entities, the foreign trade of planned economies might still be rationally foreseeable — but there are, alas, countries that would not plan centrally and whose unwillingness to do so interferes with the most carefully laid plans of the planners. [13] Such is the complaint of the "planners". From complaining of the "inconveniences" of foreign trade to advocating policies of insulation, there is only one step. Here again Fichte's doctrines are our best guide, for he was clear-headed where collectivists of today are not. What Fichte saw and they do not see are the evil consequences of *partial* insulation. Fichte's logic, as we know, led him to postulating full isolation — a proposal which is, of course, utterly impracticable and could not be seriously entertained by anybody in the modern world.

Closest to this concept of isolation comes the Keynesian notion of a country's reducing its foreign trade to a minimum so as to increase to the utmost its freedom of national economic action. As we have seen, Keynes never carefully examined the implications of his proposal. Neither have those who continued to offer it as a principle of sound economic policy at the time of international conferences drawing up a charter for the proposed International Trade Organization. Nevertheless, the concept of insulated national economies is a necessary corollary of collectivist economic planning. Because of the "disturbing effects" of international trade the former is inconceivable without the latter. The latter, of course, is essentially nationalistic and leads to policies which could not but seriously disturb the world economy and keep it in a condition of disintegration and chaos.

Today, we fortunately have at our disposal a large body of practical experience with which to support the thesis of the incompatibility of national planning with a workable international economy. But pure reasoning could settle the case beyond any reasonable doubt. I have referred already to the Fichtean analysis. Among contemporary writers, none has presented the case more clearly and convincingly than Professor Lionel Robbins, whose book *Economic Planning and International Order* appeared in 1937. It is one of the most important studies in this field and one which should be read by every student of this subject. What Professor Robbins shows very clearly is the disruptive effect upon the world economy of planning

---

[13] A very characteristic sentence might be quoted from *The Principles of Economic Planning* by Professor W. Arthur Lewis (London, 1949): "We must resign ourselves to cyclical fluctuations in international trade until such time as the U.S.A. is converted to planning for stability" (p. 72).

carried out by national states. He then examines the possibilities of international planning on a world scale and arrives at the conclusion that world planning would involve as much of a loss of liberty as does national planning. The distribution of capital and labour, no longer brought about through the market process, would have to be subjected to "some mechanism of authoritative control", while "decision with regard to these issues would tend to gravitate more and more into the hands of men not subject to democratic control." And so we should be moving into a dictatorial system in which "mass propaganda, stunt trials and secret coercion would become the normal instruments of government," while "individual freedom and variety would suffer final extinction". [14]

Luckily, world planning could only follow upon the establishment of a world state, and that is not at present on the cards. The advocates of such a political enterprise, however, might find it a sobering thought that, if established, a world state might easily lead, in certain circumstances, to world despotism. Everybody is free to pick his own daydreams and, with Professor Robbins, I should choose world liberalism instead.

IV

A planned economy that wishes to be insulated from the world economy has at its disposal a number of devices, some of them already known to the mercantilists, others introduced in more recent times. The most important are import quotas and exchange controls. The former consists in the licensing by the government of specified quantities of imports of particular goods, the latter involves the licensing by the government of all foreign payments and the obligation upon the residents of the country to surrender to the government all receipts in foreign currency in exchange for national currency. In order to arrive at a system of import quotas, the governement must establish what it regards as a desirable pattern of the country's import trade, involving the setting up of a system of priorities, the determination of maximum quantities for the importation of the

---

[14] *Op. cit.*, pp. 219-20.

various goods, and the allocation of this total among the various importers. In a more advanced stage of collectivism, there are no private importers any more, for the state has assumed a monopoly of foreign trade. Then state trading replaces the quota system.

Exchange control plays a major role in the type of collectivist planning where trade and finance are (at least temporarily) left in private hands but are subject to strict governmental supervision. In order to evolve a system of exchange control the government has again to lay down plans for foreign payments and enforce those plans through allocations of foreign exchange and other devices. The system of exchange control has many technical aspects, such as the manipulation of foreign exchange rates and the operation of multiple rates (i.e., making the national currency available to some buyers more cheaply than to others). In a free market economy, the rates at which the various currencies exchange for one another are closely inter-related and so-called arbitrage transactions lead to a uniformity of "cross-rates" of exchange in the various foreign exchange markets of the world. One of the first effects of exchange control, however, consists in a suppression of arbitrage. [15] Under a regime of free international payments and free foreign exchange markets, we obtain — as we did under the gold standard — a very close approximation to a world currency; in a system of exchange control this approximation to a world currency disintegrates into a maze of unrelated national currencies which only the most stringent regulations and draconian enforcement procedures can prevent, up to a point, from turning into the black marketeer's paradise.

It will be appropriate here to define more closely the two concepts of *multilateral trade* and *bilateralism*. We call multilateral trade a system in which a country seeks the appropriate monetary policies to keep its payments with the outside world in balance without expecting them to balance with any particular country. The surplus achieved in trade relations with one country or group of countries is used to pay off debts incurred in commercial and financial transactions with other countries. In order that this multilateral system may operate, any

---

[15] These rather technical matters are discussed at greater length in Chapter III of my *Trade of Nations,* and in Chapters VI and X of my *International Monetary Economics,* already cited.

country which earns a credit balance in its dealings with a second country must be able to use that balance freely to pay a debt to a third country. [16] Hence the freedom of international payments is a condition of multilateralism, while the introduction of exchange control tends to limit greatly its scope and eventually destroys it altogether.

What takes its place is bilateralism, a trading system in which every country seeks to balance its payments with every foreign country taken separately. Both reasoning and experience show that bilateralism tends to erstrict trade below the level it would achieve under a system of multilateral payments. Normally, transactions are not in balance between any two countries. If surpluses earned in one place cannot be used to pay off deficits incurred somewhere else, accounts must be balanced either by expanding the exports of the "deficit" country to the "surplus" country, or by reducing the former country's imports. In practice, the second is the more likely course, for it is far easier to use controls for the purpose of restriction rather than of expansion. That such a bilateralist system would tend to place the weaker country at the mercy of the stronger is pretty obvious and has been amply verified by the experience of Nazi trade in the thirties and of Soviet trade more recently. The system of controlling and restricting imports is frequently combined with measures that promote exports artificially by subsidy or by exchange rate manipulation. [17] The entire fabric of international trade relations becomes distorted and subject to arbitrary decisions; it is, indeed, a strange paradox that the more countries plan and control their foreign trade, the less previsible becomes the pattern of world trade for each and every one of them. The relative stability of trade currents in a liberal world is replaced by the wilfulness of governmental decisions.

Bilateralism brings again into the foreground a wide acceptance of one of the mercantilist fallacies, against which Adam Smith protested with particular indignation, the notion that a country should

---

[16] It is this kind of reasoning that resulted in the frequently used term "triangular trade"; because in practice there are more than three, the term used became in due course "multilateral".

[17] Reference has been made in the previous chapter (p. 110) to the Macmillan Report, in which Keynes and others argued for a combination of trade restriction with export promotion, both by artificial means.

buy from countries that buy from it rather than from countries where it can obtain the goods it needs on more advantageous terms. [18] Thus, by seeking insulation from the world economy, the economic nationalists of today have evolved a system which combines some of the least excusable fallacies of the mercantilists with the grimmest aspects of the Fichtean blueprint. At the same time, they make the world rife with economic conflict.

So that the reader, appalled by what he has read, should not think that I am building up a man of straw for the only purpose of knocking it down, I shall now quote some specific comments from the collectivist literature of the last fifteen years.

V

In 1944, having already acquired world fame as author of what is known as the "Beveridge Report", [19] Sir William H. (later Lord) Beveridge published under the title *Full Employment in a Free Society* a most comprehensive blueprint for a planned society. His concern is with the maintenance of what he calls full employment (and what most people would call overfull employment). His proposals are for a comprehensive government regulation of economic life, wich can be classed under the following six headings:

(1) A long-term programme of planned public expenditures including the regulation of private business investments, subsidies to consumers, etc.

(2) State control of banking, including the nationalization of the Bank of England: "The banking system must clearly function in accord with the general financial policy of the State." (page 178.)

(3) Control over the location of industry, which "must be exercised ultimately by a central authority making a national plan for the whole country." (page 170.)

---

[18] See above, pp. 79-80.
[19] *Report on Social Insurance and Allied Services*, published by the British government in November 1942.

(4) "Organized mobility of labour", involving a compulsory use of employment exchanges for all young people under eighteen, who "should be fitted into occupations adapted to their capacities" by these governmentally run agencies. "It is desirable to put an end to the aimless, unguided search for work ... there can be no opposition of principle to ... requiring the actual engagement to be made either through the exchange or an approved agency such as a trade union." (pages 171-2.)

(5) Permanent price control: "Price control ... will concentrate upon essential goods and services and upon those in the supply of which there is a temporary scarcity." (page 203.)

(6) State control of foreign trade: "The whole trend of the argument of this Part of the Report [dealing with international implications of full employment] is towards a management of international trade, in place of leaving it to unregulated competion." (page 238.) [20]

The Beveridge blueprint is a very consistent one. Although the words "free society" appear in the title of the book, and although its author is a faithful member of the British Liberal Party, he lets fall by the wayside, one after another, all the tenets of a liberal society, including even the principle of private property. The list of "essential liberties" which he enumerates in his book "does not include liberty of a private citizen to own means of production and to employ other citizens in operating them at a wage. ... if ... it should be shown by experience *or by argument* that abolition of private property in the means of production was necessary for full employment, this abolition would have to be undertaken." [21] A strange statement for a liberal to make! It throws some light on the contemporary crisis of the British Liberal Party and may explain why liberals have had to look for a home in recent years either in the "progressive" wing of the Conservative Party or in the "conservative" wing of the Labour Party. Are we not right, in the light of his own statements, to regard Beveridge as a collectivist? His programme is certainly

---

[20] William H. Beveridge: *Full Employment in a Free Society*, London, 1944.
[21] *Ibid.*, p. 23. Italics added.

one that any collectivist could adopt and that every liberal should scorn. However tempting it would be to analyse it at length and to examine in detail the concept of "full employment" from which the whole trouble started, let us turn to Beveridge's views on international trade. He offers a very good case-study of a collectivist approach to that subject.

No British writer in his senses could, of course, adopt in 1944 the Fichtean formula for an isolated economy. "Britain must have imports; she must have exports to pay for the imports," Beveridge wisely remarks, and then adds: "She must have international trade *up to a certain minimum.*" [22] The words which I have underlined are characteristic. Foreign trade is indispensable for Britain but only "up to a certain minimum" — beyond that, never mind. There follovs a discussion which it is important to quote in full:

> The first point to realize is that Britain's chances in international trade are not unfavourable. ... The countries which produce food and raw materials need markets and have largely developed their economic systems to supply markets of which Britain is, for many articles, the largest and most important. They are not only willing but anxious to sell to us. Should we then try to make specific bargains with them — bargains advantageous to both parties — so that we shall take their goods and they ours? Should we confront them with the clearcut alternative: we give you a stable market here, if you give us a stable market for our exports; but if you are not prepared to do the letter, you cannot have our custom? This type of arrangement is normally called "bilateralism"; it is a form of barter, although all actual transactions are made in the currency of the countries concerned. But the currency which either country surrenders in payment for its imports is a blocked currency; it cannot be used only to pay for the purchase of goods of the country from which it was issued. Should we on the other hand, attempt to return to a "multilateral" system — to a system along the lines of the gold standard, under which countries make their purchases wherever they find them cheapest and sell their exports wherever they can, and do not attempt to balance the purchases from one particular country against the sales made to that particular country? Under a multilateral system, the currency received for exports to one country can be spent on imports from any other country. No one can say: "the currency I have given you for your goods must be considered as blocked; you can spend it or keep it; but if you

---

[22] *Ibid.,* p. 215. Italics added.

want to spend it you must spend it on my goods and on nobody else's". [23]

This is an excellent statement of the dilemma which was confronting Great Britain at the end of the war and which confronts every country when it tries to take stock of its international position and evolve a rational foreign economic policy. Indeed, Beveridge's definition of the alternatives is a gem of clear definition, but what of his actual recommendations?

"It is obvious", he says, "that a multilateral system has great advantages. Bilateralism is akin to barter, ... it is workable but clumsy." (p. 217). Indeed, he could say that bilateralism has other disadvantages than clumsiness as compared with multilateralism. These have been enumerated in the preceding section of the present chapter. Instead, Beveridge proposes three criteria, upon the prior fulfilment of which, he claims, the adoption of multilateralism must eventually depend:

> First, each of the participating nations must aim at full employment within its borders and must do so without relying on export surpluses as the principal means to full employment. Second, each of the participating nations must be prepared to balance its accounts with the rest of the world; for that purpose any nation which, for any reason, systematically sells abroad in goods or services more than it buys from abroad, and so has an export surplus, must be prepared to grant long-term loans sufficient to enable the rest of the world to pay for those exports, without losing gold or other reserves essential for international liquidity. Third, each of the participating nations must aim at a certain stability of economic behaviour — continuity in tariff, subsidy, foreign exchange and other economic policies — and must refrain from introducing important changes in these policies without prior consultation with the other participants. [24]

These are not unreasonable requirements. Much depends on how they are interpreted in terms of actual policy. No believer in a free economy will deny that economic policy should aim everywhere at the maintenance of as high a level of economic activity and employment as can be achieved without inflation. No one would argue that

---

[23] *Ibid.*, p. 215.
[24] *Ibid.*, p. 218.

a country aiming at export surpluses as a means of promoting domestic full employment is adopting a mercantilist policy entirely alien to a liberal philosophy. The balancing of a country's accounts with the rest of the world can be achieved either by giving the greatest possible scope to the spontaneous operations of the free market (in combination, as under the gold standard, with appropriate domestic policies) or by seeking to bring the credit and the debit sides of the country's foreign accounts into balance through deliberate manipulations, such as exchange control. Beveridge favours the latter as against the former alternative, but that stands in complete contradiction with the principles of multilateral trade. Finally, when speaking of stability in a country's economic behaviour, he refers to continuity in tariff, subsidy, and other policies. He includes in his list policies which stand in conflict with the principles of multilateralism, such as exchange control and export subsidies. Nor could his policies, by their very nature, be administered with an eye to continuity.

We thus find abundant contradictions in the Beveridge statement of prerequisites for multilateral trade. As any reader of paragraphs 316-35 of the book will readily see, Beveridge's heart is not really in the matter. His real attitude is found later, in paragraph 356, where he declares:

> *International trade, both for imports and for exports, will on the whole have to come under public management, in place of being left to market forces either competitive or monopolistic. The organs which serve for planning at home will serve also for planning in a wider sphere.*[25]

In spite of all the lip service paid to multilateral trade earlier in his report and in spite of having quite clearly seen the disadvantages of bilateralism from the point of view of the international division of labour, Beveridge produces in the above passage a succinct statement of the basic collectivist view on foreign trade. In this he is, even more than Keynes and equally unknown to himself, a faithful follower of Fichte. To make his position abundantly clear, Beveridge resorts to what we might call the "parable of the fire-escape". It, too, deserves quotation in full, for it, too, is a gem of its kind — albeit of a very peculiar kind:

---

[25] *Ibid.*, p. 241. Italics added.

In terms of convenience for traffic, world-wide multilateral trade may be likened to an elevator, speedy but capable of going out of action. Regional multilateral trade may be likened to a staircase, less speedy but consistent with reasonable comfort. Bilateralism is the fire-escape, clumsy but certain. [26]

This parable is so entirely and fundamentally wrong that it is surprising to see it used by so learned a man as Lord Beveridge. Everyone knows that we can have and generally do have in a building an elevator, a staircase, and a fire-escape, all three of them. We don't need to make a choice and have a fire-escape instead, say, of an elevator; we can have them all. Not so with various trading systems: we cannot have them all at once, *we must make a choice* and that choice is of the greatest importance for the future both of our well-being and of our liberties. Multilateralism is the trading system of free men and it is also the trading system which gives to the world economy maximum scope as well as adaptability to changing conditions. Multilateral trade extending to a part of the globe is the next best thing, although it lacks the long-range stability of world-wide multilateralism; it is something which we may have to put up with while conditions are not favourable to having the system on a world scale. There is no difference *in kind* between geographically limited multilateralism and universal multilateralism. The difference in kind, however, is basic when it comes to bilateralism. Beveridge's fire-escape is not a fire-escape at all; it is a prison staircase! Bilateralism is a trading system not of free citizens but of unfree subjects. It is the trading system in which individual deals are subject to government control and licensing and which minimizes the international division of labour and the advantages resulting from international commerce. We are living in an age in which the payment by vice of its homage to virtue — as de La Rochefoucauld would have it — has become so widespread as to obscure greatly the political and economic literature of the time. Instead of saying that they favour bilateralism, the collectivists of today say that they favour multilateralism *but* ... "But" has become one of the most widely used words of the dictionary and it has immensely contributed to the intellectual confusion of our days. The use of misleading analogies belongs to the same category.

---

[26] *Ibid.,* p. 241.

VI

Reluctantly or not, the incompatibility between multilateral trade and national planning is recognized, as it must be, by the advocates of the latter. In listing the main defects of the planned economy — a list which would have turned a less staunch believer in economic planning than he into a liberal — Gunnar Myrdal refers to "the tendency of our economic planning to become autarkic", and continues :

All our countries have committed themselves to full employment. It was found out during the thirties that, to some extent, it was possible to alleviate a depression by restricting imports and further, that internal expansion during an international deflationary development required import restrictions as protection. Everybody knows that internationally these national policies counteract each other and, on balance, tend to spread and deepen a depression. But, in a worldwide deflationary development, restricting imports from abroad will stand out as a financial necessity to any individual country which has to try to keep up employment at home.

If the planned economy in a country instead develops in an inflationary direction, which for reasons already given will be a more ordinary course, again this country will have to restrict its imports even if there is no general trend toward deflation abroad. The too large incomes will tend to increase the demand for import goods and decrease the supply of export goods. This is a fact which economists overlooked until very recently, that in a system of planned economies both national inflation and international deflation tend to make import restrictions necessary.

To these Professor Myrdal adds another and, to my mind, more fundamental reason why collectivist planning turns in the direction of economic nationalism or a quest for self-sufficiency (i.e. autarky):

It is possible to plan home consumption and internal demand with some degree of certainly, including the substitution of home produce for imported goods. Export is so much more difficult to calculate and investment for the production of export goods carries greater risk. It is very natural indeed, if, with the stress now given to full employment, the planner prefers security, particularly as the world is now developing. [27]

---

[27] "The Trend towards Economic Planning", *op. cit.*, pp. 38-9.

The reader might almost think that he is still reading Chapter V of the present book, where nearly the same reasons are cited that were given by Fichte, the grim prophet of national isolation! [28]

Probably the most outspoken and the most forthwright postwar statement of the collectivist position will be found in a report on

---

[28] Thus Myrdal found himself up against a dilemma: should he turn his back upon national planning as a means of promotion the objectives of full employment and economic development — or should he accept the inevitability of economic nationalism. The former he refused to do in spite of all the shortcomings of planning, even though he saw these shortcomings very clearly indeed. He accepted international co-operation, to be sure, but only as something to be achieved around a conference table, by an agreement among governments to co-ordinate their national plans and policies. But in practice this proved impossible, while the alternative, international economic integration through freedom of trade and payments, Myrdal clearly and flatly rejected. ("As a theory the free trade doctrine is not tenable"; see *Economic Theory and Under-developed Regions*, London, 1957, p. 141.) The following two quotations, from his major work, *An International Economy* (New York, 1956), show the evolution of his thinking:

"National political machinery is strong and effective and has a firm basis in people's attitudes of allegiance and solidarity ... Machinery for international co-operation is, by contrast, weak and ineffective, and it lacks a solid basis in people's valuations and expectations. ... Under these circumstances, internationalism tends more and more to be relegated to abstract utopianism. There is in the world of today so little possibility of giving reality to such strivings that they appear unrealistic and impractical; they are dreams and theories, while economic nationalism is realistic and practical" (p. 34).

"While foreign markets, determined by the actions of other governments and groups, thus increasingly involve economic risks, one of the surest and simplest means of stabilizing the conditions for production and employment at home consists in regulating imports. Such public controls usually have the political advantage — at least immediately — of shifting the effects of adverse developments on to the foreigner, while helping domestic industries or leaving them undisturbed" (p. 39).

These are typical quotations — their number could be greatly multiplied. With the western countries moving increasingly away from economic nationalism during the past decade, it is the underdeveloped countries which are nowadays its principal practitioners. To their problems the books cited above are primarily addressed. One final quotation, will exemplify the kind of doctrine they are being taught: "The advice underdeveloped countries are now often gratuitously given to abstain from interfering with foreign and from tampering with foreign exchanges is in most cases tantamount to advice not to bother about economic development" (*Economic Theory and Under-developed Regions*, p. 94). His own advice is: more planning and as much trade control and exchange control as desired! It is in these underdeveloped regions of the world that economic nationalism is fighting its supreme battle.

National and International Measures for Full Employment prepared in 1949 by a group of five U.N. experts: [29]

> While the return to multilateralism and currency convertibility is the declared aim of the great majority of nations — alongside the policy of internal stability and full employment, as laid down in the Charter of the United Nations — it is important to realize clearly how far these aim are complementary and how far one is a precondition of the other. *The system of bilateral trading and exchange control is undoubtedly a most powerful weapon for maintaining full employment and a high level of production within the countries participating in such a system, in the face of serious fluctuations emanating from non-participating countries.* It is not, however, in itself a major source of economic instability and cannot therefore be regarded as an obstacle to the successful pursuit of domestic full employment policies by any country. The justification for bilateral methods of trade will undoubtedly disappear once the present structural disequilibrium in international trade has been removed and countries have succeeded in eliminating major fluctuations in their balances of payments arising from inadequate or unstable effective demand. However, *in the successful attainment of the twin goals of full employment and the creation of a relatively free multilateral trading system, the former must certainly take precedence over the latter:* while countries can pursue full employment policies even without a multilateral trading system, the restoration of multilateralism without the attainment of internal economic stability in the trading countries is impossible. [30]

Although the usual lip-service is paid to multilateralism in the first lines of the above quotation, this is entirely nullified by the dogmatic statement with which the paragraph ends. It is the centre of the paragraph and especially the passages I have underlined which contain the meat of the United Nations experts' position. That their report, which is a monument to economic nationalism, should have been issued with high appreciation by the United Nations itself, is one of the most significant paradoxes of our time.

---

[29] J.M. Clark, Nicholas Kaldor, Arthur Smithies, Pierre Uri and E. Ronald Walker.
[30] *National and International Measures for Full Employment*, United Nations, New York, 1949, par. 65. Italics added.

APPENDIX

INTRODUCTION

It has been suggested to me that I include in an Appendix a selection from the fairly large number of articles scattered through many journals, magazines and symposiums, which I have devoted over the past two decades to the problem of economic nationalism, its nature, causes and cures. The idea was tempting and it was dangerous. It is tempting to recover some of one's past writings now largely inaccessible; but it is dangerous, too, to re-serve old dishes which have possibly long since lost such flavour as they once may have possessed!

With one exception (item 3), these essays are reprinted as originally published. The first is a wartime adaptation of my last pre-war study on "The Economic Foundations of Collective Security". The second essay, on "Prosperity versus Peace", principally debating Lord Keynes' contribution to economic nationalism may seem redundant in view of the long chapter devoted to this subject in the main body of the book (Chapter VI): but the time of the original publication (1947) and the emphasis which differs from that of the main chapter seemed to warrant its inclusion. It bridges the reader over to item 3: "An Economist's views on International Organization" (written in 1950, published in 1952), a point of view which brought many thunders over my head but has been, I think, entirely vindicated by experience.

The "Havana Charter" for the once-projected International Trade Organization has been for several years in the foreground of my academic and public activities: among the many papers I wrote on that subject, the one reprinted here (item 4) first appeared in the *Canadian Banker* for May, 1948. Also reprinted is an article published in the September, 1949 issue of *Fortune*, New York, the start of a happy and continuing association. This latter article (item 5) attempts to diagnose the reasons for which the United States, the original sponsor of an international trade code, found itself face to face with what was, in effect, a "Charter of Economic Nationalism". Conflicting, as it did, with the basic U.S. philosophy of postwar reconstruction and of peacetime life, it had to be eventually discarted.

The United States is torn to this day between the protectionist inheritance of its past and the internationalist requirements of its future. The battle has been raging for a quarter century or more and is entering into a new phase as this book goes to press. From much that I have written as participant in the *Free Trade Crusade*, I have selected two items, of 1952 and 1958 respectively. They reflect my firm conviction that only the United States can effectively slay the dragon of economic nationalism, they indicate my reasons why it is essential that the dragon should be slayed, and they briefly formulate the elements of a new American foreign economic policy. The reader will excuse their polemic and "current events" character!

1.

THE ECONOMIC FOUNDATIONS OF COLLECTIVE SECURITY *
(1943)

The achievement of political security is the basic quest of every peace-loving human group. It is even more basic than the quest for material welfare, since in an insecure world the latter is merely a passing phase. It has become clear to many thinkers and statesmen for some time past that political security cannot be attained and preserved through its own devices by one nation alone. Out of that realization developed the conception of *collective* security. The term, once widely used, now less frequently applied, is a very appropriate one since it emphasizes the collective or social aspect of the security problem. Should another terminology be adopted in the years to come, the fact will remain that no nation can remain secure alone. The opposite of collective security is individual insecurity. This was fully realized by the peacemakers of 1919 and has been fully confirmed by the tragic developments of the past decade.

The system of security devised in the latter years of the first World War and at the Paris Peace Conference and embodied in the Covenant of the League of Nations attached a great deal of importance to economic measures. Economic sanctions, referred to in certain League of Nations documents as the "economic weapon", occupied a prominent position in the plans for repressing acts of aggression. We shall see that the provisions of the Covenant were of utmost importance and that they might have become the beginning of a very fruitful course of developments. We shall see also that in setting up in the days to come an improved system of security, it will be necessary to go well beyond the provisions of Article XVI

* Published in the *Quarterly Bulletin* of the Polish Institute of Arts and Sciences in America, New York, April, 1943.

of the Covenant. oth the theoretical analysis of the issues involved in the enforcement of peace, and the practical lessons learned since 1931, point to the need for reconsidering the role of the economic factor in a system of organized security. With respect to the military factor, the lesson seems to have been learned: nobody doubts any more that an organized and peaceful world society needs a strong armed force to repel all possible future acts of aggression. But in the realm of economic relationships there is still a good deal of ground to cover. This paper leads to two conclusions: (1) that the "economic weapon" in order to be fully effective must be used as a *preventive* weapon; (2) that only in an economically interdependent world can such a weapon be at all used. In the pages that follow we shall try to show by what process these conclusions have been reached and to what sort of further implications they lead.[1]

The notion of Collective Security.

Article XVI of the Covenant of the League of Nations contains the basic definitions and implementations of "Collective security." Since some of the discussion that follows is based on that article, its most relevant parts are quoted:

1. Should any Member of the League resort to war in disregard of its Covenants under Articles 12, 13 or 15,[2] it shall *ipso facto* be deemed to have committed an act of war against all other Members of the League, which hereby undertake immediately to subject it to the severance of all trade or financial relations, the prohibition of all intercourse between their nationals and the nationals of the Covenant-breaking State,[3] and the prevention of all financial, commercial or personal intercourse between the nationals of the

---

[1] The present writer delivered in August 1939 a course of lectures on "La coopération économique internationale et la sécurité collective" before the Academy of International Law at The Hague. The publication of these lectures was prevented by the German invasion if the Low Countries and of France. Some of the material used in these lectures is included in the present paper. In the summer of 1939 everybody knew that the peace had been lost. The "lesson" referred to above was before us to learn. The present study is therefore entirely in accord with the author's Hague lectures; these were published in full *after the war* in the Academy's *Recueil des Cours* for 1939.

[2] These three articles relate to arbitration and to the judicial settlement of international disputes.

[3] The term "nationals" has been subsequently interpreted as meaning "residents."

Covenant-breaking State and the nationals of any other State, whether a Member of the League or not.

2. It shall be the duty of the Council in such case to recommend to the several Governments concerned what effective military, naval or air force the Members of the League shall severally contribute to the armed forces to be used to protect the Covenants of the League.

3. The Members of the League agree, further, that they will mutually support one another in the financial and economic measures which are taken under this Article, in order to minimize the loss and inconvenience resulting from the above measures, and that they will mutually support one another in resisting any special measures aimed at one of their number by the Covenant-breaking State, and that they will take the necessary steps to afford passage through their territory to the forces of any of the Members of the League which are co-operating to protect the Covenants of the League.

It is the provision which stipulates that the aggressor country will become *ipso facto* engaged in war with all the other members of the League that contains the essence of the collective security idea. To be sure, this means that an act of aggression constitutes the starting point of a general war. But such a war is not a *bellum omnium contra omnes*, but merely a common war against an aggressor, law-breaking state. It expresses the social reaction against a lawless use of force. True, it commits every member of the International Organization to taking part in a war even if the aggression is geographically very remote. The alternative, however, is to give a free hand to aggressors.

After 1920 the commitments under Article XVI were quickly whittled down. [4] Whatever was left, was not applied in practice when an opportunity arose or was applied only half-heartedly and partially as in the Italo-Ethiopian war. We shall not deal here with that dismal story, except as it teaches certain valuable lessons for the future. But we shall examine carefully article XVI and its implications. While it was unapplied in the past, it contains, embryonically, important principles of policy. In one way or another

---

[4] The story of it is told in William E. Rappard's *The Quest for Peace since the World War*, Harvard University Press, Cambridge, Mass., 1940, pages 219-243.

these principles, further developed and amended, are indispensable to any system of international security.

War, then, is stipulated to be indivisible, that is to say, a matter of concern to the whole international community. The aggressor is to be repelled, his designs frustrated by a common action of members of the International Organization. To that effect, they are to adopt various measures, economic and military. Article XVI gives a great deal of prominence to the former. The latter are mentioned, explicitly but in a rather secondary way. It is the "economic weapon" which is considered to be of primary importance. The reasons of it are simple: on the one hand, the great role played by blockade in the World War; on the other hand, the reluctance to resort to military measures except *in extremis*. However, the conception of efficient economic sanctions is based on certain assumptions, mostly made tacity or even unwittingly, at the time of the drafting of the Covenant, yet essential to the success of the scheme. These assumptions we must now carefully examine.

Foundations of Economic Sanctions.

The League of Nations was to be, in the hopes of its authors, a universal organization. The assumption of universality underlies to a considerable extent the philosophy of the Covenant. Once it became clear that it was not to be fulfilled in practice, certain important consequences should have naturally followed.

If the International Organization has a universal membership and if its members live up to their obligations, then the execution of the provisions of paragraph 1 of Article XVI is a relatively simple matter. If all the states of the world effectively break off relations, economic and others, with the aggressor state, then the latter is deprivedi of all accesss to desources produced outside of its boundaries [5] and is greatly handicapped in the conduct of the war. The degree of this handicap depends, obviously, upon the economic resources of the aggressor country — and this consideration opens a line of thought to which we shall revert presently.

---

[5] This can be overcome, in part, by policies of autarky and by territorial expansion carried out in the early phases of the war; both these possibilities are considered below.

On the other hand, if the International Organization has a limited membership, and such was the case of the League of Nations, the situation is completely different. Non-members are not bound by the rules of the Organization. Since they remain outside the Organization by their own will, this is presumably due to the fact that they do ont approve of collective security and of the obligations it entails. Can one, then, count on their full collaboration in times of crisis? Optimistic commentators of the early 'twenties nortwithstanding, it is safer and more reasonable to assume that some at least of the non-members would fail to collaborate. Indeed, some might line up with the peace-breaking country. It is clear therefore that in the case of a non-univerasl organization voluntary measures adopted in line with the obligations of Article XVI will not suffice. In order to prevent "all financial, economic and personal intercourse between the nationals of any other state, *whether a Member of the League or not*," measures of compulsion are indispensable, or at least very likely to become indispensable. The words which we now have italicized contain the key to the problem, if not to its solution. Members of the League had an obligation. How then was the economic intercourse between their nationals and those of the Covenant-breaking state to be prevented? There is one way only to achieve this. Its name is *blockade*. [6]

Blockade, however, is not a purely economic measure. It consists in interrupting or intercepting trade between the blockaded country and other countries which might be disposed to trade with it. This calls for naval and military measures. The blokaded country tends to fight back. And the "shooting war" is on. In the case of countries which are neighbor sof the blockaded country on the same continent, the enforcement of blockade is even more difficult. In any case when we speak of blockade we cease speaking of an "economic weapon" as distinct from military ones.

It follows that in a non-universal organization economic sanctions cannot be separated from military ones if applied *after* an act of aggression has been committed. We shall see presently that there is considerable scope for purely economic sanctions in policies aiming

---

[6] The same should hold for a member of the Organization who would fail to live up to the statutory obligations.

at the *prevention* of aggression. But ance an act of aggression has been committed, war in the military sense of the word is hardly avoidable.

Let us get back, however, to the ideas underlying the theory of economic asnctions. The basic ones is that of the importance of international economic interdependence. Modern war is a great industrial undertaking and modern industry works with materials produced the world over and secured through trade by those who do not dispose of them at home. If trade could be interrupted, the country affected by it would find it impossible to continue for any length of time the operation of the industrial machine necessary for the war. Some countries would lack certain raw materials, other countries would lack some other raw materials or some types of technical equipment, or food, or some secret of production patented abroad. Thus they would be handicapped in their war effort. In other words, owing to the economic interdependence of nations, the application of economic sanctions (as provided in Article XVI) would reduce the *war potential* of the aggressor country and thus condemn it to eventual defeat.

We see now that the crux of the conception of economic sanctions is to be found in the international division of labor. The more a country depends upon world trade, the more it is vulnerable to economic sanctions. The larger th enumber of countries which are dependent upon foreign trade for some of their basic supplies, the greater the degree of international security: in a world of interdependent countries economic sanctions could be very effective; such a world would not be therefore "safe for aggressors."

This last point has not been clearly perceived by the authors of the League of Nations Covenant. If it had been, measures would have been taken to increase the degree of economic interdependence. Instead, as we know only too well, no frontal attack was launched — or even proposed — against economic nationalism. That failure of creating an economic environment favorable to the operation of the "economic weapon" was not the least among the causes which brought about the collapse of collective security and contributed to the coming of the Second World War.

Complicating factors.

We have already emphasized one of the mots important factors which complicated the simplicity of the League of Nations scheme of security: the non-universality of the system. From that follows the need for blockade and the impossibility of avoiding military war measures alongside the economic ones. Should there be powerful outsiders and should they either be strictly neutral or take the side of the aggressor, the chances of a *quick* victory for the defenders of law would be very slim, while the prospect of a long and difficult war is often an incentive to forces of "appeasement." In the future no effort must therefore be spared to achieve a broad, universal organization. The "United Nations" are an excellent nucleus for such an organization. In order to keep them all in the peace-time system and in order to attract to it other countries as well, the new International Organization must offer important inducements to its members. Membership must not only entail obligations, it must also contribute to the security and prosperity of member states.

In order to provide security, the system must be so devised as to be trusted by the member states. It must be strong and free from important reservations. Developments such as the recommendations of the "International Blockade Commission" should not be allowed to happen again. In the first few years after the World War the League system of security was so reduced by reservations and interpretations that in 1925 a distinguisyed Swiss scholar and statesman could write as follows: [7]

> By the various interpretations adopted, these articles (10 and 16) have been so appreciably weakened, that today no responsible European statesman would venture to stake his reputation and the security of his country on the potential protection of the League in case of international disturbance.

In another attempt to establish security in the world such a situation should not develop again. In the end it is some test-case or other that will either confirm and strengthen or eles weaken or destroy the faith in the system that will have been established. That

---

[7] William E. Rappard, *International Relations as viewed from Geneva,* New Haven, 1925, pp. 143-144. This book is the text of lectures delivered in the summer 1925 before the Williamstown Institute of Politics.

faith, in turn, will determine the adoption by the various countries of certain necessary, domestic economic measures. Here, as in so many other matters, the political and the economic factors are intimately woven together.

In addition to that general confidence in the system, there is both need and scope for certain economic advantages accruing to members of the International Organization and to them alone. This is the type of advantage that would be easily understood by the man in the street, would readily appeal to him, and would make him into an adherent of the Organization which otherwise might well remain for him an unintelligible abstraction. These measures, which cannot be outlined here in detail, would consist in a preferential treatment with respect to commercial policy, international credits etc. which members of the Organization would grant to each other but which would not be extended to non-members. Since membership would be open to all states which accept the obligations entailed by it, this discrimination against non-members would in effect be a penalty imposed for non-collaboration. While we cannot do more at this place than state the broad principle, the matter should be carefully studied at the present time, in connection with post-war planning.

Within the International Organization the above-mentioned economic arrangements would tend so develop interdependence. The discriminatory treatment of non-members would, on the other hand, make it more difficult for them to achieve economic independence. Such would be the case, at least, of economically none too powerful countries. Since, however, a strong country may stay out of the Organization, there is another source of complication to be reckoned with.

Small or economically weak states are a very minor danger to world's peace, especially if there is in existence a system of collective security. An armed "revolt" of "have-nots" about which so much was being said in the years preceding World War II is an impossibility. In order to wage war with any hope of success against powerful opponents, a country has to dispose of a large war potential, adequate industrial facilities, supplies of raw materials and food as well as of technical skill. It has, furthermore, to make itself as blockade-proof as possible. All of that is beyond the reach of an economically weak country. The alleged "have-nots" of the thirties were economically and military powerful countries, strong enough to intimidate their opponents into making concessions, strong enough to face the prospect of war. All this would hardly need emphasizing were it not for the stubborn survival of the myth (or, rather, fallacy) of the "have-not nations."

There remains the fact to be counted with in the future that some powerful country might violate peace and resist economic sanctions. Should that ever happen, another major conflagration would be inevitable. Thus no complete guarantee against war can be obtained. We shall have achieved a great deal of progress, however, if we minimize the chances of aggression. After World War II after the defeat of the Axis powers, it is quite likely that the remaining powers will be members of the new International Organization. And this makes it possible to view with hopeful anticipation new developments in the direction of international security.

It will be noted that not one of the Axis powers would have been strong enough for wars of conquest had a system of security been in operation all through the twenty inter-war years. Had the United Nations been in existence as an effective grouping of peace-loving countries willing to strike at an aggressor swiftly and strongly, all the acts of violence from 1931 onwards might have been prevented or beaten back locally. The economic aspects of these speculations are also very interesting. Neither Germany, nor Japan, nor Italy are normally independent of foreign trade. All of them, and particularly the latter two are very vulnerable to blockade, unless they have had an opportunity of improving their situation through an accumulation of stock-piles of strategic materials. But this and similar policies is precisely what preceded the coming of the Second World War. Nor were these measures counteracted by appropriate moves on the part of states interested in the maintenance of peace and of the respect for international law. Policies of *autarky* were freely carried out. And these policies were a prelude to and preparation for conquest.

Autarky and Conquest.

On the surface of it nothing could sound more peaceful than "autarky," the desire of a country to be entirely independent from the rest of the world. The reality, however, is much less peaceful than that. The desire for complete economic independence cannot be motivated by the quest for higher living standards, since it is recognized that international trade contributes to the prosperity of the trading nations. The planet is so built that every nation needs resources which are not obtainable within the area it inhabits. And the "autarkic" countries were precisely those which complained most insistently about being "have-nots." Why then the policies of self-sufficiency? The answer is very simple. Just as the advocates of collective security realize the importance of economic inter-dependence and of economic sanctions against the aggressor country, so aggressors-to-be realize the importance of being blockade-proof. Policies of autarky as they were practiced by Germany, Italy and Japan in the recent past, were attempts at making these countries capable of withstanding blockade. Furthermore, by establishing state control over foreign trade, the governments of these countries could change the structure of imports in a way favoring the growth of the national war potential.

Policies of "autarky" involve certain changes in the structure of domestic industries as well as changes in the composition of foreign trade. The development of "key-industries" and substitute products, regardless of costs, at the detriment of articles of civilian consumption, with ample use of state subsidies and a reduction of living standards of the population, such is the essence of the domestic measures. Adopted in peace-times, such measures can only serve the cause of some future war.

As for foreign policies, modern "autarky" does not aim at reducing the volume of imports. On the contrary, attempts are made to expand it . More and more imports are needed to satisfy the requirements of a growing war industry and to build up, at the same time, stock-piles of imported materials of the kinds which are essential in war and impossible to replace by home-produced goods. Thus Axis imports were growing at the very time when their professed policies were autarkic. These countries were even complaining at their inability to import more — and these complaints were taken all too seriously by the statesmen of Western powers.

One of the means of expanding their imports has been found by the "autarkic" countries in the commercial penetration and domination of other countries. Germany's "bloodless conquest" are well-known and their story need nor be retold here. What needs to be said, however, is that these conquests would not have taken place if the Western powers had practiced a policy of international economic collaboration in the 'thirties, instead of a policy of economic nationalism. Countries of Eastern and South-Eastern Europe traded with Germany which most of them distrusted and feared, because they could not expand their trade with the democratic countries owing to the import restrictions of the latter. The same development started with respect to certain Latin American countries but, before it went very far, the war and the ensuing blockade of Germany by the British Navy interrupted the course of the German economic penetration of the Western Hemisphere.

Japan also was able to import strategic raw materials well after its wars of aggression in Asia got under way.

Thus what was called "autarky" was a system of policies the purpose of which was to speed up the production of war equipment and the attainment, for some years at least, of a high degree of independence from foreign sources of supply. This is something to remember in the future. Autarchy is a prelude to wars of conquest and should therefore be considered as a first step in a country's violation of peace.

Other forms of economic nationalism and their effects upon autarky.

The policies of "autarky" briefly discussed above are economic helpmates of policies of conquest. But there are other economic restrictions, other manifestations of economic nationalism which have no aggressive purposes by themselves, but help the type of developments with which we were hitherto concerned. They either are the expression of "old-fashioned" protectionism or result from fear of aggression. Thus one can speak of an "autarky of fear" as well as of an "autarky of aggression."

Fear of this type can be only eliminated through the establishment of a reliable system of international security and through effective limitations of national sovereignty. The establishment of appropriate super-national bodies, endowed with responsibilities and powers, is, of course, the road towards a trustworthy International Organization.

In the economic field this involves the creation of bodies such as an International Trade Authority, [8] an International Monetary Authority, an International Investment Board, etc. The new International Organization must have powers to counteract measures of economic nationalism on the part of individual members. Competitive tariff increases, competitive monetary devaluations, onesided defaults on international loans are all of them most detrimental to good relations between nations and to the growth of that economic interdependence which, as we have seen, is of such vital importance to the operation of collective security.

All of this is conducive to sweeping changes of international economic relations. But without such radical changes security will remain unachieved and the "autarky of defense" will remain in operation. And this will make it possible for countries contemplating eventual aggressions to prepare for them economically in the future as they did in the recent past.

Instruments of commercial policy are limited in number though their number has been expanded in the past fifteen years. The "new" instruments include quotas, exchange control, barter-clearing arrangements and various types of subsidies. All of them involve state control over the volume *and the structure* of foreign trade. Such control makes it possible for the state to promote policies of autarky. Some of these instruments have been introduced, at first, to help a country in the event of a major upset in her balance of payments. This took place in a world whose economic relations were torn apart by economic nationalism. In a world of collaborating nations other measures can be devised with the help of the International Monetary Authority and the International Investment Board. [9] On the other hand, the enumerated "new" instruments of policy should be eliminated entirely. What is also necessary is the limitation, wherever possible, of the direct control by the state over the structure of foreign trade. Whatever interventions are necessary,

---

[8] Compare on that the excellent article by Professor Percy W. Bidwell, "Controlling Trade after the War," *Foreign Affairs*, January 1943.
[9] These names are, of course, purely tentative.

should take the shape of "framework interventions" such as general trade agreements and tariffs. [10]

Concerning tariffs, it is not likely that they could be eliminated entirely. They might be, however, revised, reduced and stabilized. Also further changes of tariffs should be placed under the supervision of the International Trade Authority. It could be shown, for instance, that the "infant industries protection" which is one of the most valid protectionist measures can only then be carried our in practice if there is an international authority which could rule about the removal of protection after the protected industry has "grown up". In actual practice there has never been a way of preventing the protection of "infant industries" from degenerating into that of "vested interests." While the idea of withdrawing tariff policies from the exclusive sovereignty of individual states is certainly very "revolutionary," we shall have to adopt some such "revolutionary" ideas if we are to achieve peace in the world. On careful examination it will appear, however, that the impact of these suggestions upon the doily life of people everywhere would be advantageous rather than otherwise. It is only the intellectual adjustment that may be difficult.

Far from us the idea of offering here a blue-print for post-war reconstruction. We are concerned with these matters only in order to make it clear that some such program is necessary in order to fight effectively policies of aggressive autarky. It is only when we have made "autarky of defense" uneecessary through the establisment of a system of security that could be relied upon, and when we have placed "old-fashioned protectionism" under an international control, that we shall have isolated autarkic policies proper. And then we can proceed to fight them.

Economic nationalism is either a body-guard of policies of aggression and conquest, or the result of considerations mentioned above. [11] In the first case it is a part of international warfare. In the

---

[10] On "framework interventions" see M. A. Heilperin, *Economic Policy and Democracy, op. cit.*, pp. 14-16.

[11] One important factor is left out of consideration here because it is impossible to develop it fully within the compass of the present paper. It is the role of the national quest for "full employment." In the nineteen-thirties

second, it helps the future breakers of peace by making it impossible to prevent them from mobilizing resources in the service of their warlike designs. Economic factors are only rarely and to a minor extent causes of was; but economic nationalism, if allowed to continue after the present war is won, may well develop into the principal "Trojan Horse" of the next peace.

The scope of the "Economic Weapon".

We have seen the limitations on the use of the economic sanctions in a system of collective security. Once a conflagration has started through an act of aggression, economic measures alone are insufficient. Blockade involves military measures as well. Futhermore if the aggressor power is to be checked in its course of conquest, military help must be given to the victim of aggression, while the attacker may have to be brought into a battle on one or more additional fronts. The idea that collective security can work through the economic sanctions alone is a dangerous fallacy. While the very terms of Article XVI of the League's Covenant gives no real support to that fallacy, it gained ground nevertheless in the fifteen years that followed the establishment of the League of Nations. Thus in the Italo-Ethiopian war exclusive reliance was placed on economic sanctions — and even those were not carried out completely. Italy was very vulnerable by the "Economic Weapon," and, had that weapon been fully used, it might have proved effective. This would have involved blockade and — very likely — naval fighting on the Mediterranean. But that was precisely what the powers "enforcing" the Covenant were unwilling to undertake. If it had been fully realized that economic and military measures are inseparables once war has broken out, one would have either applied full sanctions or none. It may be suggested that either course would have been preferable to the one actually taken.

Before we try to define the real scope of the economic measures aiming at the enforcement of peace, let us digress for a moment

---

this has been one of the very important causes ot economic nationalism. Since the results were, however, far from satisfactory, it may be hoped that in the future it will be recognized that, like peace, prosperity is unattainable without a large amount of international co-operation. (This was written in 1943. See, however, Chapter VII above and Item 2 below.)

and deal with the cost of sanctions and with the requirements for collaboration among members of the International Organization.

The application of economic sanctions not only creates serious difficulties to the country against which they are imposed, but may cause substantial losses to countries which apply them. Economic sanctions mean: cessation of trade. And this means disruption of usual trade channels and of normal business dealings. The impact varies from country to country. Some may have depended heavily upon their trade with the country against which sanctions have now been declared. Others may have depended on that trade less or not at all. Some countries may make the necessary adjustments easily, while others, economically weaker, may find it very difficult. Monetary and financial complications may develop. All of this is so evident that plans should he made beforehand for co-operative coping with such a situation. Furthermore some countries, such as the neighbors of that against which sanctions have been imposed, may face aggressive acts on the part of that country, should they participate in the imposition and application of sanctions.

All that has been foreseen by the authors of the Covenant, as witnessed by paragraph 3 of Article XVI. Its provisions failed, however, to be elaborated in the years that followed, and in 1935-6 no procedure was available for dealing with these important matters. In the future this angle of the problem must not be disregarded. Fortunately, we have now an instrument of action in the shape of the Lend-Lease Program. Without going into the details of the matter, let us suggest that arrangements which are proving so efficient at the time of the present war may be very useful instruments of sharing judiciously and equitably the costs of economic sanctions and of giving economic help to countries which bear the brunt of the economic maladjustments resulting from sanctions and blockade.

Preventive economic sanctions.

With this in mind, we can now approach what is the principal contention of this paper, namely the role of economic sanctions considered as a *preventive weapon*. It is as such that they may render the use of armed force unnecessary, limit the gravity of conflict and bring about a reconsideration by an adventurous government of its aggressive plans. We know only too well how high in terms of life and treasure may be the costs of repressing and repulsing aggression. And the more one studies the twenty years between the two world wars, the more one feels that the second of them might have been prevented. Nobody can be sure what the course of history might have become had certain developments taken place instead of others. It would be idle to speculate too much about it. And yet history has a lesson to teach and one way it teaches it is to make us formulate certain hypotheses as guides to future action. In the particular case with which we are here concerned the hypothesis is the following: if the Axis powers had been prevented to organize their economic life and foreign trade so as to increase their war potential and to make themselves, temporarily at least, self-sufficient in basic war materials, they might have been unable to risk the war.

Thus the "Economic Weapon" of collective security would come into operation as soon as it would be ascertained that some government or group of governments apply policies (of the type described above) aiming at reducing their dependence on the world market. These governments would be approached by proper agencies of the International Organization with the demand to explain these measures and to abandon them in favor of others, cooperative in nature and internationally supervised. In that way, every legitimate objective could be achieved, relative to improving the economic situation of the country or countries in question, while the adoption of autarkic policies would be made more difficult. Members of the International Organization would be obliged by statute to seek international collaboration in case of domestic difficulties, rather than to resort to the "forbidden" instruments of policy. But the Organization would also keep a watchful eye on "outsiders". The latter, to be sure, would anyhow be deprived of certain advantages enjoyed by members of the Organization — but there would be ample scope for additional sanctions should they adopt autarkic policies and refuse to abandon them. The aim of these "preventive sanctions" is to make it impossible in the future for any country to repeat the recent economic feats of Germany and Japan. Thus the danger of aggression would be reduced. And should the aggression happen nevertheless, the aggressor would from the outser be weaker than if no such preventive measures were adopted.

What we suggest, then, is to consider autarkic policies are internationally unfriendly acts and to respond to them by the imposition of "preventive sanctions." This proposal calls for much elaboration. It is submitted here for discussion. It seems to result from the twenty years of experience of the interwar period.

Modern war is a complex economic venture. To be waged successfully it must be well prepared. If we want to minimize the chances of war in the future we must accomplish two purposes: make it as difficult as possible for individual countries to be prepared for war, and make the international community strong enough to repel aggression whenever it occurs. The collective security system of the League of Nations was aiming at the second objective, though in practice much too half-heartedly. The first objective was given little attention; and yet it is at least as vital as the second and it holds out the best chance for the avoidance of war. The objective can only be attained if economic nationalism is eliminated from contemporary international life. And it can best be attained through the threat and application of what we have called "preventive economic sanctions."

Conclusions.

The conclusions of the foregoing analysis can be summed up very briefly. The economic contribution to collective security is twofold. Positively, it consists in the development of a system of preventive sanctions. Negatively, and most importantly, it involves a fight against economic nationalism. This fight, let us add, in order to be successful, should probably be started already *during* the present war.

The outlawry of autarky and the establishment of a strong International Organization are necessary steps in the struggle against economic nationalism, but there must be also an attack against the more purely economic arguments for nationalist economic policies. That attack can show, as economists have indeed been showing since the days of Adam Smith, that economic nationalism is prejudicial to prosperity. In the past decade, however, the view was often voiced, under the leadership of Lord Keynes, that economic "insulation" is favorable to domestic stability, full employment and prosperity. Even if that view should be accepted (and the present writer strongly dissents from it), it would still be true that economic interdependence is to be prefered on the grounds of security and peace. Adam Smith was willing to make concessions to protectionism on the assumption that it might help national defense. Today, in a changed world, it is the internationalists rather than the nationalists who have a right to make the claim that "defense . . . is of much more importance than opulence," for defense — or security — calls for a well integrated world economy. And if the teachings of an important body of economic doctrine are correct, that way lies also the prosperous economic development of all the nations of the world.

2.

PROSPERITY VERSUS PEACE:
THE POLITICAL CONSEQUENCES OF A NEW
ECONOMY FALLACY (1947)*

A new economic fallacy came of age in the course of the last prewar decade and threatens to play havoc with the future peace of the world. This fallacy consists in saying that a country's national prosperity depends, essentially, upon a centralized planning of its economic life. Those who propound this point of view usually confuse full employment with prosperity and state the problem in terms of the former rather than of the latter objective. They do not object, in principle, to international trade or to such measures as might improve international economic relations. They claim, however, that so long as the world economy is unstable, a country can best serve its own interests and those of the rest of the world by pursuing its own full employment program. They often go on to say that, if only each country adopted a full employment program suited to its particular circumstances, a great step forward would be taken on the path to world economic stability. They argue that the greatest source of barriers to world trade is to be found in depressions and in the fear of depressions; should that fear be eliminated by appropriate measures of national planning, it would be much easier for a country to let down barriers to imports, since those imports would not interfere any longer with national economic stability. Most of these spokesmen are unwilling to accept any limitations on the freedom of national action in planning for full employment.

The doctrine briefly described in the preceding paragraph can be attributed to many contemporary writers. Its chief intellectual sponsor

* Published in "Conflicts of Power in Modern Culture", Seventh Symposium of the Conference on Science, Philosophy and Religion, New York, 1947.

has undoubtedly been John Maynard (later Lord) Keynes. In his *Tract on Monetary Reform*, published in 1923, Keynes emphasized the conflict which, in his opinion, existed between internal and international monetary stability, and cast his influential ballot in favor of the former. Turning from monetary to general economic issues, in 1933 he espoused the cause of national self-sufficiency. In his last major work, which was to become the *vade mecum* of the "Keynesians," he launched another vigorous attack against world trade. "It nations can learn," he wrote, "to provide themselves with full employment by their domestic policy... there need be no important economic force calculated to set the interest of one country against that of its neighbors." [1]

One hundred and thirty-six years earlier another book had appeared which linked together self-sufficiency and peace. It was *The Closed Commercial State* by Johann Gottlieb Fichte, the German philosopher and first *Rektor* of the University of Berlin. Fichte, however, realized that individual countries would have to expand their territory and, therefore, go to war to achieve self-sufficiency, whereas Keynes did not even realize that the lovely fruit of national self-sufficiency, which he so glowingly described, concealed the ugly and poisonous worm of war. On the contrary, he was obsessed by the fallacious idea that in the past international trade had been a source of wars. If nations would only provide themselves with full employment by their national policy, he argued, "there would no longer be a pressing motive why one country need force its wares on another. ... International trade would cease to be what it is, namely, a desperate expedient to maintain employment at home by forcing sales on foreign markets and restricting purchases ... but a willing and unimpeded exchange of goods and services in conditions of mutual advantage." [2]

These conceptions of international economic relations are based upon several misapprehensions; their net outcome is an intensification of economic nationalism. Indeed, it can be said that by placing in a faulty perspective the problem of national prosperity, these doctrines lead us inescapably to a conclusion which surely their authors would be the first to repudiate, namely, that prosperity and peace are contradictory objectives, that the quest for the former places the latter

---

[1] *The General Theory of Employment, Interest and Money, op. cit.*, p. 382.
[2] *Op. cit.*, pp. 382-383.

in jeopardy, and that mankind can be prosperous only in a world living in a shadow of war.

Yet Keyne's views have been taken up by followers throughout the world. In the United States, *e.g.*, Professor Alvin H. Hansen of Harvard propounds the view that if all countries would secure full employment at home, the stage would be set for a liberalization of foreign trade. America's principal contribution to world prosperity, he argues, is to maintain full employment at home. [3]

No one would disagree with the statement that the world cannot be prosperous unless the United States is prosperous and that an American economic depression would cast a shadow upon the prosperity of the world. But the question arises, what else is necessary on the part of the United States to promote world prosperity besides being prosperous herself? We know from the experiences of the thirties that measures aimed at national prosperity can lead to an increase of trade barriers and other obstacles to international economic intercourse. In order for American prosperity (or that of any other important country) to promote effectively the prosperity of other countries, it is indispensable that the national market should be wide open to the produce of other countries and that national capital should be free to seek investments in foreign countries. Thus American prosperity is a condition of international prosperity, provided it is sought by measures which are favorable to international trade and capital movements. It is also a mistake to argue as if world prosperity were dependent upon American prosperity, but American prosperity depended only upon America's own domestic economic policies. Actually, as a careful study of the 1929 breakdown would clearly show, the causal factors underlying that breakdown were not all located within the United States but were widely spread throughout the world economy. The fact that America's prosperity in the years preceding the crash was accompanied by a growing precariousness of the international economic equilibrium rendered the depression, when it came, worse both for this country and for the rest of the world than it might have been, had the United States imported substantially more during the twenties and lent quite a bit less, especially on short term.

---

[3] See *America's Role in the World Economy*, New York, 1945.

In brief, a proper conception of the relationships between American prosperity and that of the rest of the world would place them in a relation of mutual dependency rather than imply that American full employment planning is necessary for the welfare of the world, regardless of what forms that planning takes.

The Keynesian notion of prosperity attributes an excessive importance to the level of employment as against that of living standards. "Full employment" (whatever that ambiguous term may statistically mean) can be attained at various levels of well-being and within various types of social organizations. We can have full employment in a slave society in which the majority of people live on a subsistence level, and we can have full employment in a free society in which people enjoy high and rising standards of living. Were it not for the seemingly indestructible specter of the mass unemployment of the thirties, we would realize that political freedom and economic well-being, rather than full employment, are the real objectives of our quest. In a prosperous economy, to be sure, there are adequate opportunities for employment for all men and women willing and able to work. But an economy in which there is full employment need not necessarily be prosperous. If the international division of labor is a source of prosperity and well-being, then its curtailment reduces national prosperity below the level it might otherwise achieve. And since the days of Adam Smith economists and their readers have been made increasingly aware of the connection between this division of labor and the growth of standards of living.

The Wealth of Nations proved a time bomb which several decades after publication blasted out of existence the controls and restrictions on international trade which England inherited from the mercantilist period, and which had become a serious handicap to her economic growth. One hundred and seventy years after the publication of Adam Smith's immortal work, Keyne's *magnum opus* devoted many pages to a brilliant, if unconvincing, attempt at rehabilitating mercantilism, by showing that its spokesmen were in reality very farsighted men from whom much could be learned that was of great value in our own days. This Keynesian "rehabilitation" of mercantilists was a sign of the times. For the mercantilists were economic nationalists *par excellence,* that is to say, they subordinated all considerations of economic policy to the fundamental *desideratum* of national power. The mercantilist period was a period of recurrent warfare, and the economic doctrines of that time were very much concerned with the problem of making a country strong for war. Today we know that political sentiment dictates economic policies, that economic nationalism is merely an aspect of nationalism *tout court,* and that in a world dominated and obsessed by nationalism, policies aimed at better international economic relations are like tender plants at the mercy of strong northern winds.

Perhaps the mercantilists were not unaware of the importance of the international division of labor as a source of prosperity and well-being. But, since their concern was mostly with national power, they paid less attention than we do to the problem of national welfare. In the mercantilist revival of our own days, however, we are faced with a brand new fallacy, which consists in linking national prosperity with national full employment planning and in minimizing the importance of foreign trade. Much more importance is attached to national planning than to the international division of labor as a basis for national well-being. To seek prosperity within an insulated national economy rather than within a closely integrated world economy is a fallacy which arises by attaching an exaggerated importance to short run aspects of the problem and by ignoring the long run effects of these short run process. As Henry Hazlitt has emphasized in his recent book, *Economics in One Lesson,* most economic fallacies are due to such failures to take the "long view" of economic processes. What our neomercantilists, taking the "short view," usually offer as a choice is full employment at home with limited foreign trade as against freer international trade tied up with domestic unemployment. In doing that they draw false conclusions from the historic evidence that is before us. In particular, they tend to mistake the desperate attempts, in the thirties, to fight unemployment by promoting exports while keeping down imports, with the normal operations of internaitonal trade. But the "beggar-my-neighbor" policies of the depression years were in themselves a consequence of the economic nationalism of the twenties and of the failure to achieve in the thirties enough international collaboration to develop joint policies in fighting the depressions. The effect of the nationalistic ways of curing national depression was to increase the obstacles to international trade, to precipitate a further disintegration of the world economy, and to place each country's economic life upon a very uncertain basis.

The disintegration of the world economy, far from being attributed by them to economic nationalism, was then used by the neomercantilists to justify the adoption of still more nationalistic policies. In a disorganized world economy, it looked as if each country had its "own" business cycle, the elimination of which was the proper objective of national policy. Policies of national planning had the effect of disturbing the relations between the country's economy and the currents of the world economy. In consequence, the erroneous notion gained increasing acceptance that the business cycle is a national phenomenon, and that a country may best preserve its prosperity by insulating itself against the evil disturbances originating in foreign lands. Prosperity thus came to be regarded as a national virtue and depression as an imported evil. Considering that economic theory clearly shows the organic connections that exist between the upward and downward phases of a business cycle, this political dissociation of prosperity from depression strikes one as utterly nonsensical. Nonetheless, it has exercised a profound influence upon the course of economic policy and theoretical discussion.

What made the issue between economic nationalism and internationalism in our own time sdifferent from what it has been in the past, is the emergence of collectivism. In its various forms, collectivism represents a growing control by the national government over the country's economic activity. Such collectivism promises prosperity through centralized planning. Since, however, the national government can only plan economic activity (and nationalize resources and industries) within the national boundaries of the state, international relations become inevitably subordinated to national plans. Hence the impatience with international relations evidenced by collectivists.

Thus collectivism promotes the segregation of countries from one another; it emphasizes the importance of national boundaries. Indeed, it makes territorial expansion once more worthwhile because, within the wider area, there are more resources and a greater scope for planning. Thus collectivism takes us further and further away from the kind of world envisaged by the liberal thinkers of the nineteenth and twentieth centuries: a world in which political boundaries would gradually become mere administrative divisions; a world of free trade, free capital movements and free migration; a world in which peace as well as prosperity would be indivisible and sought by common action of all mankind. Such a world seems today much further removed from the realm of practical realizations than it had been in the days of Richard Cobden. But, whereas Cobden, his predecessors, and his followers, all inspired by the *Wealth of Nations,* realized that the same road leads to prosperity and to peace, the collectivistic and neomercantilistic writers of today seek prosperity along a road which necessarily takes us further and further away from peace. Only a reversal of policy, a return to the Smithian ideas, can save us from a further exacerbation of economic nationalism.

The suggested reversal of policy does not involve, of course, any return to *laisez faire.* As society grows more complex and economic problems increase in scope and variety, economic policy becomes more and more important as well as increasingly difficult to plan. This is not the place to discuss in detail the problem of *laissez faire.* It will be enough to ugsgest that in its more extreme formulations that philosophy was the symptom of a violent reaction against the excesses of state interventionism and state control in the mercantilist era, when economic life was all but strangled by a maze of regulations and red tape. In actual practice we never had a situation in which governmental economic policy was fully absent. In our days, those interest groups which advocate *laissez faire* have in mind more often than not what ought really to be called "*laissez* moi *faire,*" meaning "let *us* act as *we* please." That attitude has been and occasionally still is characteristic of business, but more recently it can also be observed among labor leaders opposing any state regulations of union activities.

The return to Smithian ideas suggested before involves the abandonment of *centralized* and *national* planning of economic activity in favor of an *international* approach to economic problems. It is indispenasble, if we are to seek prosperity within a framework which is also favorable to peace, that we should acknowledge the fact that economic cycle sof prosperity and depression are a worldwide phenomenon with national manifestations. These manifestations may vary from country to country, just as they vary, within one and the same country, from one region to another, but the phenomenon itself is international in scope. It is also indispensable to reduce the emplitude of these cyclical swings of economic activity which bring in their wake so much hardship and so much social trouble. But the endeavor to secure more economic stability in the world must be carried out by concerned international action and not by nationalistic policies. The fallacy which this paper has set out to denounce consists in expecting that enduring economic prosperity and stability will result from nationalistic policies, uncoordinated with and unrelated to those of other countries. The proper policy would consist in promoting international action for the purpose of reducing economic instabilities throughout the world. In doing so, it may be necessary, as Professor Jacob Viner suggested at the 1945 session of the Harris Foundation of the University of Chicago, to establish a new international financial institution, the sole purpose of which would be to attenuate business cycles wherever and whenever necessary.

We can seek economic prosperity and stability by methods of nationalism and through the instrumentality of a social strait-jacker. By doing so, we increase international friction, while reducing individual freedom at home. Or we may seek the solution by means of internationally designed measures so as to respect freedom and flexibility within the various national economies. It is along this second road that we are more likely to find enduring prosperity in a world of free and friendly nations.

3

AN ECONOMIST'S VIEWS ON INTERNATIONAL ORGANIZATION *
(1950)

It is difficult not to be impressed by the fact that the quest for world organization carried out since the end of World War I was accompanied by a continuous growth of restrictions placed by governments of the various countries upon the economic intercourse between their residents and those of other countries. In consequence, the breakup of the world economy has been going *pari passu* with a growing concern over international cooperation in the political field. Therein lies one of the most basic contradictions of our times, a contradiction which is at the bottom of the frustrations of the past thirty years in the international sphere.

It is an elementary, but often forgotten, fact that policies of national governments have always been the principal obstacle to economic relations between people living in various countries, and that whenever these relations were free from governmental restrictions, equilibrium and balanced growth would follow by virtue of the spontaneous and anonymous mechanism of the market. Adam Smith clearly understood and brilliantly explained these relationships in *The Wealth of Nations*, but, of course, he did not invent them: the market is one of the oldest human institutions, and over centuries and millennia of experience one of the most successful ones. The fact that in recent years many politicians and even a number of economists lost confidence in the effectiveness of the market mechanism has not been due to the impact of new and decisive experiences. On the doctrinal side, the market mechanism has been the object of persistent

* This paper, written in 1950, was published, somewhat obridged in "Foundations of World Organisation", Eleventh Symposium of the Conference on Science, Philosophy and Religion, New York, 1952.

attack by collectivist thinkers who prefer "rational" and "purposeful" planning by a centarl government to the "uncertainties" and "accidents" of the market place. Their faith in planning has, by the way, as little support in experience as has their distrust of the market mechanism. On the empirical side, the intricate mechanism of markets and prices has been interfered with increasingly by governments, and has therefore been less effective in the past two or three decades than it used to be previously and than it could be again. The results of these governmental interferences are not such as to encourage the belief that deliberate planning serves the cause of economic growth and prosperity better than the unplanned processes of the free market place. Indeed, to any dispassionate observer the opposite would appear as a far more likely conclusion to be drawn from recent economic history.

II

The growth of collectivism has led to a great increase in the scope and virulence of economic nationalism. There is nothing in that to surprise us. The collectivist philosophy places in the hands of a national government the powers of planning and directing the entire economic life of the country. These powers are limited to the territory over which that government is sovereign. Within that territory it can plan, it can persuade, and it can enforce; outside of that territory it has very little effective control. Is it surprising then that a collectivist government becomes impatient with the outside world and the developments which take place in it and which are beyond its own direction and control? Is it surprising that it wishes to "insulate" its territory from the rest of the world by all kind and manner of economic barriers, such as exchange controls, import quotas, and the like?

John Maynard Keynes, the great modern prophet of national self-sufficiency, expressed that philosophy of "insulation" very clearly in his essay on "National Self-sufficiency".[1]

Even though Keynes himself has turned his back, toward the end of his life, upon those earlier flights of his fancy, they have remained the inspiration of the more sophisticated collectivists

---

[1] See above, Chapter VI.

throughout the Western world. The Keynesians, whom, had he lived
longer, he would very possibly have disowned, are promoting the
notion that national planning is the mainstay of national prosperity,
as well as of the security of individuals in each and every country.
This all ties in with a collectivist approach to the problem of full
employment, according to which, when it is stripped of its technical-
ities, jobs, and not goods and services, are considered the principal
purpose of economic activity, and not, as in the classical liberal
doctrine, the result of brisk and balanced activity of which the primary
object is to satisfy human wants and needs.

In terms of internal relations in the collectivized or semi-collectiv-
ized countries, planned full employment is paid for in terms of
important human liberties. [2] Nor is it at all certain that, short of
going the whole way in the direction of totalitarianism, the governments inspired by collectivist doctrines will prove successful in
maintaining full employment and economic stability by the means they
are currently using or proposing to use. One of the reasons is that
no country can fully achieve economic insulation from the rest of the
world. Another reason is that people, being what they are, will not
submit for any length of time to regimentation and cumbersome
controls, unless they are forced to do so. It has often been said that
the path of collectivism is the road to serfdom, and this seems to be
confirmed by the growing empirical experience. That experience also
shows that whenever collectivists have not succeeded in destroying
the democratic freedom of their fellow citizens, these tend to rebel
against regimentation and force extensive economic decontrols. The
experience of Western European countries, including Great Britain,
in 1945-1950 is very striking in that respect.

III

Cumbersome at home, collectivism is disruptive in the international field. During the past twenty years, depression and war helping, it has succeeded in destroying the delicate network of world
markets and international prices, disrupted the stability of international monetary relations, broken up the economic integration the

---

[2] See F. A. von Hayek, *The Road to Serfdom*, London, 1944; John Jewkes,
Ordeal by Planning, New York, 1948, etc.

world had achieved to such a large extent prior to World War I and which it had regained, albeit very imperfectly so, in the mid-twenties. Human relations across boundary lines have become increasingly difficult. Cultural intercourse has been restricted by the effects of exchange control, and so has been one of the important human freedoms, the right to move from place to place, whenever national boundaries are involved. What an environment in which to seek world organization!

Having done a great deal to make international relations between individuals more difficult and less frequent, governments have set out to promote international cooperation among themselves. That the results have been disappointing, we well know and, again, there is little ground for surprise. Intergovernmental cooperation is acceptable to those concerned only if it infringes in no way upon their sovereignty. So limited, it becomes a mere bandying about of words and phrases. International conferences, whenever the hurdle of sovereignty appears, work on texts — not on policies — and agree on ambiguous phrases which can be all things to all men. No better example of this process could be given than the extraordinary document produced, as a result of three long international conferences, to serve as a charter for the proposed International Trade Organization. The purpose of that effort, it will be recalled, was to set out the "rules of the game" in the field of world trade, in view of promoting freer and more abundant commercial relations among nations. But whenever any government felt that one or another of its nationalistic policies might have to be discontinued or changed in view of the "rules of the game," it insisted on appropriate amendments, qualifications, or exceptions to be made with regard to the rules themselves. The result was a document which codified every evisting economic malpractice in the name of "realism."

What actually happened was that no government wished to commit itself to changing its policies or accepting limitations on its future freedom of action. It would have been far more candid had the ITO conferees rejected as impracticable the whole idea of drawing up a world trade charter. Instead they decided to pay lip service to the very principles which the detailed charter provisions violate in every practical application. The Havana Conference turned into a very illuminating and enlightening seminar in present day nationalism, and highlighted the role of collectivism as an obstacle to reaching meaningful international economic agreements.

IV

If national collectivisms and semi-collectivisms do not and could not add up to world organization, can it not be argued that the collectivist policies should be applied in a world politically united through federation or otherwise? This is a line of thought which is not infrequently encountered, one which puts political organization ahead of economic organization and assumes that the latter will take care of itself — presumably under the regime of centralized planning — once political unity has been achieved. If anybody has any doubt as to what such an international collectivism might produce in practice, he need only cast a glance behind the Iron Curtain and he will see what extremes of oppression and enslavement unbridled collectivism leads to, when it is backed by the power of a strong totalitarian nation. World organization based on economic collectivism, were it at all susceptible of achievement, would become the worst tyranny the world has ever known. When we speak of world organization, we surely do not regard that as an aim in itself, but merely as a means to safeguard the peace of free individuals. Peace at the expense of freedom would be the kind of peace that exists in a prison or in a concentration camp, and this, surely, is not what we are aiming at.

It world collectivism is to be discarded, and if economic nationalism is to be recognized as being a source of international division and friction, what then is the pat hleading to world organization as it may appear to a student of economics?

If international organization is ever to be successfully achieved under conditions safeguarding the freedom and the opportunities of the human individual, the importance of national boundaries, in terms of the everyday life of people living on either side of them, must be radically and drastically reduced. If national boundaries become mere administrative demarcation lines, if national governments have only limited powers over their populations, then one may hope to achieve international arrangements that are really meaningful and helpful. The first step then would appear to lie in a progressive but rapid suppression of economic barriers. This may sound like a reversion to free trade. It is, within reason. It may be considered as an attempt to revive the "dodo bird"; it may be branded as unrealistic or utopian. But is it not more unrealistic and more utopian to expect world order and individual freedom to be preserved under a regime of economic nationalism and collectivism? Is it not folly to expect governments which do all in their power to restrict, hamper, and frustrate international economic relations between individuals (and individual concerns), to advance, in conference with other such governments, the cause of a well knit and "integrated" world economy?

One of the most persuasive arguments used by collectivists relates to the pursuit of full employment. Because the world economy has been so broken up by restrictions and barriers, it becomes possible, superficially at least, to regard a country's economic prosperity or depression as a national matter. The business cycle of the world economy, with its many regional manifestations, has been broken up into a number of national business cycles. Collectivists believe that they can maintain a high level of economic activity and of employment at home by means of centralized planning, provided they can keep out disturbing influences coming from abroad. National prosperity thus becomes the fruit of the national government's wisdom, while depression comes to be regarded as an imported evil. Such an approach stands in sharp contradiction both with economic thought (which regards prosperity and depression as two organic, connected phases of the business cycle) and with experience, which shows how intricately economic developments which occur in one area of the world are linked with economic developments occurring somewhere else.

The public is led to believe that its economic condition can be made prosperous and secure by centralized planning, and is led to regard with suspicion foreign economic developments. Economic insulation, to which reference has already been made, thus becomes the politically accepted pattern of national economic life. The importance of the internaitonal division of labor, in terms of economic progress and of rising living standards everywhere, is being underplayed or brushed aside. Yet, this is the price which the "beneficiaries" of centralized planning have to pay for insulation.

Nor is it possible for any length of time to ignore the physical structure of the planet. Facts of life have a way of coming back with a vengeance. Those "undesirable" outside foreign disturbances, about which collectivists complain, are the inevitable result of the country's being a part of the planet. Attempts are made at present to brand countries that experience economic depressions or setbacks as bad neighbors and a source of difficulties for all. Outside of international friction such an approach can bring no other results. In United Nations circles pressure is being put upon countries which have so far resisted collectivism, such as the United States, to adopt, in turn, the road to planning. Should this ever occur the results will be more than regrettable for those very countries which, like Great Britain, are able today to engage in collectivist planning, because they are recipients of foreign aid — aid which the United States is able to extend, because the dynamism of its economic life has not been crippled by centralized governmental planning. It is because the United States, Canada, and several other countries have resisted the collectivist drive, and because elsewhere — as in continental Western Europe — collectivism is receding, that the world economy is not in a worse condition than that in which it finds itself — and which, even so, is very precarious. Should the doctrine of centralized economic planning in the name of, say, full employment be accepted by each and every country, including the United States, the disintegration of the world economy will be completed, with a great aggravation of international frictions.

V

In terms of present day conditoins, it may be "unrealistic" to talk about a reversion from collectivism to liberalism. But it may be well to remember that it is the "realists" of today — and their elder brothers — who have brought the world economy into a condition of greater disruption and chaos than it has ever known. How far can one trust them then as advisers and counselors regarding the future?

To the present writer at least, it appears as quite certain tbat unless the power of governments to restrict international economic relations is curtailed, indeed unless the notion of centralized national economic planning is abandoned, we shall never achieve an integrated well functioning world economy, and the political organization of the world will lack its economic foundations. Experience would seem to indicate that these excessive powers of government cannot be effectively restricted by international conferences and conventions. The necessary conditions for a return to economic liberalism on an international scale can be achieved within the various nations only through internal political developments. Public opinion must be made to understand better that in the longer run growing standards of living depend upon the dynamic qualities of private business enterprise, upon the international division of labor, upon foreign investments and an expanding volume of international trade. Public opinion must also come to realize that high and sustained employment is the necessary outgrowth of high levels of economic activity; whenever it is regarded as an aim in itself, it has to be paid for in terms of both freedom and prosperity, whereas no such price need be paid when it results spontaneously from the free and smooth functioning of economic forces throughout the world.

In the past two decades far too much emphasis has been placed on institutional arrangements, and far too little emphasis on the actual policies pursued by those who participate in these arrangements. Too much has been expected from international conferences and international bodies and too little attention has been paid to the national policies of the participating countries. Yet, it is upon these policies that the success of the international arrangements — or their failure — ultimately depends. If the quest for world organization has been so frustrating so far, it is because outward professions of the wish to cooperate were rarely, if ever, matched by appropriate policies of the various national governments.

In the economic sphere it is government policies which have erected the greatest barriers on the path of international relations between (human) individuals. It is the market mechanism which creates world unity out of a multitude of business transactions. Let this market mechanism be revived, let economic forces regain the freedom to function, and a decisive step will have been made toward world organization, economic and otherwise. To say this, does not imply the acceptance of an extreme *laissez-faire* position either internally or internationally. Internally there are many functions that the government has to perfarm even in a liberal non-collectivist society. [8] In

---

[8] See the present writer's "Economic Policy and Democracy," *op. cit.*

the international field there will also be scope for a great many arrangements made jointly by the various national governments for the purpose of making the operation of world markets easier and smoother and the framework within which they operate more resilient and stable. But these are tasks for the future: the first task before those who wish to endow world organization with solid economic foundations consists in joining in a struggle against collectivism and economic nationalism in its various forms. In that struggle the first and foremost battlefield is that represented by the public opinions of the various countries of the democratic world.

4

NOTES ON THE HAVANA TRADE CHARTER (1948) *

The signing in Havana on March 24th 1948 of the Final Act of the United Nations Conference on Trade and Employment brought to a close three years of negotiating and drafting successive texts of the Charter for an International Trade Organization. The results of that long and painstaking effort are now before us and will become, undoubtedly, the object of very careful scrutiny throughout the world, in chancelleries, universities, business organizations, etc. It is not my intention in this article to provide a detailed analysis of what is henceforth to be known as the Havana Charter. However, having been fortunate enough to be able to follow from very close quarters, though not in a governmental capacity, the Geneva and Havana conferences devoted to the drawing up of the Charter, I shall endeavour in the pages that follow to explain the basic reasons for the Charter's present form and to appraise its significance in relation to the future shape of international economic relations.

ECONOMIC NATIONALISM AND THE I.T.O.

Probably the most striking impression that an observer could obtain at the Geneva Conference of last summer or at the Havana Conference which has just come to a close was of the strength of economic nationalism throughout the world. Not only did most delegates constantly and consistently emphasize the need of their respective countries to practise trade restrictions of considerable scope and variety; the very concept of a *world economy* was almost completely missing from the discussions. Clearly, it was the duty of

---

* Published in *The Canadian Banker*, Toronto, May 1948.

national delegations to be guided by the national interest of their respective countries; what was striking, however, was the fact that national interest was nearly always viewed only against the background of the particular problems and conditions of each country, without reference to the operating characteristics of a wellfunctioning world economy. Instead of the answers to particular national problems being sought within the broader framework of an international economic system, attainment of the latter was given the status of a secondary, not a primary, goal. Most arguments advanced followed the pattern of showing how a particular set of trade restrictions might benefit the country interested in operating them; no serious effort was made to contrast the benefits received by that country with the disadvantages for other countries resulting from such restrictions. True, the Charter provides that a country adversely affected by trade restrictions imposed by another country may complain to the Organization and, under certain circumstances, may even retaliate in kind. But, whereas these provisions open the doors wide to international recrimination and conflict, they do not add up to a "universalist" or world-economic approach to the national policies of particular countries. The Trade and Employment Conference provided ample opportunity for each participating country to defend its largely nationalistic point of view; but no pattern of international co-operation made its appearance, and no real set of international "rules of the game" in the realm of commercial policy emerged from the long debates.

Whereas the Preparatory Committee of the Trade and Employment Conference included 17 countries, the full Conference had 59 participants. Some members of the United Nations, including the USSR did not take part; some countries which are not members of the United Nations, e.g. Switzerland, attended. The nearly universal character of the Conference undoubtedly became one of its major drawbacks. Even though they depend so greatly upon the rest of the world, the smaller or, at least, economically less developed countries are inspired nowadays by a most ardent spirit of economic nationalism. These countries formed a large majority of the participants in the Havana Conference and their attitudes not inconsiderably contributed to the weakness of the final document. "Protection of economic development through trade restrictions" became the battle cry of the so-called "under-developed countries" which include the Latin-American republics, the Asian countries of the Near, Middle and Far East, as well as several others, with Australia (which could hardly claim for itself an under-developed status) assuming a very effective leadership of the group. In addition to provisions introduced into the Charter to satisfy under-developed countries, there are two other groups of provisions, the effect of which is greatly to weaken that document. These are: (1) provisions inspired by the concern experienced by certain countries such as Great Britain, France, etc., over their balance-of-payments difficulties and (2) provisions arising from the importance attached by certain countries such as Australia, New Zealand, etc. to leaving full scope for national planning for "full employment."

These three vital issues — economic development, employment, balance-of-payments difficulties — can all be dealt with, of course, in an internationally-minded way. In actual fact, however, the approach to their solution at the London, Geneva and Havana conferences was invariably nationalistic. The attitude taken, generally speaking, was like this: "Such and such are the policies we, Country A, would like to adopt — or might like to adopt — to deal with our balance-of-payments deficit, with our employment problem, with our industrialization program. The rules of the I.T.O. must be so written as to enable us to carry out such policies as we choose to adopt." An attitude more conducive to international co-operation and to a sound world economy would have been: "Such and such are the requirements of an equilibrated world economy. Our particular national problems must be dealt with by methods compatible with the necessary international 'discipline'." In addition, to make things worse, no serious attempt was made to draw a sharp and clear dividing line between the long-range principles incorporated in the Charter and its short-term transition-period provisions. As a result, the long-term principles included in the Charter are so qualified by numerous exceptions, "escape clauses" and interpretative notes that they can hardly become effective guides to practical governmental action, even in the long run.

This is an unhappy state of affairs but it could in no way be described as surprising. A world trade charter favourable to the growth of non-discriminatory multilateral trade could result only from the adoption by the great trading nations of the world of a point of view in which the choice of their particular national policies would be subordinated to a well-operating world economy. So long as the maintenance of freedom of national action is considered to overrule the essential requirements of international economic solidarity, no satisfactory agreement can be reached and the future of international economic relations remains precarious. The maintenance of a country's foreign payments in a condition of long-run balance, the maintenance of economic activity and employment at high levels, and the furtherance of economic growth are, all of them, entirely compatible with the maintenance of substantial freedom of international trade. Economic literature provides plenty of material to support such a contention, though it is certainly necessary to proceed to a new demonstration of it because of both the widespread acceptance nowadays of the doctrines of economic nationalism and the influence these doctrines exercise over the governmental policies of most countries of the world.

For purposes of practical action, the absence of an international approach to economic stability, to development and to balance-of-payments equilibrium comprises the most important and urgent "unsettled issues." They should evidently have been settled before the drawing up of the final draft of the I.T.O. Charter. Even though the Havana Conference adopted a charter it still remains important that these issues be thoroughly explored, so that the document may gradually be amended and eventually become an effective instrument of international co-operation — instead of remaining what it now is, a striking testimony to the ubiquity on our planet of strong economic nationalism.

TRADE RESTRICTIONS UNDER THE I.T.O. CHARTER

When the project of establishing an International Trade Organization was first formulated by the United States, its purpose was to provide the world with an instrumentality for gradual achievement of a significant reduction of tariffs and elimination of quantitative trade restrictions·and discriminatory treatment in international trade. A first major exception was introduced into the original *Proposals for the Expansion of World Trade and Employment* (December 1945) to enable countries in balance-of-payments difficulties to limit their imports by means of quantitative trade restrictions. In the further work on the Charter of the I.T.O. this provision grew into the very elaborate Article 21 of the Havana text. In addition, quantitative trade restrictions have been admitted in a number of other cases by virtue of Articles 13 and 20 (paras. 2 and 3). The former of these is particularly important, referring as it does to the protection of "economic development" by means of quantitative trade restrictions. In the London version of the I.T.O. Charter (November 1946) exceptions under Article 13 could be applied only after obtaining prior approval from the I.T.O. This most important prerogative thus given to the Organization was limited in scope in the Geneva draft of the Charter (August 1947), whereas the final or Havana draft whittled it down to almost nothing. When the process of "erosion by amendments" had been completed, all that remained of the principle of "prior approval" was its purely verbal affirmation, though in most of the cases likely to arise in practice the Organization will have to grant its approval, once the applicant country has shown that its case falls under one of several comprehensive headings listed in Article 13 of the Charter.

The principle of non-discrimination was forcefully stated in the early versions of the Charter. It has been qualified by important exceptions in the Geneva draft to enable countries in balance-of-payments difficulties (a) to give priority to essential imports over less essential ones and (b) to use their "weak currencies" in a manner entailing discrimination against "hard-currency" countries. At Havana this question came up for very considerable discussion resulting in the final and very complicated draft of Article 23. It is of interest to note that this article, in its final version, is one of the few provisions of the Charter in which a clear-cut distinction is made between the transition-period and the long-term arrangements. For the transition period there is now a great deal of latitude regarding discrimination, whereas in the long run discriminatory applications of quantitative restrictions will have a considerably more limited scope. The original idea of attogether eliminating discriminatory treatment from international trade relations has now been so altered as, in effect, to admit the principle of discrimination for a number of carefully defined situations.

Preferential agreements also are now admitted in a number of cases, in connection with the establishment of customs unions and with more limited trade agreements designed for "free-trade areas" (Article 44), as well as to promote economic development (Article 15). This is a complete departure from the original intention of prohibiting all new tariff preferences, while eliminating gradually all the existing ones. The scope of export subsidies has also been broadened in Geneva and in Havana (Articles 25 to 28). The most-favoured-nation clause is maintained as a principle of commercial policy by virtue of Article 16, with qualifications resulting from the maintenance of preferences. This would be a more important provision if the scope of quantitative trade restrictions were less than it is under the Havana Charter. The original intentions of the authors of the I.T.O. project notwithstanding, quantitative trade restrictions will remain under the Charter a far more important instrument of commercial policy than tariffs; since the most-favoured-nation clause does not apply to quantitative restrictions, its significance is correspondingly limited.

Under the Charter any country that has balance-of-payments difficulties or has embarked on a program of industrialization may resort to a substantial use of quantitative trade restrictions without obtaining prior approval from the I.T.O. This is the weakest as well as the most characteristic feature of the trading system defined in the Havana Charter. Because it results from the way in which the three previously-mentioned "unsettled issues" were handled by the authors of the Havana Charter, it is most important to analyse these issues more fully in the pages that follow.

UNSETTLED ISSUES

Employment Policies

One of the most vexing economic problems confronting the world is how to reconcile with the requirements of a world economy policies aiming at stable economic activity at high levels of production and employment. If we had a better understanding of the issues involved and an adequate degree of economic co-operation, we could approach the problem on a world scale. In the absence of both that knowledge and that co-operation, individual countries frequently incline towards planning of thier economic policies independently of one another. Sooner or latter they find that foreign economic developments affect their domestic plans. One speaks then of external deflationary or inflationary pressures and takes steps to prevent these pressures from interfering with domestic economic plans. By adopting policies of "insulation," however, one disrupts the normal currents of international trade and capital movements.

It is a curious comment on man's inability to learn from experience that there should be in the world today so much support for independent national planning for economic stability, considering how badly all such plans failed during the decade of the '30's. True, the League of Nations published as one of its "swan song" reports a study, *Economic Stability in the Post-War World*, which appeared in 1945 and outlined an approach to the problem that was full of promise; but this pioneering effort has not been followed up since. In the long course of the work preparatory to the Havana Conference little was said about an international approach to the problem of economic stability; instead, independent national planning carried out behind a screen of trade restrictions has been accepted as legitimate.

The concern over full employment dovetails, in many cases, with the adoption of state socialistic planning of the economic life of the country. Such planning is possible, of course, only within the territory over which the particular government exercises sovereign power. What happens beyond the boundaries of that country is outside the control of its government, and may be frowned upon as an unwanted foreign interference with domestic planning. It is sobering to reflect that socialism, which started its career under internationalist slogans, is now firmly wedded to political nationalism. By one of those curious turnabouts, which the sardonic Muse of History seems to enjoy so much, it is now socialism which invokes national sovereignty in support of its national planning.

Economic Development

The most widespread progress in economic growth of the underdeveloped areas of the world has been achieved when the flow of international commerce was freest and capital movements from the more advanced to the less advanced countries were most abundant.

At the end of the second world war, concern over economic development had become very strong throughout the world, but by a curious intellectual and political distortion this has led, not to the adoption of more liberal trade policies but, on the contrary, to a great accentuation of economic nationalism.

It is true that nearly a century and a half ago a great American statesman propounded a theory that the growth of young industries could be assisted by protective tariffs. But Alexander Hamilton was thinking of moderate and, most of all, of temporary restrictions. He would certainly not have acquiesced in the way in which today the most drastic and intransigent restrictionist policies are defended on the grounds that they protect new industries. At the same time, the countries most concerned over their economic development tend to under-estimate the importance of securing an adequate influx of foreign capital; their governments show the greatest possible reluctance to grant to foreign investors such assurances of fair treatment as would make them willing, in spite of painfully recent memories of past defaults and new threats of nationalization, to venture into foreign lands. One might well ask: "If trade restrictions are all that is needed to promote economic development, why is it that the so-called under-developed countries are not much further along on the path of economic growth?" To that question no satisfactory answer can be obtained.

As in the case of employment policies, it is not the goal which is questioned here but the means by which individual countries propose to attain it. In the Havana Charter for World Trade, economic development as well as employment is used as justification for the adoption of new restrictions on international trade; in neither case have any provisions been inserted which would indicate a realization that productive employment, high levels of efficient production and promising economic development all depend upon the achievement and maintenance of a soundly expanding world economy.

On the contrary, we are faced today with a "myth of economic development," a myth according to which a country can best promote its economic growth by the use of stringent trade restrictions, free from any major international commitments in the realm of commercial policy. Such a concept is sheer fallacy. It ignores not only the teachings of economic theory but also the century-long experience of economic practice. Instead of being used as an argument in favour of more abundant investments and freer trade, economic development is being used as an argument for breaking up still further the already very precarious world economy.

Balance-of-Payments Difficulties

The depression of the '30's and the second world war have resulted in widespread and deep-rooted dislocations of international trade, in the liquidation of many foreign assets and in new international indebtedness. The most dramatic case, and one which presents the world with an extremely difficult problem to solve, is that of Great Britain. As a result of the depression and war-born dislocations, serious balance-of-payments difficulties are experienced by most countries of the world; they are unable to pay for their current import requirements (and financial commitments) with the proceeds of their exports (and the income derived from their foreign investments, if any). In addition, the difficulties of many countries are increased in consequence of their policies of economic "insulation," to which reference has been made before.

In order to gradually liquidate the balance-of-payments difficulties that are so upsetting at the present time, two lines of policy are evidently necessary: (1) economic assistance such as envisaged by the Marshall Plan to bridge for war-torn countries the period of essential and difficult readjustments and (2) the adoption by these countries of policies which would tie their economy more closely to that of other countries and would increase the flexibility of their cost-price structures. What is necessary, in addition, is revival of the spirit of competitive enterprise which has always been a vital factor in the expansion of foreign trade. Only by making its economy more productive and more flexible and by integrating it more closely with the world economy can a country achieve lasting improvement in its international economic position.

It is characteristic of the present condition of economic thought and statecraft that these considerations seem to have been absent from the councils in which the Havana Trade Charter was elaborated. Instead, a different concept has been applied, the simplicity of which is equalled only by its fallaciousness. What it boils down to is this: if a country is in the throes of balance-of-payments difficulties, it must be allowed to protect its international position by means of import quotas and the like. That balance-of-payments difficulties may be due to the domestic policies of the countries suffering from them is recognized in the Charter of the I.T.O., but only obliquely and with wrong conclusions. According to Article 21, para. 4 (b), members of the I.T.O. recognize that, as a result of its domestic employment or development policies, "a member may find that demands for foreign exchange on account of imports and other current payments are absorbing the foreign exchange resources currently available to it in such a manner as to exercise pressure on its monetary resources which would justify the institution or maintenance of restrictions under paragraph 3 of this Article."

If the Charter were inspired by the concept of an organic world economy the above recognition would lead to a rule that countries should pursue their domestic employment or development goals in a manner that would not upset their balance-of-payments equilibrium. The exact opposite, however, appears to be the Charter's philosophy. Just after the sentence quoted above, Article 21, para. 4 (b) (i) goes on to say: "No member shall be required to withdraw or modify restrictions which it is applying under this Article on the ground that a change in such [employment or development] policies would render these restrictions unnecessary." This is re-enforced by the provisions of Article 6 of the Charter, devoted to "safeguards for members subject to external inflationary or deflationary pressures." This article amounts to an explicit acceptance of the principle of economic "insulation" with respect to business-cycle policy — a principle which is the very negation of the concept of a world economy.

In this connection Professor D. H. Robertson's observations in a recent article appear to be particularly pertinent: "What are politely called 'balance-of-payments difficulties' do not necessarily drop like a murrain from heaven ... any nation which gives its mind to it can create them for itself in half an hour with the aid of the printing press and a strong trade union movement." [2]

---

[1] Cf. *Economic Journal*, London, December 1947.

In the whole modern armoury of economic nationalism no argument is more superficially plausible, more misleading, and more devastating in its applications than that which justifies import restrictions by the need to eliminate balance-of-payments difficulties.

CONCLUSION

It is because these great "unsettled isues" have not been settled in an international spirit that the Charter has acquired its present form. It follows from the foregoing discussion that the prevalence of economic nationalism is to a considerable extent due to the effect of the war upon many countries and upon international economic relations. When, with the help of the European Recovery Program and other measures throughout the world, the war damage is finally restored, there may be a good chance to revise and improve the I.T.O. Charter. That document itself (Article 101) provides for "a general review of the provisions of this Charter" by a special session of the I.T.O.'s Conference about the end of the fifth year after the entry into force of the Charter. This will be the first major opportunity for a fundamental revision of the Havana Charter and those who have at heart the prosperous growth of friendly international economic relations must hope that this opportunity will not be missed. In the meantime, much preliminary work should be done on the subject of "unsettled issues."

HOW IHE U.S. LOST THE ITO CONFERENCES (1949) *

It is not my present purpose to engage in a detailed discussion of the Havana Charter, nor to give reasons why I believe, as I do, that it is a harmful document which should not be ratified by Congress. What I purpose to examine is another aspect of the problem: the course of action that resulted in American delegates' signing a document which denies rather than confirms the basic objectives of American economic policy.

The ITO project has its origin in the fact that in the U.S. (and in the State Department in particular) an important lesson had been learned from the economic frustrations of the interwar period. A dismal fate epentually befell the American initiative, however, because our authorities have not learned certain other, equally important lessons of those years.

The first lesson, which we learned, was the importance of adopting, immediately after the war, agreements that would definitely commit the signatories ot abstain from policies of economic nationalism. This was recognized in documents such as Article 7 of the master lend-lease agreement, which carried precise commitments by the recipients to work with us, after the war, for the elimination of major trade barriers and all discriminatory trade practices. The second lesson, to which little or no attention seems to have been paid, is that no meaningful international economic agreement can, in an ideologically divided world, be secured on a universal basis. The failure of the London Conference of 1933 and of the mission undertaken in 1937 by Paul Van Zeeland, on behalf of the French and

---

* Published in "Fortune", New York, September 1949.

British governments, illustrates the futility of a universalist approach and the need for a selective one.

There were two basic flaws in the State Department's *Proposals for Expansion of World Trade and Employment,* which it published simultaneously with the Anglo-American loan agreement in September, 1945, after extensive confidential negotiations with the British Government. One flaw was strategic, the other intellectual. I happen to know that attention of high State Department officials was directed to these flaws soon after the publication of the *Proposals* and that they were warned of the bad effect they might have upon the further course of ITO negotiations.

Let us start with the strategic flaw, of which the intellectual one was a consequence. Instead of publishing its own concrete proposals, the Government of the U.S. decided first to negotiate with the British Governement to get a mutually acceptable text. Had this plan, good or bad, been consistently followed through, an original Anglo-American statement would have been presented to the world by the two governments acting in unison. But such was not the case. The document was an Anglo-American compromise. It included, in particular, a section authorizing the protection of balance of payments through import quotas, which was clearly of British inspiration, and brought into the fine project of an International Trade Organization the "Trojan horse" of mercantilist restrictionism. Nevertheless, the document, vitally weakened by compromise, was then presented to the world as a purely American declaration: *"Proposals for Expansion of World Trade and Employment* — Developped by a Technical Staff within the Government of the U.S. ... and Presented for Consideration by the Peoples of the World."* To be sure, an Anglo-American joint statement was issued at the same time announcing that "the government of the United Kingdom is in full agreement on all important points in these *Proposals* and accepts them as a basis for international discussion" — that much, but no more. The *Proposals* were given very great publicity and were elaborated into a *Suggested Charter for an International Trade Organization,* which the U.S. presented to the London meeting of the Preparatory Committee in October, 1946. Thus, instead of having a clear-cut statement of the American position that the American delegates could defend at the London Conference and the gatherings that followed, our delegates in London found themselves defending an Anglo-American compromise as if it had been an undiluted statement of American aims.

The principal intellectual flaw in the *Proposals*, the result of this strategic error, is found in Section C.2: *Members confronted with an adverse balance of payments should be entitled to impose quantitative import restrictions as an aid to the restoration of equilibrium in the balance of payments.*

This short statement, through the process of elaboration in the successive ITO conferences, became Article 21 of the Havana Charter. There it occupies four closely printed pages and contains some of the most devastating provisions of that document. The phrase that accepts the use of import quotas as "an aid to the restoration of equilibrium in the balance of payments" was the Trojan horse. It expressed the basic mercantilist conviction that a country is justified in restricting its imports by quotas in order to influence its international accounts in a desired way. Due to the exertions of Adam Smith and his followers, this notion became justly and widely discredited in the nineteenth century as it was increasingly realized that import restrictions (and indeed export subsidies as well) can give only short-lived relief of the country that practices them and this at the cost of harming other countries and disrupting sound trade.

From having discussed this problem time and again with our State Department officials and some of their advisers, I judge, for my part, that the real significance of that British-inspired provision escaped them at the time of drafting the *Proposals* — and later. I generally met with the attitude that I was taking too gloomy a view of this "exception." The memory of these conversations leads me to believe that the American intention may have been to regard the balance-of-payments exception as a transition-period clause, but this was never explicitly stated and the consecutive texts of what is now Article 21 of the charter are clearly permanent provisions and not transitional ones. Had the *Proposals* been issued as an Anglo-American document and had the dangerous implications of Section C.2 been acknowledged, the U.S. negotiators might have fought this exception at the London, Geneva, and Havana conferences. But as far as I am aware these provisions have never been challenged by the American delegation; indeed they have been looked upon as entirely legitimate. Therein lies, I should suggest, one of the reasons for the failure of the ITO effort.

The missed turning point

To be sure, the U.S. insisted on a number of exceptions and escape clauses of its own in the interests of agriculture, of shipping, and of tariff-protected interests. Even weakened by these concessions, however, the original American position could have been quite strong had we made it clear that our interests in the establishment of an ITO depended pretty much on the contents of its charter. But by and by our bargaining position was destroyed by the excessive eagerness of our negotiators to reach a wide agreement on *a* charter and their insufficient stubbornness when it came to defending basic principles. In Geneva and in Havana the generally accepted view was that the U.S. delegates were so anxious to get a charter that they would, in the end, accept all those changes in that document that would prove indispensable for obtaining its general acceptance.

I must note one important occasion that might have become the turning point in the ITO conversations. On December 23, 1947, at Havana, Clair Wilcox (vice chairman of the U.S. delegation) delivered a very strong speech to one of the conference's principal commissions. He warned the delegates that they were too complacent about quantitative trade restrictions and were too easily assuming that the U.S. would never introduce such restrictions an its own trade even if they were to be declared acceptable and legal. That speech came close to breaking up the conference. Had it been followed by a shift in the entire American strategy, the whole course of the Havana Conference would have been altered. It might have wound up with a charter conforming better with American ideals; it might have adjourned for the time being without a charter; or again thé entire project might have been abandoned. The last-named course would have been the likeliest, I think, since it appeared very clearly by that time that the overwhelming majority of countries represented at Havana were far more interested in their freedom of action in respect to applying import quotas, discriminatory practices, and the like than in a general suppression of those instruments of restrictive commercial policy. Unfortunately the Christmas spirit that enveloped the conference soon after Mr. Wilcox spoke brought in its wake a wave of mellowness and the road of compromise was resumed early in 1948, never to be abandoned again.

The Anglo-American *Proposals* elaborated by the U.S. into a *Suggested Charter for an International Trade Organization* became, as mentioned before, the basic working paper of the London Conference. But after this initial "success" of the U.S., the leadership in the drafting of the charter seems to have passed into other hands, the U.S. assuming a defensive position — defending the Anglo-American compromise as if it had been an exact expression of America's views and desires, and giving in on very fundamental issues to delegations from state-socialist countries.

The British attacked the *Proposals* in an attempt to widen the balance-of-payments escape clause, to safeguard imperial tariff preferences, and to protect national freedom of action in the field of economic planning. They were very ably seconded by Commonwealth delegates, two in particular, Dr. Coombs of Australia and Walter Nash, Deputy Prime Minister and Finance Minister of New Zealand. The shift of emphasis was best illustrated by the way two chapters — the one on employment policies and a new chapter on economic development, very effectively sponsored by Dr. Coombs — took on more and more importance in the structure of the charter, in contrast to the chapter on commercial policy, originally intended to be the core of the entire document. Although these chapters on employment and economic development contained no positive guidance concerning the achievement of "full employment" or economic development, they became a significant source of exceptions from the rule of freer multilateral trade that the charter was originally intended to serve.

Later, in Geneva, Dr. Coombs told me that he regarded these chapters as *the two pillars of the ITO* and that he felt quite confident trade would move briskly and freely between countries once they have reached the condition of secure full employment and once they have set in motion effective programs of economic development. Far from sharing so optimistic a forecast, I asked Dr. Coombs how he reconciled these anticipations with the fact that national economic plans, whether inspired by the concern over employment or over economic development, generally lead to balance-of-payments difficulties and to the adoption of restrictive trade and payment policies by governments that practice them. I received no answer to that question at the time but found it in the final draft of the charter as adopted in Geneva and again in the definitive text adopted in Havana. These provisions (Article 21, paragraph 4b) acknowledge the fact that national economic planning may lead to balance-of-payments difficulties and then proceed to draw conclusions eminently favorable to such planning. To quote from Mr. Nash's report to the New Zealand Parliament, the provisions of Article 21, paragraph 4b mean that:

... *when a conflict arises between the desirability of pursuing policies of economic development and full employment on the one hand and the desirability of avoiding quantitative restrictions on the other, the domestic policies will take precedence. Thus a Member cannot be required to* alter *or suspend its policies of economic development or full employment on the grounds that such action would remove the cause of the balance of payments difficulties and render the restrictions unnecessary.*

Note the world "alter," which I have underlined. It indicates that by becoming a member of the ITO, a country assumes no obligation whatever to shape its domestic policy so as to avoid disrupting international trade through the application of import quotas, and that it should not even be invited to *alter* its policies if they are prejudicial to international economic order. In this provision the shift of emphasis in the charter that started in London was brought to full fruition. It is noteworthy that the American delegates didn't dissent from it at either Geneva or Havana. The only public protest came from the Benelux countries.

In addition to the very successful offensives conducetd by Great Britain and the Commonwealth countries in London, there was formed at that conference an informal bloc of underdeveloped countries largely led and influenced by Dr. Coombs and the active Indian delegation. Later, at Havana, the South American countries suported it on most occasions. The underdeveloped countries were primarily interested in the right to use import quotas as a means of protecting their "infant industries." Somehow they seemed to attach more importance to that than to ways and means of securing an adequate influx of investment capital from abroad. At Geneva the U.S. and Great Britain formed an alliance against this bloc of underdeveloped countries. Great Britain, to be sure, claimed the right to use quantitative trade restrictions but did so on balance-of-payments grounds, fully realizing the dangers for its export trade in the use of the same devices for protective purposes by the so-called underdeveloped countries. Instead of opposing *all* import quotas in pursuance of its own view, the U.S. delegation remained faithful to the 1945 compromise with Britain (even though Britain did *not* stand by it) and limited itself to fighting the claims of the underdeveloped countries. These countries eventually reached, as a matter of fact, an almost complete victory by the process of numerous amendments. At Havana they had an overwhelming majority behind them, while our delegates, whether they admitted it or not, were desperately anxious to have *a* charter and didn't match the stubbornness of their opponents.

Gradually and imperceptibly, indeed, our delegates seem to have been won over to quite a few of the points of view of their opponents. At Havana they accepted the notion that the ITO "shall have regard, in the exercise of its functions under other Articles of this Charter, to the need of Members to take action within the provisions of this Charter to safeguard their economies against inflationary or deflationary pressure from abroad" (Article 6). This provision was originally introduced in London and referred only to "deflationary" pressure. In Havana a proposal was made to take into account "inflationary" pressure as well. Our delegation briefly and unsuccessfully fought this extension of the scope of the article. Yet is was entirely logical that it should cover both the inflationary and deflationary phases of the business cycle. What was wrong was the fact that such an article was included in the charter *at all*. My frequent suggestions to the effect that the U.S. should try to get rid of it met with no favorable response, as our delegates seemed to see nothing basically wrong with it. And yet this article represents another victory of the principle of "economic insulation" over that of international economic interdependence. It was this very principle of "insulation," through trade restrictions, that contributed so decisively to the disintegration of the world economy in the thirties.

A tale of frustration

The initiative in the drafting of the charter slipped away from the American negotiators in London and was never regained. In Geneva they defended the London draft of the charter, at Havana they de-

14

fended the Geneva draft. I have it on excellent authority that between the Geneva and Havana conferences Mr. Wilcox was earnestly urged to reopen at Havana such basic issues as the right to use import quotas for the purpose of protecting a country's balance-of-payments equilibrium. I understand that this suggestion was considered impractical because it would disrupt the unity of the seventeen members of the Preparatory Committee which had reached agreement in Geneva, thereby causing other countries to reopen many issues as well. What happened is a matter of record. In the opening phase of the Havana Conference 800 amendments were presented. Most of them were written by countries not represented in Geneva, but members of the Preparatory Committee proved far less devoted to the contents of the Geneva text and to the maintenance of a united front than the State Department anticipated. So the Havana Conference became a tale of frustration. Our delegates did not launch any imaginative campaign for the drastic improvement of the Geneva draft. They did not even stand pat on that draft but allowed it to deteriorate still further.

That is should so deteriorate was inevitable, considering the broad membership of the conference and the ideas emanating from the great majority of delegates. There was no interest in freeing international trade from its shackles. Opinion at Havana was very favorable to import quotas, to tariff preferences, to discriminatory practices, and to exchange control. Along with a few countries, such as Canada and the Benelux group, we were isolated in our desire for free multilateral trade. What was *not* inevitable, however, was the placing of the American signature under the Havana Charter. Our delegates might have made it clear that we would not accept a charter which deviated too far from the principles of non-discriminatory, multilateral, free-enterprise trade. No such statement was made, with the sole exception of the above-mentioned and quickly forgotten pre-Christmas speech by Clair Wilcox.

It easy to extol the virtues of compromise, but compromise is a dangerous instrument and has to be handled with the utmost care. In 1874 the great English liberal statesman John (later Lord) Morley published a now famous essay, "*On Compromise.*" Here are his conclusions:

A principle, if it be sound, represents one of the larger expedi-

ences. To abandon that for the sake of some seeming expediency of the hour, is to sacrifice the greater good for the less, on no more credible ground than that the less is nearer. It is better to wait, and to defer the realization of our ideas until we can realize them fully, than to defraud the future by truncating them, if truncate them we must, in order to secure a partial triumph for them in the immediate present. It is better to bear the burden of impracticableness, than to stifle conviction and to pare away principle until it becomes mere hollowness and triviality. What is the sense, and what is the morality, of postponing the wider utility to the narrower? Nothing is so sure to impoverish an epoch, to deprive conduct of nobleness, and character of elevation.

Had Lord Morley's essay been read by our delegates before they embarked for London and reread from time to time in the months that followed, we might have been spared the necessity now of deciding whether or not to ratify the charter.

6

ECONOMIC NATIONALISM AS AN OBSTACLE TO FREE WORLD UNITY (1952) *

I

It is one of the jobs of historians, when they look back upon past events, decades or centuries after they have taken place, to ascertain when the destinies of countries and nations have taken fundamental turns, for better or for worse, in the course of their history, what the causes of these turns were — and their consequences, whether they could have been avoided or reversed, in brief, whether nations through their leaders and their public opinion have acted wisely or otherwise in the face of external forces and events.

Contemporaries lack, of course, the perspective from which alone the tides of history can be properly appraised and fairly judged. An interpreter of the contemporary scene, be he a journalist, a commentator, a political analyst, or an economic counselor, cannot do the work, which will only be performed, years after he is gone, by dispassionate and detached historians. When living, however, in the midst of great changes and violent commotions, when facing an uncertain future against the background of a troubled past, how can we avoid the temptation to take stock in our present situation, to try to appraise the exact position we have reached along the road we are travelling and to make a guess, however hazardous, as to the course that is ahead of us.

Deliberately, I am yielding to this temptation. I am doing so because my reading of contemporary events leads me do the con-

* An address before the Commonwealth Club of California, San Francisco, Calif., Sept. 12, 1952, published in *The Commercial and Financial Chronicle*, New York, September 18, 1952.

clusion that our nation and the entire free world are on the threshold of one of the great turnings of history. This I believe not so much because of the clouds of war which are hanging over us, clouds which are not getting any lighter because many of us turn our eyes away from them in the hope that they will disappear, and not so much because of the great danger of communist influences which, even without war, can undermine our society, our civilization, and our freedom.

The reason why I think that our destinies are about to take a major turn is that I am convinced that the unity of the Western World is threatened from within, as much as its security is threatened from without, and because I believe that the next *months* will show whether that all-important unity will be growing stronger or weaker in the *years* that lie ahead.

The imperalism of the Soviet Union, the pernicious infiltration of communism, these are the enemies whose power we must destroy. In order to do so, we, the nations of the free world, have to be strong, purposeful, and united.

The Western world through the North Atlantic Treaty Organization and other arrangements has achieved by now a considerable degree of military and political cohesion. The edifice of Western unity lacks, however, solid economic foundations. It is still divided by major economic barriers and by national policies which do little to promote unity and a great deal to prevent it. If the all-important cohension of the Western world is to endure and it solid economic foundations are to be built underneath the military and political arrangements, one major obstacle must be got out of the way. Its name is economic nationalism.

In the world as it exists today there is only one power which can conduct successfully a struggle against economic nationalism: the United States. We have the means if we have the will to do to the world of our time what England did to the world of a century ago: break down trade barriers, establish a stable international monetary system, promote a steady flow of foreign investments.

To be able to exercise this leadership, we in America have to give up one of our most traditional attitudes in the field of foreign economic relations. This attitude, although it has long since become obsolete in view of our own growth and of our position in the world economy, has still a great many adherents throughout the land. It is an attitude which goes back to the beginnings of the Republic and to Alexander Hamilton's famous *Report on Manufactures.* It looks upon a protectionist tariff policy as a foundation of American prosperity.

This protectionist outlook may — I say "may" — have been beneficial to America's growth in the 19th century. If it was, this was less due to the tariff itself than to the fact that, under Great Britain's leadership, a large part of the world has moved away from protection and that from the middle of the 19th century onwards free trade was the prevalent "climate" of the world economy. A protectionist nation, in a freetrade world, may conceivably have derived some benefits from its tariff. It would not have derived them in a protectionist world or one in which our own tariff measures would have been countered by foreign restrictions against our trade.

It was realized even before the First World War broke loose that this attitude and this policy was becoming obsolete. When the United States emerged from World War I as one of the world's most powerful economies, protectionism should have become confined to history books. Instead, it came back more virulent than ever.

In 1934, under the influence of the then Secretary of State, the great Cordell Hull, the United States entered upon a course of trade liberalization by adopting the Reciprocal Trade Agreements program. But the world was being increasingly torn by conflict and by the impact of totaliterianism and was moving inexorably towards another world war. The time was not ripe for an effective exercise of our leadership and the Second World War was upon us before we could make any impact upon the tidal wave of economic nationalism which was sweeping the world.

The history of our endeavors and frustrations of recent years is too long to be recounted here; it is, however, familiar and calls for only one comment. Instead of launching an all-out attack on economic nationalism, our Administration compromised with it. Instead of playing the role of St. George to the deadly dragon of economic nationalism, we temporized and compromised in quest of a *modus vivendi.* A little later we found that the role of Santa Claus was more comfortable than that of St. George: we fed the dragon dollars hoping he would turn into an amiable beast. Need I say that the dragon did nothing of the kind, much as he enjoyed our dollars!

Now, however, as 1952 draws to a close, we are moving towards a very important turn of the road. The year that lies ahead of us will, I feel, be a year of great opportunity. It may prove in the annals of the future to have been a year of great achievement. It may prove to have been a year of another great frustration. In the former case, 1953 will have been the year of an all-out frontal attack against the forces of economic nationalism, a year in which great strides will have been taken in the direction of currency convertibility and international monetary reconstruction, a year in which we will have called a halt to the protectionist tendencies which are again on the rampage, a year in which we will have told the world, friends and foes alike, that we are aware of our place in the world economy, of our leadership, of our opportunities, and of our responsibilities.

Failing this, 1953 may be the year in which hope for a sound world economy will have been decisively dimmed, in which new international economic crises will destroy what is left of the endeavors of the past few years, in which our friends will be disillusioned over our leadership and our foes cheered by our failures; a year in which it will become apparent that the free world is moving away from unity rather than towards it, because of the growing, not declining, influence of economic nationalism.

The situation strikes me as being serious in the extreme. Whether we shall move towards success or towards disaster depends largely on us in this country.

In Western Europe a new wind of good economic sense is blowing with increasing strength. Governments in power today in Western Europe are led by moderate people, wholehearted believers in the virtues of individual freedom, of private enterprise, and of the market economy. They are people endowed with great common sense and who have given proof in recen tyears of both daring and wisdom. They are trying very hard to put their houses in order even if that means a temporary decline in living standards.

I had long conferences with many of these statesmen as recently as May and June of this year. They are willing to be our partners in a common pursuit of a sound world economy. They are awaiting our cooperation and our leadership. They want trade rather than aid, they want to earn their prosperity rather than to get it as a gift.

The world doesn't stand still. Opportunities come and go. A new Administration is going to come into office next January. The stage is set for great positive accomplishments in the international economic field. Will the American nation as a whole overcome the protectionist tradition in favor of a dynamic new outlook in international trade? It is harder, I know, to change habits of thought and long-standing patterns of emotion than it is to accomplish anything else in the world.

There are, I am sure, many people who would heroically fight for their country, who would sacrifice their health and their wealth alike for national survival but who will cling emotionally to the last shreds of a worn-out policy, such as protectionism, not wanting to admit that the future of their country depends upon its being overcome and reversed. To these I say: think well, think fast, for time is running out on us!

II

"Economic nationalism" is then the arch enemy of free world unity, but what exactly is economic nationalism? So far in this address, I have used the term without definition, assuming that we have, all of us, an intuitive understanding of its meaning. The moment has come where a precise definition is of essence. To be successfully fought, an evil must be well understood. Part of our troubles since the war has consisted precisely in allowing the contours of our problems to get blurred; consequently our policies lost both sense of purpose and dynamism.

In order to perceive clearly the nature of economic nationalism, let us reflect for a moment upon the contrast which exists between the physical structure of our planet and its political organization.

In physical terms the planet is a single unit which cannot be subdivided into equivalent or selfcontained parts. Politically, however, it is divided into a multitude of separate states, all bent on independence, often seeking at least partial economic self-sufficiency, and, throughout the course of history, moving in an ever-changing pattern of alliances and conflicts.

Neither the earth's surface nor its interior can be divided into fully or partially independent sections. The distribution of fertile soil, of climates favorable to human well-being, of land and sea, mountains, rivers and lakes, does not favor the kind of politiacl division which prevails on our planet. The interior of the earth, in so far as it is open to human exploitation, is not as homogeneous as, for example, an apple nor divisible into equivalent and selfcontained portions as is an orange. There is no way in which the political division of the planet can be reconciled with its physical structure by apportioning in some way or other the surface and the resources of the globe among individual states. The alternative is to reduce the imoprtance of political divisions in terms of economic relationships.

Here we get into the heart of the problem. Given the multiplicity of nations and states, on one hand, and the fundamental natural unit of the planet, on the other, governments can, through their policies, foster unity or increase division. In some areas, such as trade, government can best promote unity by standing aside and allowing individuals to work things out among themselves. This was the doctrine and the practice of free trade. In other areas, such as international monetary relations, positive measures on the part of public bodies, governments and central banks, are necessary to create an international system out of the multiplicity of national currencies. How this can be done was illustrated by the long and highly successful experience of the gold standard.

Division, on the other hand, is fostered willfully or unwittingly whenever governments interfere in trade transactions between residents of their country and people living elsewhere in the world; whenever they restrict migrations and travel; whenever they limit the freedom of people to buy and sell foreign goods or to invest capital in foreign lands.

From Adam Smith till 1930, economists have been well-nigh unanimous in recognizing the virtues of unfettered, unhampered trade relations between people living in the various countries of the globe. Whenever departures from free trade were advocated, this was done for reasons of a political or social character, such as military strength or the diversification of industries, or the maintenance of high-cost farming, for example. These military, political, or social aspirations had then to be paid for by the loss of some of the benefits of international trade and of the international division of labor.

Such — apart from the "protection" of special vested interests by means of tariffs — were the major motivations of the relatively mild form of economic nationalism which was experienced in some countries (including the United States) during the ninetheeth century. The fact that individual freedom was greatly respected in those days and the powers of the state were limited, and the fact that a large part of the world, under leadership emanating from England, was on a free trade basis, tended greatly to mitigate tendencies toward economic nationalism.

More recently the situation changed very dramatically. The rise of collectivism in the 20th century and the widespread (and only too well founded) sense of political insecurity have played into the hands of economic nationalism. Economic planning became the intellectual fashion of the twenties, and the reality of the thirties and the forties; currently it shows, for the first time since the Great Depression, signs of receding.

Centralized economic planning is a typical feature of the totalitarian state; but it *can* be advocated also in the name of wellbeing or in the name of security. The economists of the Keynesian school have been at pains to demonstrate that national planning fosters prosperity — even though it breaks up the world economy. Both reasoning and experience shows them to be wrong; their influence, however, although it has passed its zenith, it still considerable. The popular appeal of the full employment slogan is still very great in certain countries as is the appeal of the economic development slogan in some areas of the globe. It is one of the tragedies of our age that these slogans should have become the weapons of economic nationalism; actually those who use these weapons are incapable, in the end, of delivering the promised goods, but by the time this is discovered much harm has been done.

Actually, governmental planning for full employment can only result, in an economy insulated from the rest of the world, in regimented poverty. Prosperity is a child of freedom and of enterprise. Economic development, too, is jeopardized by governmental regulations and restrictions; it calls for the best possibe utilization of ressources and is stimulated by the availability of foreign capital and imported skills.

In a growing world economy there are jobs enough for all. In a world economy free from restrictions economic development of any one area can be carried out with the help and the resources and skills of other, more advanced, areas. There is actually no conflict between full employment and economic development, on the one side, and the freedom of international economic intercourse, on the other. It is a tragedy that millions of people all over the world have been misled into believing the opposite.

It is up to those who believe in the virtues of private enterprise and individual endeavor as against the paternalism of an all-powerful state to fight against the fallacies that are being spread in the world by the adherents of economic nationalism and its siamese twin, collectivism. Actually, this is a task for Americans, in the performance of which we can count, at this point, upon the able partnership of our friends from Western Europe. They are the people who have awakened — or are in the process of awakening — from the day-dream turned nightmare of the "Welfare State" and who are today in the front ranks of the defenders of sound, time-proven, principles of "old-fashioned" economic liberalism.

A fake promise of welfare is one of the propaganda weapons of economic nationalism today; the other is the promise of national security. That promise, too, is unfulfillable. Two world wars have abundantly demonstrated the hopelessness for any country to be strong in and through economic isolation from the rest of the world. National strength requires the use of resources, many of which are outside of the country's territory. Only a group of countries working freely together can achieve strength. This is the basic concept of NATO and it is in urgent need of an economic implementation.

It is when one examines a common endeavor such as that of NATO countries that one is most forcibly struck by the folly of economic nationalism. Here we are, a group of friendly nations, seeking by common effort protection against outside aggression. We are working towards a common foreign policy. We are working towards a joint military force. And yet we continue having economic policies which create division amongst us. Unless we decide to abolish the use of exchange controls, import quotas, high tariffs and discriminatory trade practices, all of them tools of economic nationalism, we, the countries of the Western World, will most certainly fail to achieve the unity upon which our common survival depends.

Nor does the practice of economic nationalism allow the governments of the underdeveloped areas of the world to join with the United States and Western Europe in a common endeavor for a richer and more abundant life. Economic nationalism of the underdeveloped countries of Asia, of Latin America, of other areas, discourages today most effectively a large and sustained influx of capital and know-how from abroad without which no major economic advance can rapidly be made.

The security and the prosperity of the free world alike demand that an end be put to policies of economic nationalism. We alone in America can provide effective and dynamic leadership towards that end. We are strong and young and prosperous. We are the leaders of the free world in the fight against tyranny and aggression. We alone can be its leaders in the fight for economic unity and against economic nationalism.

How can we do that? This is the big question before us and one which we must answer fast if we are not to miss our chance of making our leadership effective. The following, in conclusion, are some positive suggestions for an American foreign economic policy aimed at the unity of the free world.

III

Our fight against economic nationalism must begin at home. As was suggested earlier in this discussion, we ourselves still have the protectionist virus in our system. It frustrates our commercial policy by our insistence upon escape clauses which make it possible to reverse tariff concessions granted to foreign countries (should it be shown that these concessions hurt some established industrial and agricultural interests at home). It creates in the world a great deal of uncertainty as to the American market, since our tariff increases can destroy long, painstaking, and costly, efforts on the part of foreign producers to sell their products to the American public. Thereby it destroys all the effectiveness we might have when urging other countries to liberalize their own trade policies. The example we are giving is what matters!

Protectionism is not only an *obsolete* policy for a country that leads the world in productive efficiency and in managerial skill, it is also a very *costly* policy for the great mass of American consumers and taxpayers. Consumers often fail to realize it, but they are paying more for a great many of the things they buy because the competition of foreign goods in the American market is interfered with by the imposition of high import duties. We all favor competition — but many want to stop it where foreign goods are concerned. This makes, of course, no sense — and it is a very expensive form of nonsense.

In the second place, we have been maintaining, for a number of years now, an export surplus financed through gifts and grants to foreign countries made at the expense of the American taxpayer. There has been much justification for these grants at the immediate aftermath of the war — but one should not mistake an emergency action for a new way of life. The American taxpayer is getting tired of the load he is bearing: the "dollar shortage" is a familiar complaint in a great many American households and there is a growing feeling that Santa Claus ought to be a sporadic event in the life not only of children but of nations!

If we are, however, to balance our foreign payments without making gifts or grants, there are only two ways by which this can be achieved:

(1) We can allow our exports to fall to the level of our imports. This would follow automatically upon the cessation of foreign aid. This solution would cause widespread difficulties in our export industries, which are among our most efficient ones, and it would deprive the rest of the world of American-produced goods of which there is great need. This, then, is a bad solution, for it is prejudicial to our own prosperity and to that of the world.

(2) We can, on the other hand, expand our imports so that foreign countries could *earn* the dollars needed to pay for the goods they are buying from us. This solution can maintain the prosperity of our export industries while allowing foreign countries to expand their production and trade. Because it favors both our own prosperity

and that of the rest of the world, I should regard this as a good solution.

To open more widely the American market to foreign goods is then the *first* and major requirement for our foreign economic policy. This calls for a number of measures on our part. While a new and low tariff is being worked out, we should "bind" our present rates (in our relations with friendly nations) and we should pass through Conugress, as soon as possible, the presently pigeonholed Customs Simplification Bill. We are keeping out goods from the American market not only because tariff rates are high but also because the administration of the tariff involves many elements of arbitrariness and of uncertainty, as well as an excessive amount of red tape. When we get a new and low tariff, we should use it as an instrument of trade negotiation in order to bring about a reduction of trade barriers by the other free countries of the world.

The *second* major objective of our foreign economic policy should be the re-establishment of convertible currencies throughout the largest possible part of the non-Sovient world. This process could best be started in Western Europe and the Sterling Area. The United States has had no really active foreign monetary policy since 1947. In that year an attempt to restore the convertibility of the pound sterling had failed through had preparation and premature action, and ever since then we have avoided pressing this basic objective of our foreign economic policy.

Exchange control, however, is one of the most devastating instruments of economic nationalism. It insulates, more effectively than any other device, a country's economy from the rest of the world. It provides a wall behind which the country's internal prices can develop out of touch with the course of world prices, thereby creating balance-of-payments difficulties. And by appearing to protect a country against the consequences of mistaken domestic policies, it encourages scomplacency towards infernal inflation and the growth of economic maladjustments. Furthermore, exchange control combined with the use of import quotas restricts international trade and payments and leads in the direction of bilateralism *à la* Doctor Schacht. Until exchange control has been eliminated, multilateral trade based on private trading and individual enterprise cannot be restored.

It has been my conviction for a number of years now that the Marshall Plan might have become an instrument of monetary reconstruction. This has not, however, been the case. Now, we must adopt a number of important measures if we are to benefit from the outlook in Western Europe which is currently very favorable to the removal of exchange control. What stands in the way of realization along that line is the lack of adequate reserves with which to buttress the position of central banks once convertibility of currencies has been restored.

Together with Switzerland and Canada, but much more importantly so, the United Sattes is the source from which additional reserves could be obtained by foreign countries. We must design a program which would create a monetary reserve fund of substantial magnitude and make it available to our friends in Western Europe first, elsewhere afterwards. It would be tedious, at this point, to go into a welter of technical detail. Let me indicate, however, my personal conviction that the solution of this problem calls for a major upward revision of the world price of gold, as a part of a comprehensive, many-faceted, program.

Let us now turn our attention to a *third* aspect of our foreign economic policy: the problem of foreign investments. Much has been said on this subject in recent years. The U.S. Government has been greatly concerned over methods of encouraging private foreign investments. Rivers of ink have flown concerning the "Point Four" program. And yet capital movements have not been revived to anything like the hoped-for extent. In spite of the very successful operations of the International Bank for Reconstruction and Development, of the activities of the Export-Import Bank, and of a certain amount of private investment, economic development of many areas of the world has been slower than it might very conceivably have been with a more abundant supply of capital.

Another frustration? Indeed, yes! And why? Essentially for two reasons: the prevalence of economic nationalism among the governments of underdeveloped countries and the prevalence of exchange controls. The combination of the two has resulted in an atmosphere which is most unfavorable to the expansion of private investments in the underdeveloped countries. The problem is ours, for we have a stake in an expanding world economy. It is our problem, too, for we don't want the dissatisfied masses of the under-developed countries to be led astray by communist blandishments. But the problem is not ours alone. Indeed, it is first and foremost the problem of the underdeveloped countries themselves. They stand to gain very much by the speed-up of their growth and they stand to lose their very freedom it the lack of growth gives way to dis-content and despair.

It is the governments of underdeveloped countries which have the greatest responsibility in the matter and the government of the United States should make this abundantly clear to them and to the rest of the world. It should be made abundantly clear, as the International Chamber of Commerce urged as recently as last May that governmental loans or grants could never be a *substitute* for private capital. Such governmental funds as could be made available from time to time to underdeveloped countries should go preferably in the direction of countries whose governments have taken positive measures to attract private capital.

So long as private investors are discouraged from going abroad by a hostile attitude of foreign governments, international capital movements cannot revive. Here is a wall which the United States could very effectively help to break down. It could do so by an adroit combination of the proverbial carrot with the proverbial stick, by rewarding fair treatment of private investments and by penalizing acts of arbitrary nationalism.

These three aspects of our foreign economic policy are very closely tied together. Unless we have monetary reconstruction in the world, we can achieve neither the liberalization of trade nor the revival of foreign invetsments. Nor can monetary reconstruction endure if our commercial policies result in a chronic "dollar gap" and balance-of-payments difficulties for foreign countries. The revival of foreign investments must not be regarded, as it sometimes is, as an alternative way of resolving the "dollar gap" problem. Capital exports are not a substitute for merchandise imports. If our foreign loans and investments are to be secure, we have to accept foreign goods and services more abundantly than heretofore.

It is greatly to be hoped that the new Administration of the United States which will be inaugurated in January will put high on its agenda the formulation of a comprehensive program for a foreign economic policy. This program must be a deliberate and bold attack against economic nationalism, both our own and that of other countries. It must be a program based on the realization that, unless we open our market more widely to foreign goods, we are incapacitated in our struggle against economic nationalism and the division it creates in the free world. In contrast with what has been the case for the past quarter century, our foreign economic policy must be acutely aware of the importance of a sound international monetary system for our own prosperity and for that of the other free nations of the world, and for the unity of us all.

A comprehensive tour of Western Europe conducted early last summer has persuaded me that there is a very good opportunity for restoring currency convertibility in Western Europe in the course of the next 12 months and for bringing to an end the widespread use of import quotas. If these goals are to be reached, we shall have to act fast and act forcefully. Time will be of the essence. Even if we win the Battle of Convertibility, there will be a hard struggle ahead of us in the war against economic nationalism — but the chances of eventual victory will then be bright.

Prosperity is a wonderful objective. Even more wonderful is the objective of human freedom. Both of these are within the reach of the Western World if — and only if — that world achieves internal cohesion and unity. After the many tribulations, disappointments and frustrations of the past, will future historians be able to record that by the end of 1952 we Americans — and the free nations of the world — have learned the lesson that we must all prosper together if we are not to go down separately in misery and distress? The answer is in our hands!

7

U.S. FOREIGN ECONOMY POLICY (1958) *

I

Unless the U.S. wishes to give its export surplus away indefinitely, it should aim either to expand its private overseas investment, or to expand its imports, or both. As will presently be shown, there is much scope for the further growth of U.S. investment, given a favorable international environment, but it is not in itself a substitute for the expansion of U.S. imports: no country has ever been prepared to reinvest all of its foreign earnings on past investments, and add on top of it a new export of capital. This may be typical of a country's early phase as a capital exporter, but once a sizable foreign investment has been built up (and direct U.S. investment abroad now runs to about $25 billion), an increase in imports is necessary to allow for increasing dividend payments. But neither this fact nor the importance of the U.S. export trade is the final reason for favoring a much more liberal import policy. The ultimate purpose of foreign trade, after all, is not to maintain any predetermined level of exports. It is rather to get imports back in return that will enrich the national economy and benefit the ultimate consumer.

Such benefit will result whenever goods are brought into this country that enjoy a comparative advantage in costs and prices over domestically made products, and this comparative advantage exists in many lines including both raw materials and manufactured goods. The argument that if the U.S. opens its doors to imports it will be "flooded" with cheap goods from overseas because foreign wages are generally lower than U.S. wages is, of course, specious. National wage levels are determined by productivity, and wages are generally

---

* Excerpts from an article published in *Fortune*, New Yorn, June, 1958.

high in the U.S. precisely because productivity is high. What is true is that it pays nations, like individuals, to go in for a certain degree of specialization. Indeed, it is through such specialization that all trade has been built up over the years not just between the industrialized nations and the raw-material producing nations but also between highly industrialized countries such as the U.S., Canada, Britain, Germany, and other nations in Europe.

II

The expansion of U.S. imports, however, requires knocking down a whole series of obstacles that now impede their flow into this country. Under the Reciprocal Trade Agreements Act, which gives the President limited power to negotiate tariff changes, the level of U.S. tariffs has undoubtedly been lowered, but the act itself is now hopelessly cluttered up wit hprotectionist amendments. Under its Peril Point provision the U.S. Tariff Commission examines all items on which tariff reductions are contemplated and reports to the President. Under the Escape Clause producers may appeal to the Tariff Commission *after* tariff reductions have been made, and the commission then makes its recommendations to the President. While these recommendations are not binding on him, it should be noted that both the President and the Commission are bound by the general language of the act, which states that tariff reductions shall not be permitted to continue in effect if they "cause or threaten serious injury to domestic" producers. Since any competition from abroad must cause some injury to someone, this provision is highly protectionist in its effect.

The greatest objection to the Escape Clause in whatever form is, of course, that it introduces a profound element of uncertainty into the whole U.S. tariff structure. Foreign producers usually work many years and invest many millions of dollars to set up adequate sales organizations within this country before their products can make a dent in the American market. At any time this investment may be nullified by Escape Clause action. In addition, foreign producers are up against other hurdles. The Reciprocal Trade Act gives the President power to restrict imports if such goods enter the U.S. in such quantities as to threaten the national security. The Buy-American

Act, passed in 1933, forbids government agencies to purchase equipment from abroad unless its price is substantially below (6 or 10 per cent) U.S. prices. Finally, it should be noted that under various agricultural and other enactments, the government is empowered to invoke quotas against foreign products. Such quotas now apply to various types of cotton, rye, and wheat as well as peanuts and butter substitutes, and some industrial producers want the same treatment.

A sensible U.S. trade program should make a clean sweep of these obstructions. Specifically it should (1) eliminate the Peril Point and Escape clauses from present law; (2) liquidate the Tariff Commission, which has become an instrument of protectionism; (3) set up in its place a Tariff Liquidation Board, which would deal with true hardship cases resulting from tariff reductions and, if the facts justified, give temporary compensation for their effects; (4) repeal the Buy-American Act and eliminate the security provisions of the Reciprocal Trade Agreements Act; insofar as specific strategic goods need protection, they should get it directly from the Defense Department in straight military subsidies; (5) eliminate present U.S. quotas, which are infinitely more restrictive and dangerous than tariffs.

These critical and difficult reforms — especially the elimination of U.S. quotas — would pave the way for a still larger step. The great defect of the Reciprocal Trade Act as now drawn is not just its hampering amendments, but the fact that the U.S. can normally reduce its tariffs only as others give equal concessions. In many cases, however, the U.S. would gain by reducing tariffs and trade barriers unilaterally, and its long-term objective should be to dismantle the tariff wall altogether. What is needed is new legislation whose declared aim would be a free-trade policy for the U.S. In carrying out such a policy the U.S. would conclude new trade treaties with other nations that provide certain minimal conditions as a *quid pro quo*. These conditions need not involve the complete elimination of foreign tariffs; they should involve the gradual suppression of foreign quotas and exchange controls, fair treatment of private foreign investment, American and other, and fair opportunity for private enterprise. Trade with countries having state trading monopolies — including all of Russia's satellites — would continue, of course, to be regulated and restricted as at present. But the aim of the new policy would be to free up both trade and payments throughout the Atlantic world and with all non-Communist countries, with the U.S. leading the way.

III

Such a change in American commercial policy from one of growing protectionism toward one aimed at complete free trade would have far reaching effects. On some estimates it might raise the level of U.S. imports by $1 billion to $2 billion even at the present level of national income. Insofar as the goods were cheaper than comporable goods made here, they would tend to stabilize the U.S. cost of living and benefit the consumer. They also would provide foreign nations with additional means of payment for a possible expansion of U.S. exports and additional employment in the export industries. But beyond this, a policy looking toward freer trade would help practically and psychologically in resolving three other problems that need to be attacked simultaneously in any reform of comprehensive foreign economic policy. These are (1) the gradual enlargment, *were profitable,* of U.S. foreign investment; (2) the redirection and reorganization of our foreign-aid program; and (3) the promoiton of full convertibility of other currencies with the dollar.

As to U.S. private foreign investment, expansion for profit has already been considerable. In the decade ending in 1955, the net outflow of private capital from the U.S. averaged $1.6 billion per year. In 1956 and 1957 direct and portfolio investment rose to an average of some $4 billion per year (a figure that includes $1 billion of reinvested earnings abroad which does not show up in the balance-of-payments figures). Large as this expansion has been, it deserves some qualifications. The bulk of our investment has been flowing to Canada, Europe, and Latin America, and only about 15 per cent of it in 1956 and 1957 went to the great underdeveloped areas of Asia, Africa, and the Middle East. And in the Middle East as well as in Latin America a large proportion of our investment goes into the extractive industries — notably oil — rather than into the light and heavy manufacturing industries that many nations say they need.

Hence it is entirely natural that there should be constant discussion of how investment, particularly in these backward areas, can be speeded up, taking the place where possible of U.S. foreign aid. Yet the plain fact is that the answer is largely in the lap of foreign countries.

Confiscation, unfortunately, did not end with the famous Mexican oil seizures. In our day Bolivia has seized foreign-owned tin mines. Nasser nationalized the Suez Canal with impunity. Sukarno has driven the Dutch from Indonesia with large and tragic consequences for his countrymen. Even where confiscation is not outright, many countries — notably Italy, Brazil, and Argentina — have put up the "not wanted" sign with respect to oil development. Finally, many countries that cry most loudly for capital have adopted inflationary development programs which in effect impede rather than promote capital formation.

In the face of all this, U.S. policy, however, need not remain passive. In a speech delivered last autumn in San Francisco, Vice President Nixon stated: "The government of the United States would never presume to tell any other government what its policy should be toward foreign investment, but the owners of private capital will inevitably take note of the investment climate before moving abroad." The latter statement is, of course, true; the former leaves something to be desired. The U.S. Government has every reason not only to protect its nationals abroad but by every means at its command — both diplomatic and commercial — to impress on foreign governments that if they want U.S. private capital they must earn the right to it. We should make new investment treaties with foreign nations, paralleling our trade treaties, which would lay down minimal conditions for the fair treatment of capital and for the prompt remittance of dividends. Finally, the U.S. might well give its support to the idea promulgated by Hermann J. Abs, German banker, for a new Magna Charta that would seek to protect private investment abroad and set up a new kind of World Court for the adjudication of disputes. In sum, we should stand for the spread and enforcement of international law, and the recognition that private property, domestic or foreign, is basic to progress and to human liberty itself.

IV

This whole effort to stimulate private overseas investment must be accompanied, however, by a thorough reorganization and redirection of America's foreign-aid program, which is today completely unhinged from America's long-term objectives. Of the $3.9 billion that the President requested early this year for all forms of foreign aid, about $1.8 billion is mainly for arms to our allies; $865 million is for socalled "defense support" operations, chiefly to help countries like South Korea and Formosa; and the remaining $1.3 billion is variously divided between a requested authorization for a new economic development loan fund ($625 million), technical cooperation ($164 million), and various forms of special assistance.

To begin with, straight military aid, plus most of the "defense support" money, should clearly be taken out of the foreign-aid program entirely and incorporated in this country's regular military budget. In addition, firm distinction should be drawn between funds requested for obvious political purposes — as in the case of money we are spending in the Middle East to support the Eisenhower Doctrine — and true economic assistance for development purposes. From time immemorial, governments have used money to influence and cajole other governments, and, so long as the cold war lasts, the President and State Department may need a kitty for such maneuvers. But this should not be confused with money appropriated for economic development, which should be kept under completely separate administration.

Once foreign economic aid has been really sorted out in this fashion, rapid progress might be made both in reducing its scope and in using it as a lever rather than as a drag on our efforts to free up world trade and payments. Undoubtedly the newly created U.S. development fund may be able to make some loans that will help recipient nations build what is called the "infra-structure" of economic development — i.e., roads, harbors, health facilities, and the like, which cannot well be undertaken by private enterprise. But there is an enormous difference between making such loans to countries that exercise a due degree of fiscal prudence and giving them to countries that say they need these facilities after they have used up all of their own public funds in building steel mills and other facilities far better left to private enterprise. In his address last autumn at San Francisco Eugene Black noted that today the governments of many underdeveloped nations do need so-called "overhead capital." But he significantly added: "What government faced with these great tasks has the capacity, financial and administrative, to preempt the directly productive sector [of the economy] as well?" In short, economic aid, to the degree it is necessary at all, should be given on the firm conditions that recipient governments balance their budgets, control credit, and in general obey the well-tested rules that, in the U.S. and other once-poor nations, have allowed economic progress to go forward over the centuries.

This turning about of the whole philosophy of foreign aid, plus the encouragement of private investment, plus the wide-scale reduction of America's own tariff barriers, would go a long way toward solving the final great problem that confronts our foreign economic policy — namely, the problem of currency convertibility and the lifting of exchange controls.